Being Human in Digital Cities

Being Human in Digital Cities

Myria Georgiou

polity

Copyright © Myria Georgiou 2024

The right of Myria Georgiou to be identified as Author of this Work has been asserted in accordance with the UK Copyright, Designs and Patents Act 1988.

First published in 2024 by Polity Press

Polity Press
65 Bridge Street
Cambridge CB2 1UR, UK

Polity Press
111 River Street
Hoboken, NJ 07030, USA

All rights reserved. Except for the quotation of short passages for the purpose of criticism and review, no part of this publication may be reproduced, stored in a retrieval system or transmitted, in any form or by any means, electronic, mechanical, photocopying, recording or otherwise, without the prior permission of the publisher.

ISBN-13: 978-1-5095-3079-3
ISBN-13: 978-1-5095-3080-9(pb)

A catalogue record for this book is available from the British Library.

Library of Congress Control Number: 2023936994

Typeset in 11 on 13pt Berling
by Fakenham Prepress Solutions, Fakenham, Norfolk NR21 8NL
Printed and bound in Great Britain by CPI Group (UK) Ltd, Croydon

The publisher has used its best endeavours to ensure that the URLs for external websites referred to in this book are correct and active at the time of going to press. However, the publisher has no responsibility for the websites and can make no guarantee that a site will remain live or that the content is or will remain appropriate.

Every effort has been made to trace all copyright holders, but if any have been overlooked the publisher will be pleased to include any necessary credits in any subsequent reprint or edition.

For further information on Polity, visit our website:
politybooks.com

Contents

Acknowledgements vi

1 The Digital Order of Cities: For People, by the People? 1

2 The Competing Humanisms of the Digital City 40

3 Popular Humanism: The Sociotechnical Imaginaries of the Digital Order 70

4 Demotic Humanism: The Liminal Subject of the Digital Order 99

5 Critical Humanism: Against the Digital Order 141

Notes 166

Bibliography 168

Index 196

Acknowledgements

The journey towards the completion of this book was long, exciting, sometimes difficult. But, more than anything, it was a journey with amazing companions – colleagues, participants, friends, family. This project has truly benefited from intellectual insights generously offeredby a number of colleagues. I am grateful to Lilie Choularaki for inspiring conversations and thorough feedback throughout the project; to Nick Couldry and to Wendy Willems for their close read of chapters in the making and their challenging but encouraging feedback; to Giorgia Aiello, Christoph Lindner, John Downey, Scott McQuire, Alison Powell, and Scott Rodgers for sharing thought-provoking feedback at different stages of my writing. I am indebted to colleagues who invited me to discuss the ideas and research behind the book at the University of Melbourne, the University of Stockholm, the University of Southern California, the University of Oregon, and, of course, at my home institution, the LSE. The Urban Communication Foundation and its co-directors, especially Susan Drucker and Gary Gumpert, have been wonderful co-travellers in the long journey of researching and debating urban communication. The colleagues who shared their expertise and showed patience and generosity of spirit while we were working on the project Digital

Acknowledgements

Makings of the City of Refuge have brought great inspiration and support to the development of some of the ideas and material discussed in this book. I am particularly indebted to Deena Dajani, Suzanne Hall, Giles Lane, and Marcia Chandra, as well as to Kristina Kolbe, Afroditi Koulaxi, and Vivi Theodoropoulou for sharing research experiences in Athens, Berlin, and London. My ySKILLS colleagues Alia Zaki in London and Leen d'Haenens, Veronica Donoso, and Emilie Bossen in Belgium, and also the Athens journalist and good friend Ioanna Niaoti, through her support of my fieldwork in Greece, were wonderful partners in respectfully engaging with young refugees at Europe's urban margins.

Many of the intellectual conversations behind the book took place during my travels and were conducted with the colleagues who showed me incredible generosity and hospitality, while helping me to recognize the connections of the urban world, and also the many layers of their particular cities. The Annenberg School at the University of Southern California has been a welcoming host during my Leverhulme Trust International Fellowship, and I am particularly thankful to Sandra Ball-Rokeach's encouraging spirit and her always big heart in sharing her ideas, her office, and her home. Sarah Banet-Weiser offered warm encouragement and intellectual stimulation, and so did dear colleagues François Bar, Matt Bui, and Hernan Galperin, while Tanita Enderes provided great research support during my fieldwork. Saskia Witterborn hosted me in Hong Kong and helped me to understand the city as a distinct and global site of communication, while Yong-Chan Kim facilitated my discovery of the many complex and contradictory sides of Seoul and Songdo. I cannot thank them enough for sharing ideas and for offering invaluable guidance and mediating fieldwork support that helped me to conduct research in those locations. I am also indebted to Alejandro Medina for his support in Havana, which was instrumental to my getting to know the city beyond the surface. And Laura Guimarães Corrêa was both an insightful co-traveller to Havana and a generous host during my visiting professorship at the Universidade Federal de Minas Gerais, Brazil. I am grateful for your hospitality and inspirational conversations. And, of course, my biggest appreciation goes to the many participants in the research behind the book; it is their agency, their intellect, and their experiences of injustice and resistance that kept reminding me who it is that we do research for.

The intellectual and ethico-political challenges I encountered across cities drove this project, but I would not have managed this journey without the love and friendship of those close to me. Many of them are the colleagues already mentioned – good and trusted friends. I am also deeply thankful to Rosslyn Bender, Gareth Dale, Wendy Dembo, Amira Lopez, Lucy Nabijou, Andreas Onoufriou, Nancy Thumim, and Natasa Vourna for their amazing friendship in Athens, London, and Los Angeles. My warmest thanks go to my wonderful family, Kevin, Leon, and Elektra, who never stopped encouraging me and holding my hand, and to my parents, Clara and Aris, whose love and commitment to justice taught me how to engage with the world and how to never lose hope.

1
The Digital Order of Cities
For People, by the People?

Today, like almost every day now, I leave my car at home and go for a local walk. What has become a daily routine is the most ordinary response to some of the acute crises of our times: environmental, economic, epidemiological.

While walking, I listen to a podcast debating humanism, and at the same time I keep tapping 'deny', 'deny' on my phone screen, as apps keep asking to locate my movement in the city. Soon after, the haptic technologies I carry on my body start vibrating with reminders of my next Zoom meeting.

As I walk down the street, I come across billboards that advertise stuff, different stuff, but most of them share a common imagery: happy smiley people on their phones or on screens. When I turn into a side street, I am faced with graffiti that take over the commercial billboards and that signpost with hashtags their expansive intended audience: a fading #MeToo and a colourful #BLM are only two of the powerful reminders that the city is an agonistic space of material and symbolic struggles.

I then return home, which is not only where I live but also where I now work for the most part. As I browse through online resources on digital cities, I read 'Of the people, for the people, by the people' on a headline praising smart cities in the *Telegraph* (2019) – a British newspaper. I then notice how Google (2021) advertises its jobs: 'Googlers' ... insight, imagination, and a healthy disregard for the impossible'. And alongside those I come across the promise of Centre for London (2021), a major thinktank, to digitally advance 'a shared vision for London with Londoners'.

This is all very interesting, I am thinking, as I observe how the media, corporations, and the state promote digital change by talking about people, not about technology. The thought is interrupted by the human in the next room: my daughter, who keeps pinging me with selfies of herself and the cat.

The banality of what I described here is familiar to many – though not to everyone, not everywhere. These descriptions represent a glimpse into the ordinary – especially, but not exclusively, in the metropoles of the global North. In their ordinariness, they reflect a life that cannot be acted upon or imagined outside digitization. Yet these banal descriptions also call for reflection on a much larger problematic: the uneven but deep entanglement of technology, power, and urban life that we take for granted but still do not fully understand in its implications – both for cities and for the humans (and other beings) who occupy them.

The city I'm talking about is the kind of city now ordinarily referred to as 'the digital city'. This is far from being an unexplored area of scholarship, of course. Inspiring and influential research on what is now called 'smartcitization' (the process of making cities technologically 'smart'), on infrastructural change, and, more broadly, on platform urbanism has tackled critical questions about the transformation of cities into networked, platformized spaces of constant tracking, surveillance, and commodification of life within them. While learning from this literature, broadly labelled digital urbanism, I also note how much it situates its central enquiry on data, infrastructures, and automation. Humans often appear on the receiving end of digitization and its data-driven economic and spatial order. Humans are less studied as agents involved in the making of digital cities – cities that are imagined, regulated, and experienced through technological innovation – unless they are in positions of authority. Urban humanity often remains an opaque category, often silent, often passive, often irrelevant to explorations of the relationship between urbanization, technology, and power. Relegating humans to being mere recipients rather than agents of change displaces questions of power but also of the right to the city. Seeing the human again is an urgent responsibility, if we are to understand what is at stake in studying cities and technology, especially at times of racial, gender, and transphobic violence often intensified through technologies of surveillance, control, and data extraction. How we live, live together, but also apart; how we write the stories of our lives or how our storytelling is dismissed; and how we enjoy or are being denied the right to the present and future urban world are all questions that we need to recentre in our research on digital change.

This book argues that recentring the human in digital scholarship is a necessity if we are to fully understand the workings of power, if we are to fully grasp digitization's embeddedness in the making of urban structures *and* superstructures. We will see how an unstable but tenacious urban order is planned, performed, and sometimes resisted on platforms and networks in order to sustain social peace in cities that experience perpetual crises – economic, environmental, epidemiological. Paradoxically, while configured digitally, this order is constituted not by displacing, but by reclaiming the human.

The enquiry into what it means to recentre the human and why we need to decentre technology comes out of my own observations across the urban world. The question that drives the book is this: what if we start from the human rather than from technology when we study digital cities? The book delves into the exploration of the digital city, being driven by this fundamental, if paradoxical, observation: that humans, not innovation, now appear as the driving force of order. Why is this shift – imagining and planning digital cities through the human rather than through technology – happening? And why now?

Ridden by crises – economic, environmental, epidemiologic – cities are fragile. We see the urban poor pushed out by gentrification, which is at the same time celebrated on social media and their selfie testaments of 'authentic' city 'discoveries'; we see urban migrants' rights diminished, as automated surveillance filters access to health and education; and we even see how AI threatens to replace so much of what humans do in terms of work and decision-making, generating panic on cities' material and digital streets. How will humans be and become urban, if their sense of security in neighbourhoods and cities fades away? What future can they imagine, when they are subjected to predictive policing and to automated decisions, made for them but without them? And how will they share the city, if the rules of engagement with friends, neighbours, lovers, and co-workers become algorithmically mediated?

Paradoxically, the more power seems to slip away from urban humans' control, the more important the human becomes. The more datafication and AI threaten to displace human actions and intelligence, the more prominent the ontological and philosophical questions about the future of humanity become, and not only academically but also in conversations that expand from the media to the dinner table. Discourses of fear and hope for cities full of either parasitic humans or laidback consumers served by robots are captions not of a mere distant fantasy, but of a fast-approaching future. At least that's what we hear on news media, see in fiction, and experience in everyday conversation.

In conditions of such fast change and uncertainty, social peace and consensus also become fragile. Even as digital advancements – from tech-driven gentrification to surveilled cities – raise fears of humans losing control, another wave of change appears to emerge: protesters around the world demand humane futures, cities where dignity, safety, and respect for life supersede greed and economic and patriarchal domination over existence. Most prominently, Black Lives Matter – par excellence an urban movement that comes out of long histories of urban marginalization and violence, but also of protest – puts human life at the core of its struggle. But this is not a struggle for bare life; as so many movements show, be they feminist, LGBTQI, or environmental, the struggle for the present and the future of cities is one for dignity, autonomy, and freedom.

Given the fragility of a city where fears and hopes for the future converge, where dissensus and consensus are precariously balanced, a new order is being mobilized. This is an order that has to work with and for fragile times, that entangles the promise of diverse, sustainable, and open urban societies to technologized futures. This is what I refer to as 'the digital order'. It is in the name of better and more inclusive urban societies, an always-to-come better city, a 'present future' (Kitchin 2019b), that investment in infrastructures of connection and control is now promoted; it is by centring urban humanity in digital urban futures that sociotechnical imaginaries gain their high currency; it is in the promise of progressive cities through mediated sociality, joy, and work that platforms and networks become seductive, not threatening, technologies to users.

Recentring the human

As the possibility – or impossibility – of order is now recentred on humans, 'for people and by the people', the city becomes a site where claims to life and values for twenty-first-century humanity are gaining centre-stage. As I will show, digital cities have emerged as exemplary sites for an urban world of revamped and competing humanisms: a popular humanism through which the digital order is articulated, a demotic humanism through which the city is lived, a critical humanism through which life and freedom for humans and other beings are and can be reimagined. We will thus see how corporate and state actors aim to maintain hegemony via a popular humanism. Popular humanism mobilizes techno-solutionist promises for and on behalf of the people: technologies are seemingly necessary for better, more sustainable, and equitable cities. This is, in Mosco's (2005) words, the digital sublime: the myth that technology, transcending time, space, and politics-as-usual, will transform society. We will also see how urban humans' everyday reveals the contradictory workings of human agency that operate through demotic humanism; demotic humanism is expressed through ordinary and creative digital practices in which what it means to be and become human is played out in everyday uses of the digital, from TikTok performances of urban identity to hashtag activism. And we will conclude by examining how the political risks and potentialities of the digital city's revived humanisms demand a critical humanist resistance and response; critical humanism will be discussed as a conceptual and political alternative to the false promises of popular humanism, one that sets forward pathways and values of dignity, autonomy, and freedom for being and becoming human in the current historical, spatial, and technological conjuncture.

Drawing on research across eight cities over a period of seven years, I will show why, in the urban stories of digital change we tell, we need to pay more attention to humans, both as representations and as actors. Of course, recognizing humans as actors of technological change is not a new claim. Humans always mattered, and the tension between them and technology has shaped key debates in social sciences, especially within media and communications scholarship – since its birth. In this book I start by advocating scholarship that investigates how deeply, even if differentially, *the human* is entangled in the social, economic, and political struggles of digital cities. This claim is central to the urban world – a world where most of the world population lives (UN Habitat 2019), where inequalities are most intense (United Nations 2022a), and where, even if unevenly, order is now advanced through technological innovation.

Throughout the book I deliberately speak of humans, and more particularly of urban humans, as against other categories of analysis, such as users or audiences, consumers or citizens, subjects or selves (though I use all of these as secondary and explanatory concepts when I refer to particular kinds of human acts and representations). Privileging the human is intentional and situates the book within trajectories of critical social sciences and humanities that recognize human agency and embodied and reflexive action as fundamental to understanding societal, cultural, and political change. Specifically, I understand the human as an important concept, even if it is always unstable and plural, or precisely because it is so. The human, in the plurality of the concept's significations, is a subject with whom and through whom research is conducted. As Ingold (2006: 259) reminds us, we cannot assume a natural definition of humanity, as there is 'no human nature that has escaped the current of history'. The meanings of 'the human' are shaped through action and through discourse. Activity, Ingold (2006) argues, shapes humans; and it does so alongside 'a collective social nature of being human ... connected, relational, valued', adds Plummer (2021: 5). At the same time we need to understand how the human is always discursively constituted and claimed for within social order and through 'highly problematic assumptions at cognitive, theological and normative levels' (Chernilo 2017: 11).

The dyadic constitution of the human through action and through discourse (as well as their inevitable entanglement, of course) drives the conceptual and methodological orientation of this project. First, the book understands humans through their critical and creative capabilities to act, even in contexts of momentous technological and corporate power. Methodologically, this means seeing but also understanding how humans are being but also becoming under conditions of always limited possibilities, through embodied but also narrative acts that generate stories and feelings about the self and about human and non-human others. Humans are subjects *with* whom this urban story is written. Second, the book conceives of the human as a discursive category, mobilized to impose, but also to resist, the digital order. Methodologically, this means studying the manifestations and consequences of how the human becomes a discursive category used by different actors, from advertisers to protesters, to make specific claims and to justify specific ideologies at particular times and spaces. The human, as actor and as a discursive category, is of course differentially constituted within and across the colonial, postcolonial, and capitalist geographies of non-isomorphic distribution of power and of claims and access to rights and resources. As many city governments, for example, set digital skills at the heart of their social inclusion policies, they reframe the causes and effects of social inequalities by promising that the lives of those at the margins will become better through 'digital integration'. As corporations invite consumers to put their faith in smartphone affordances to support their healthier and safer lifestyle, they advance imaginaries of cities made by and for digitally capable individuals. And when local activists call neighbours to sign online petitions to save their local park, they enhance imaginaries of urban humans who now think and act as digital citizens. As these examples show, the humans of the digital city are anything but a singular, natural category. Rather, urban humans are subjects of competing humanist claims made for them and on their behalf.

Humanism (or rather humanisms, in the plural) becomes an important category in this book, alongside the human. Unlike the human, who is experienced and imagined, humanism is a stance – a set of beliefs and practices, 'a human search for meaning' (Plummer 2021: 5). I did not anticipate, or even imagine, the importance of humanism(s) when I started this project. However, in my research I have repeatedly observed the persistent return of the human in the many ways in which cities are imagined, regulated, and claimed – from centres of governance all the way to the urban street. While antihumanism and posthumanism have hugely influenced digital urbanism scholarship (which I will discuss later), I here call for renewed attention to the human, both as an empirical category of significance – asserted in the hegemonic and counter-hegemonic discourse and practice of technologized cities – and as an analytical category of importance – captured in the contradictory mobilizations of humanist values of diversity, equality, dignity, and freedom to affirm or challenge order, and consequently power.

Humanism, as we will see in detail in the next chapter and across the book, becomes a site of ideas, representations, and performances that capture fundamental struggles for the future of urban societies. These are struggles between a revamped liberal or, more accurately, post-neoliberal, western-centric, and inevitably exclusionary promise of human liberation through technological progress on the one hand and, on the other, a renewed ethical imperative for equality, freedom, and respect for all life – what Fassin (2019: 37) describes as a humanism after posthumanism and antihumanism: a 'post-posthumanism'. I thus recognize the need to reflect rather than ignore the return of the human in digital societies, especially in cities. With Fassin, I recognize that this requires a 'critical approach to human worlds in a time when they are faced with multiple menaces that affect both humans and non-humans, capitalism's victims and destroyed environments, war casualties and ruined cities, displaced populations and threatened species, refugees and the planet', all of which 'is the result of human actions and therefore involves human responsibility – notwithstanding the ambiguity of the word *human*' (ibid.).

The proposed analysis might seem out of sync with antihumanist and posthumanist critiques centred on the infrastructural ordering of the city through platforms and their aggressive profiteering, or with the rising concerns about AI replacing human work and agency. Yet, I claim, this is a necessary reshuffle of our conceptualization of both the digital and the human. This is even more so in times of crises, when, as I observed in my research, the struggles between securing order *in* crisis and finding hope for a life *beyond* crisis become recentred on humanistic values, as these are revived, revamped, and reimagined through competing claims to democratic and free societies. In developing my argument, I highlight the symbolic and material constitution of digital cities as more than merely infrastructural or corporate projects led by platform- and machine-driven rationalities. Cities, I argue, are uneven and complex spaces of life, meaning-making, and also hope; they are not just spaces for technological applications and experimentations. As Natale and Guzman (2022: 627) argue, we need to 'move toward a conceptualization of culture in which machines are intertwined within human systems of meaning-making', a research field that has become marginal to scholarship, since the latter is often fixated on the machine and its own 'distinct' power and agency. Yet, while scholarship often spotlights the machine, powerful actors make claims to life and agency through the promise of technologically induced human progress, reminding us that digital change is a complex project with intertwined economic, social, and cultural stakes.

Why now? Technological and humanistic convergences

The digital city's currency and appeal have grown at times of urban and global crises of the status quo – economic, political, ethical. As one of the major contemporary undertakings promising urban transformation, the digital city is par excellence a post-neoliberal project, as will be discussed later in more detail. Characteristic of many post-neoliberal projects is their ability to bring together otherwise contradictory ideals (Davies and Gane 2021). For the digital city, this is the paradoxical convergence of market economics and platformization's extractive datafication on the one hand, and the promise of diverse, sustainable, and inclusive urban societies on the other. The paradox explains why mistrust – public, political, academic – towards platforms and their digital economy is on the rise while at the same time citizens as well as elites invest in infrastructures that secure their domination across public and private urban life. What sustains this contradiction, I argue, is not infrastructural capabilities alone but also the symbolic power of digitization, persistently represented as a force for good.

This symbolic power contradicts the realities of technologically enhanced inequalities through gentrification, predictive policing, and automated rationing of public services and elevates technology still further, to the role of a believable generator of positive change. Such power becomes apparent, we will see, as so many urban actors – corporations, the state, the media, but also civil society – promise a technologically enabled rehumanization of the unequal city. What digital cities bring, we are now told, is not profit, economic growth, and controlled societies, but instead progress, openness, and sustainability. These promises turn into a diffused popular humanism that redefines the project of digital change away from neoliberalism's technocratic and technodeterministic discourse and instead moves towards a reimagined human-centric technologization in which technology is narrated as working for humans and not the other way around.

It is important to understand these new promises of progress and freedom, both within the history of capitalist modernity, including in its critique (an example is Marx's confidence that industrial machinery advances human liberation), and within and against the ideological bankruptcy of neoliberalism, expressed most intensively in financial, environmental, and epidemiological crises. Across the world, the rise of the populist right, with its post-truth and nationalist doctrines, has challenged the ideological domination of neoliberalism, reflecting the most visible and threatening forms of post-neoliberalism (Davies and Gane 2021). The appeal of the populist right may reveal the ideological and economic crisis of neoliberalism at the level of the nation. Yet, at the level of the city, we most vividly see the contradictions of this crisis in the urban manifestations of post-neoliberalism. Advancing an order that seamlessly produces consumers and only selectively citizens, platforms, data, and AI encroach on all elements of political, cultural, and social life in the city, promising freedom and autonomy through digital artefacts and infrastructures. Cities have become agonistic sites where the ideological and economic dominance of neoliberalism is both powerful and under attack (Parnell and Robinson 2012). In fact, cities reveal post-neoliberalism as a contradictory, rather than as an altogether new, phase of neoliberalism. Progressive and radical movements contest urban inequalities, as we see in the case of the Black Lives Matter (BLM) revolt across American cities, the feminist acts of disobedience across Latin American and European cities, and city governments' own defence of the rights of migrants and minorities from Barcelona to Los Angeles. At the same time, it is in cities that commodified expressions of hashtag activism and corporate sponsorship of justice causes mostly emerge, with fashion brands and digital companies incorporating the language and symbols of anti-racism, feminism, and LGBTQI rights in their strategic communication. As cities become hubs for challenging the authority of the racial and neoliberal market and state, the language and means of power and resistance are claimed and reclaimed by different actors. Technology becomes intrinsic in this process, not least as digitization makes the vision of greener, more inclusive, and democratic cities believable. Or this is what the dominant discourse of progressive urban futures claims.

The first aim of the present book is to show how, at times of perpetual economic, environmental, health, and political crises, order is fostered, not through the projected force of technological control or thriving markets, but through a post-neoliberal promise of rehumanized cities. This promise, the argument goes, depends on humancentric conceptions of technology – conceptions that push aside public suspicion of Big Tech and instead promote notions of technology as necessary to a more equitable, inclusive, and sustainable urban world. The second aim is to show what is at stake in the rise of competing humanisms that turn the city into a revamped site of social and political struggle for and against order. On one side of this struggle we can see the incorporation of humanist values into digital strategies for the regulation of the city and for the establishment of order against (or within) the fragility of neoliberalism. On the other side we see public, activist, and scholarly discourses and practices that unsettle and sometimes challenge this order, not by dismissing humanist values altogether but by rethinking what it actually means to be and to become human in cities of intense inequalities, forceful datafication, and growing threats to all forms of life. Thus this book examines how the promise of digitally enabled humane urban futures and its contestations are embedded in claiming the right to the city and the right to be and become human in it.

Defining the digital city

I here focus on *the digital city*, as I understand it to be a symbolic and material construct, constituted differentially and hierarchically across regions of the world, through the convergence of three distinctive forces: an adaptable strategic model for the governance of the city and the development of infrastructures such as fibre-optic and wireless networks and bureaucratic data and connected services; a sociotechnical imaginary that ties human betterment to technological innovation and does so differentially, by linking digital progress to each city's specific aspirations and problems; and lived experience, in cities where lifeworld and the economy are increasingly but unevenly mediated through digital infrastructures, data, and networked communications. This means that the actors that make the digital city are many: powerful authorities such as governments and corporations, which regulate the city through policies, investment, and profit-generating activities; media, which narrate the city through images and texts that define what is digital and optimal; and urban humans, who experience the city through everyday uses of technologies to manage their needs, desires, and fears.

In developing this discussion, I learned from the literature on digital cities, which brings together observations and debates on infrastructural planning, datafied governance, and sociotechnical imaginaries (Barns 2020; Halegoua 2019; Kitchin 2019a, 2019b; Powell 2021; Rose et al. 2021). This literature moves away from earlier conceptions of the 'smart city' as a technocentric project determined by bureaucratic governance and profit-driven infrastructural transformations alone. Instead, it examines how 'the actually existing smart city' (Sadowski 2021) brings together rationalities and techniques associated with data, ubiquitous computing, and AI to produce 'a shift in how societies are managed and controlled' (Kitchin et al. 2019: 7). Specifically, governmentality in the city moves away from disciplinary top-down governance towards social control, where human behaviour is 'explicitly or implicitly steered or nudged' (ibid.) – in other words, where humans' mobilities, affect, and embeddedness in the city are ordinarily mediated through digital media affordances (Halegoua 2019).

Against the narrow lens of the smart city, I understand the digital city as both disrupting and building upon pre-existing infrastructures of governmental, economic, and social relations. That means two things. First, digital infrastructures alter certain modes of working, socializing, and imagining cities and people through distinctive systems and their affordances – such as platforms, data, AI, and wireless networks. Second, like all infrastructures, they are situated within wider economic, social, and governmental systems through which cities are ordered – for example the market economy, the family, local governance (Halegoua 2019; Larkin 2013). My conception of the digital city also locates its sociotechnical constitution within longer histories of mediation, order, and disorder, as analysed in media and communications and in urban studies literature. Critical urban theory reminds us of the long histories of colonial capitalist economies, which have served the interests of elites through infrastructures of exploitative material conditions, including underpaid and unpaid migrant labour and dispossession of minoritized and indigenous populations (Brenner, Marcuse, and Mayer 2012; Cowen 2020). Reminded as we are, in this literature, of the complex and long sociotechnical trajectories of capitalist urban economies, we can understand digitization as an unexceptional, even if distinctly important, form of technologization within longer histories of innovation, and as a form embedded in capitalist structures and superstructures for the accumulation of profit (Mason 2020). I am thus inspired by non-media-centric media studies (Couldry 2004; Krajina, Moores, and Morley 2014) and by research that highlights the situatedness of digitization within histories of mediated and technological urbanism (McQuire 2008, 2016), as well as by research on the many ways of knowing and living the city – which, as Mattern reminds us, 'is not a computer' (Mattern 2021).

These interdisciplinary intellectual trajectories allow me to understand digital urbanism as a non-isomorphic, non-teleological process that involves technologies, actors, and differential local, national, and transnational spatialities. The digital city is not singular and homogeneous, but a distinct formation situated within temporal and technological trajectories of digital change. For Sadowski (2021), these transformations involve an initial phase of establishing smart cities as governmental applications of new technologies; a second phase in which platforms attempt 'to snatch sovereignty' from government; and a third phase, 'the most straightforward and most uncertain', in which corporate and state actors both converge and compete for sovereignty over the city's territory. This is the city that critical scholarship on smart cities and digital urbanism debates (see Barns 2020; Kitchin 2019a, 2019b; Sadowski 2021; Safransky 2019; Rose et al. 2021). From this interdisciplinary perspective, I also contest conceptions of digitization (and its variations through the language of datafication and platformization) as a unique force that radically changes *what was there before*, since a 'pure', unmediated city has never existed in modernity and a fully programmable city does not exist now either.

From CCTV cameras to news media cameras and, more recently, to smartphone cameras and tracking apps, technologies have become entangled in networks of control and witnessing that have long shaped order and disorder in the city. For Merrifield (2014), what we now observe is the renewal of ordered cities through 'neo-Haussmannization':

the advance of infrastructures of control and the policing of space and people, especially those at urban margins. Effective infrastructures acting as systems of control are expanded through digital connectivity, which represents more than the mere optimization of surveillance. What we witness, with digitization, is the emergence of an odd pair: control and openness. On the one hand, the infrastructures of surveillance advance and refine urban control as a new form of 'neo-Haussmannization'. On the other, the infrastructures of content creation, sharing, and decentralized communication promote urban imaginaries of post-Haussmannization, that is, allow us glimpses into the possibility of open or disordered cities. While the contradictory forces of infrastructural connectivity diverge in their distribution and consequences, what brings them together along the converging global trajectory of the digital city is the resolution of state, corporate, and media sectors to promote technological optimization (Horan 2000; Mitchell 1996; Powell 2021). From India to the United Kingdom and from Egypt to Greece, governments now prioritize urban connectivity above many other urban infrastructures, for example those of safe, inclusive, and accessible public space (Datta 2020). We are thus reminded that infrastructures reorder cities and, in their situated formulations, shape the meaning of order itself.

The digital city is built upon present imaginaries, investment, and planning for digital futures, but of course is also situated within the longer trajectories of modernity and conceptions of technological change as a force of good. As wireless networks enable smooth smartphone communication, secure banking exchanges, and fast access to services, different urban actors, from governments to corporations and, of course, to urban humans, commit themselves to enhancing an exciting, functional, and also controlled urban space. But cities are more than infrastructurally controlled spaces. As the subsequent discussion will show, especially in Chapter 4, global trajectories of technological urban transformation are more than corporate and governmental projects. Across boundaries, digital cities are realized through meaning-making processes that call for recentring the human. Urban humans, not technology, have become – or, to some extent, remain – the primary representations; they are agents, ethical subjects who desire, fear, or are expected to enact order though digital work, consumption, and play.

Writing digital cities through the intertwined geographies of humanity

The story this book narrates comes through my research journeys across eight cities of the global North and global South over seven years. The digital city, I was constantly reminded, is an imaginary and a differentiated manifestation of urban and digital change, situated in global geographies and histories of colonial and postcolonial struggles as much as of technological transformations. As such, the digital city is both particular (i.e. historically and spatially situated within local and regional geographies) and global (i.e. designed, desired, and imagined across borders and within the unequally situated trajectories of neoliberalism and people's digital lives). While recognizing how important particular materialities, technical systems, and histories are in the formation of specific digital cities, the book privileges a decentred conception of the city. It does so because its primary focus is on understanding the manifestations and consequences of imaginaries that tie technological and human progress across both urban and transurban geographies.

The book also privileges a transnational and transurban vision and practice. My research journey was initiated from a space of familiarity – the intellectual and geographical space of Europe, where I have spent most of my life and conducted most of my research. My own personal and professional biography calls for a reflexive recognition of the incomplete outlook of this project and of the positionality from which I speak. However, my own subjectivity as a migrant born both in Europe and at its postcolonial periphery, as well as my deliberate effort to move beyond familiar spaces of research and life while I carried out this project, generated an account that, in its biases and limitations, still questions assumptions about a rigid binary between a homogeneous global North and a homogeneous global South. As I was soon to discover, the digital city neither is generated by, nor belongs to, a set geographical imagination.

Arguments about the wholesale export of colonial sociotechnical discourses and the aggressive imposition of Big Tech's interests on the global South often dominate critical literature, as if the North has agency and the South always lacks it. Yet much less is understood about the ways in which these aggressive strategies of domination become entangled with regional imaginaries and local histories that engage humans in class, gender, and race struggles of power and resistance (Datta 2020, 2023; Willems 2014a, 2014b). Digital cities also reflect the contradictory ideologies of colonial domination and the imaginaries of regional knowledge production and economic autonomy, as seen in the case of many African digital cities (Jali 2022). In its transurban and local manifestations, the digital city's promise – along with its unequal delivery – of autonomy for people and cities requires a realization of the existence of divides that cut across axes of inequality, and these are not only geographical but also situated in systems of class, gender, and race and in their regional manifestations.

Assumptions about the global North–global South binary are also challenged if we are to pay attention to the city as a site of human experience, and not only of control. When focusing on order and surveillance alone, urban humans disappear and become agentless, as if they come from nowhere and have no voice and no history outside platformization and datafication. However, my research with urban humans repeatedly showed how the global South is always embedded in the cities of the global North, as much as the other way around. Urban histories and trajectories of migration, diasporization, and marginality are constant reminders that the relationship between the global North and the global South is not determined by Cartesian coordinates.

Relations of power as well as of resistance divide but also connect regions, through histories of violence but also of human migration. López (2007: 1) invites us to understand the global South through the shared condition of inequality across regions, but also through the 'mutual recognition among the world's subalterns of their shared condition at the margins of the brave new neoliberal world'.

The cities I examine are situated within the differential, incomplete, and converging trajectories of urban digital transformation – where innovation is privileged and where people are called to embrace it for their own benefit. The cities this book engages with include some of those with established histories of economic and symbolic power upon which advanced digital infrastructures and digital economies have been built – London, New York, and Los Angeles; newer players that have benefited from neoliberal globalization and public investment in digital economies and infrastructures – Berlin, Seoul, and Songdo; and cities at the margins of Europe and the Americas, caught between the contradictions of neoliberal economies, global crises, and underinvestment – Athens and Havana respectively. Of course, we'll find more differences than similarities between these cities if we approach them from the angle of their particularities; yet, within the transurban economies of imagination, representation, and infrastructure that shape the digital order, they reflect distinct manifestations of advanced, aspirational, and peripheral digital cities. I draw inspiration from Massey (2007: 10), who argues that we should understand how 'the global is as much locally produced as vice versa', and I follow her invitation to reflect on how our analysis can be *about* specific cities but can also arise *from* them so as to address wider problematics, in this case the digital order of the urban world and its humans.

The promises of technologized betterment discussed here coexist with the multiple crises of their politics and economies – such as the 2008 financial crisis, the global pandemic, the environmental emergency, and the growing mistrust of digital industries' power. In the cities studied here, the visuality of urban landscapes constantly built the optimal humans: the always connected, digitally savvy individuals who drive urban change and who seemingly reap its benefits. These humans are present in (self-)representations and billboard advertising on social media, all the way up to incarnations of the ideal consumer of technologies that promise better lives in the form of smart homes and haptic technologies for health monitoring. At the same time, intimate and public urban spaces are redesigned as ambient commons (McCullough 2015), digitally augmented and tagged spaces made to accommodate these same humans: those who stay always connected (through public Wi-Fi and ubiquitous charging stations), those who 'care' (through shared working spaces, cafés, and restaurants that promise state-of-the-art connectivity with low carbon emissions and humane green and mindful environments), and those who thrive on the city's openness (through apps that speak to the gendered, ethnic, and sexual diversity of the city and not just to homogeneous categories of buyers, even if they are always oriented to consumers rather than citizens).

Conducting research on digital lives, from London to Seoul and from Athens to Havana, I was reminded of the limitations of technocentric conceptions that privilege platformization and datafication as determinants of urban life. In some of these approaches, platformization and datafication are perceived as uniquely powerful sociotechnical and economic processes, which are incomparable with other technological innovations, from the factory to photography and broadcasting, while they often belittle the long genealogies of urban struggles – class, racial, gender, spatial. I explore here how urban humans and cities are constituted through discourses and practices of digital promise, as these discourses and practices are made through, and make themselves into, urban cultures and histories. I thus hope to contribute to a multiperspectival outlook on digital urbanism in which the entanglement of all actors, human and non-human, in creating the meaning of order and disorder is better understood. I examine the particular moment of advancement of

The Digital Order of Cities 21

AI and data systems of control and communication, while always paying attention to the layered city (Marcuse 2002) produced through social and spatial relations embedded in the past and in the present.

Over the period of the study, from 2015 to 2022, I observed practices and interviewed people who live in global cities such as London and Los Angeles, in aspirational cities such as Berlin, and in struggling cities such as Athens. Without trivializing the huge differences between cities (and I will return to some of them throughout the book), I kept observing certain repetitive patterns in their imaginings and regulations. The regulation of urban life starts with the ordinary. Most obviously, this happens through the progressive saturation of all elements of urban life with digital objects, platforms, and infrastructures. For example, smartphones, while far from being universally available or equally distributed technologies, represent the digital objects that most urban humans carry across the city, as they use them ordinarily for navigation, socialization, and safety. Social media such as Facebook, WhatsApp, TikTok, Weibo, Cacao, and IMO have become banal urban communication infrastructures for learning and speaking of and to the city of consumption, love, and work. Alongside the regulation of the ordinary, technologies of control have also become points of global convergence of systemic order, even if in apparently asymmetrical ways. From closed-circuit cameras and street corner sensors to drones and consistent resident data collection by corporate and state actors, the digitization of urban governance and policing is systematic and cumulative. In some cities these technologies are deliberately made hypervisible, as is the case in Seoul, while in others, for instance London, they seem as deliberately kept out of sight (and thus out of mind). For all their differences, these technologies now represent a staple in the governance of everyday life in all the cities I have studied.

Beyond the visible and the invisible workings of order through the wide distribution of technological objects, networks, and platforms, I have been most intrigued by the growing symbolic power of technology in regulating the city. This power is expressed as deep and unchallenged faith in technology as progressive force. But this is not just a familiar technodeterminism. Importantly, technology matters, not as a *deus ex machina* any more, not as the magic bullet of fully functioning and controlled urbanism that the projects of smartcitization promised in the early 2000s. Instead, technology is now imagined as being at the centre of power, but also on the urban street – a force of progressive change that is or should be integral to all the planning and living that take place in cities. Importantly, in these sociotechnical imaginaries, cities should not be controlled and ordered; instead they should be enjoyable as well as diverse, open as well as sustainable. Faith in technology, I have observed, drives sociotechnical imaginaries in which digital pathways lead to more humane cities. In practice this translates into significant state, corporate, and individual investment in digital infrastructures, which often sticks out against reduced investment in public services, contracted economies, and individual cutbacks to consumption. How does this disproportionate investment in digital infrastructures come about? How come the technologization of the city remains largely unchallenged, when other forms of public investment, for example in social housing, public schools, or green policies, are regularly contested? Why do so many actors of the city put their hopes in technological solutions for urban problems?

In my research I have tried to find some answers to these questions by studying how the digital city is constituted, both in discourse and in practice – and also in their inevitable entanglement, as will be discussed later in the book – and both via hegemonic and via counter-hegemonic discourses and actors. My empirical interrogation of the hegemonic planning and imagining of technologized cities is grounded in analysis of the discourses produced by powerful actors such as the state, corporations, and the media and manifest in policy documents, advertisements, corporate strategy documentation, and news stories. The significance of hegemonic discourse became clear in the first phase of my research, when I came across headlines such as those presented at the beginning of this chapter, repeatedly promising digital change *for* and *by* humans. I was surprised to see how a curious humancentrism is now driving media narratives, corporate narratives, and policy narratives of digital urbanism. Again and again, in city after city, the discourse of progress towards order became evident. As humancentric narrations of the digital city seem to gain transurban resonance, the concept of a city driven by technology looks already outdated.

To understand why and how discourse that privileges life, freedom, and well-being is gaining such prominence, I expanded my research across the sites where urban life is narrated, but also experienced. And, being driven by the ethics and the practice of ethnographic imagination as pathways to understanding the meanings of change and not just its symbols, I turned to urban humans. I adopted a multimethod approach that made use of interviews, observations, and also creative and participatory methods, so as to develop an intersectional perspective that records the range of performative and reflexive digital lives. I engaged with people whose digital lives sometimes converge and sometimes diverge, as they exist in the uneven geographies of class, race, gender, and spatial divides. The discourse of progressive, open, and diverse cities was shared by many, yet the contradictory meaning of this discourse revealed itself in their differential practices: from social media performative curations of the self to enactment of collective agency on digital commons, humanist values are revived and reconfigured digitally and performed with their contradictions.

Realizing how much digital cities are now driven by humanist, if contradictory, conceptions of technology, demands that we ask why and how smartcitization and urban infrastructural transformation have gained such high currency across the world – being embraced, albeit differentially, by both the left and the right – by the state, corporations, the media. Is this convergence of digital promise the result of corporate visions of maximizing profit? Is it the outcome of governments' attempt to control people and territories? Or is it merely the inevitable result of technological progress? The more I studied cities and their people, the more I realized the limitations of these questions: they pay little attention to the complex entanglement of the discourse and practice of digital urbanism. The making of the digital city, I found out, does not seem to be all about technology. But it does not seem to be a mere reflection of neoliberal capitalism either.

Ordering the digital city

More than a merely economic, infrastructural, or governmental affair, the technologization of urban life, I argue, needs to be understood as a process and as a system of urban order. Interest in and concern with the ordering role of media and communication technologies are not new; the topic has in fact been tackled in scholarship across the social sciences. My starting point in reading the power intricacies of digital urbanism is a reference to three key sets of debates on the order of digital cities that take it to be respectively a symbolic, a spatial, and an infrastructural framework.

The studies in the first set, rooted as they are in media and communications, examine the digital city's *symbolic order* and, specifically, the generation and regulation of urban imaginaries by its different actors (Aiello 2021; Georgiou 2013; Gordon 2010; Krajina 2013; McQuire 2008). Emphasizing the multiplicity and the competing nature of these imaginaries and the possibilities for communicative conformism and subversion, this literature situates discourse and experience within broader enquiries on the concentration or contestation of the symbolic power held by cultural industries and urban governance. More specifically, it analyses technologies of representing the city throughout modernity, for example by highlighting how the camera – from photography to film – has shaped the modern city as a spectacle and, relatedly, the identity of the urban human as spectator (Gordon 2010; McQuire 2008). With digitization, this literature emphasizes, the symbolic power of the media has been diffused, especially through the multi-perspectival view of the city produced by a variety of users – filmmakers, journalists, advertisers, social media influencers – and through multiple technologies – satellite technologies, drones, broadcasting, smartphones (McQuire 2016). This literature contests the functional, technocentric conception of digitization that drives corporate and planning visions of transformed cities and instead analyses the urban as an asymmetrical and contradictory cultural and communicative space.

Spatial order, which is rooted in the geographical imagination, focuses on the digital production of space and on the technological impact of innovation on urban governance and on the right to the city – or, in Halegoua's (2019: 5) words, the process of 're-placeing the city'. In this scholarship, the city is a fundamentally spatial formation and technology becomes implicated in this spatiality by enhancing governmental processes of surveillance and monetization in networked cities (Kitchin et al. 2019; Krivý 2016) and experiences of surveilled, collective, and sometimes subversive urban action. This scholarship has drawn attention upon the 'conjunctural geographies' (Graham 2020: 453) that reconfigure power relations in the city but also produce multiple geographies, imaginaries, and 'forms of value' (Rose et al. 2021), especially as the experience and the meanings of technology are differentially shaped in the 'actually existing smart city' (Shelton, Zook, and Wiig 2015). Such approaches capture the diversity and situatedness of spatialized politics and experiences of digitization that are implicated in histories of placemaking and urban governance.

The third, and perhaps most influential set of arguments focuses on the city's *infrastructural order*, drawing on and contributing to the interdisciplinary concerns of science and technology studies (STS) and political economy. Infrastructural transformation is understood as fundamentally reconfiguring the dynamics of social life (Amin and Thrift 2017; Mitchell 1996), especially through the overconcentration of economic and infrastructural power in platforms, the reorientation of choice and information through algorithms, and the extraction of data or appropriation of human life for profit (Couldry and Mejias 2019; Gillespie 2010; van Dijck, Poell, and de Waal 2013). Scholars who work at the border between geography and infrastructural change emphasize the 'co-generative dynamics between platforms and the urban' (Rodgers and Moore 2018) but also raise concerns about the data-driven decision-making involved in 'algorithmic violence' and the entrenchment of inequalities through discourses and practices of digital solutionism (Safransky 2019). Extractivist economies of technology-driven urbanism, Mosco adds, intensify 'surveillance, shift urban governance to private companies, shrink democracy' (2019: 1). In dialogue with critical data studies, this scholarship analyses data-driven urbanism, how cities are instrumentalized as producers and products of data (Kitchin 2011; Powell 2021), and how infrastructures (including platforms and the datafication of urban life) are used by corporate and state actors as technologies of oppression, to reproduce and congeal gendered, class, and racial inequalities, especially through algorithmic bias and the datafication of everyday life (Benjamin 2019b; Eubanks 2018; Noble 2018).

While this brief overview is far from capturing the nuances and cross-currents that can be found in these three approaches to the mediation of order, it highlights key conceptions and concerns about the shifting performativity of power in the context of digital urbanism: together, these approaches identify assemblages of power that emerge from and are strengthened through technological innovation. Invaluable as they are, however, by privileging technology, these approaches often assume the silent subjection of humans to systemic domination, because 'other things matter' more – representations, infrastructures, data. Consequently they pay less attention to processes of subjectivation, that is, to what comes to be called, recognized, and lived as human in contexts of intense digitization and differential urbanization. Drawing on these approaches and reflecting on their limitations, my proposal is that we cannot assume that humans are on the receiving side of ordering technologies. Never has this been less true than now, when a new order emerges throughout cities that visibly and assertively bind together technology and urban humanity. This is not just a social order *mobilized* through technology. It is an order *constituted* through a set of discourses and practices that tie the human to deep and lasting digital transformations of social, economic, and cultural life in the city. This is the digital order.

From mediations of order to the digital order

At the heart of my proposal lies the idea that the digital order is already central to the life of the city as a system of knowledge at once symbolic and material, discursive and enacted, a system that routinely enlists agentive and affective human capabilities to normalize and legitimize controlled cities – what Foucault (1970) calls an order of discourse. This is an order that assertively ties human life to technology. I focus on the digital order, as I observed it emerging across the world, from London to Seoul and from Los Angeles to Athens, as a rising system of established knowledge that organizes and disciplines the twenty-first-century city. As I conceptualize it, I'm learning from social theory of order as well as from phenomenological, empirically informed analyses of digital urbanism (Cardullo et al. 2019; Rodgers and Moore 2018; Rose 2020). A strong influence on my conceptualization of the digital order is Couldry and Hepp's (2017: 190) notion of the social order, which they define as 'a relatively stable pattern of interdependences' between individuals, groups, institutions, and relations of 'larger stabilities of resource and infrastructure'. These infrastructures are increasingly digital and have networks and data that operate now as key components of functioning societies, against urban chaos and societal instability (Couldry and

Hepp 2017; Wrong 1994). Order, according to social theory developed along these same trajectories, is not imposed from above but becomes embedded in human 'endowments and capacities' and in dispositions that motivate and materialize urban life (Wrong 1994: 5). Thus order is not coercive, not simply good or bad. Instead, it represents a distributed, open-ended and diffused system of knowledge of what is appropriate and 'just' (Boltanski and Chiapello 2005). Order does not preclude the competition of values but implies 'the higher-dimensional "settlement" that enables a minimal level of stability' (Couldry and Hepp 2017: 191).

Digitization makes order particularly seamless, as it embeds its rationalities and techniques (Foucault 2007) in every element of urban life, from everyday communication on social media and use of digital technologies – for example to navigate the city via Uber, Google Maps, and Airbnb – all the way to invisible but ubiquitous datafication – which takes place through algorithmic profiling of CCTV and data-sharing employment and leisure networks (Shelton et al. 2015). This advance in datafication is where Couldry and Hepp (2017: 191) see a shift in order, from an openly contestable system of norms and values to 'an authoritarian structure of compulsion'; and this is also an unsettled space, where urban scholarship identifies multiple registers and geographies of connectivity (Barns 2020; Rose et al. 2021).

The digital order is historically and spatially situated within the capitalist city of perpetual crises and technological possibilities, as mostly (but not exclusively) observed in major metropolitan centres of the global North. Specifically, this order emerges under three contemporary conditions. First, it surfaces at times of growing suspicion against Big Tech. Currently public trust in social media is at its lowest ebb worldwide (Edelman 2021), and increasing numbers of people in the global North are reducing or even completely suspending their use of social media (Business Insider 2020; Hutchinson 2021). Thus, technologized cities cannot exist any more as projects of platform domination, as the collapse of the Google-led project of a digital city in the Quayside district in Toronto has vividly demonstrated. Specifically, the deeper public mistrust of Big Tech, the market, and the state grows, the less do urban sociotechnical imaginaries constitute themselves around the promise of a technocentric capitalist future: automation, growth, and profit are values attacked by many in the city, from urban governments to grassroots movements for urban and digital rights. Popular narratives of freedom, biodiversity, cultural diversity, and openness are rising against the retreating technocentric imaginaries. Second, the ideological hegemony of neoliberalism is under attack and the market-driven language of profit and individual success through perseverance and resilience seems now less believable than ever. In many societies, and especially since 2008, neoliberalism has lost its hegemonic ability to induce 'a minimal level of stability' (Couldry and Hepp 2017: 191). Third and largely in response to the previous point, justice movements that contest racial, gendered, and spatial hegemonies are on the rise, with cities being the epicentres of their grassroots mobilizations, progressive and radical. The advent of these movements has brought the discourse of rights, freedom, dignity, and equality back into the heart of the urban world. In many cities, the awakening of a collective consciousness of rights means that top-down impositions of digital systems, which quite openly serve the market and the state, are just not viable any more.

These conditions also highlight the particularity of the city vis-à-vis the nation as a site of order (and of its contestation). Mistrust of neoliberalism, nationalism, and datafication is most visible in cities, whose progressive politics are on the rise (Douglass, Garbaye, and Ho 2019). Examples include contradictory voting attitudes in US states and US cities (Graham 2017), growing municipal movements that contest nationalism in Europe (Bloomberg 2019), and the establishment of transurban movements such as the international Cities Coalition for Digital Rights (2022). Against the post-neoliberalism of the populist right, which cashes in on the bankruptcy of neoliberalism to promote racism and hateful nationalism, cities often promise another post-neoliberal future: one of inclusivity, diversity, and sustainability. In the rising movements against racial, gender, and environmental injustice on the digital and material street, the fragility of this order is exposed. The crisis of the neoliberal dogma becomes obvious in the progressive politics of the city's political actors that promote sustainability, digital integration, and (digital) corporate accountability, be they urban governments or transurban initiatives. But how much these actions present an alternative to neoliberalism is indeed debatable.

The digital order and its contradictions

The digital order has become a post-neoliberal response to neoliberal crises, which are most exacerbated at the level of the city, with its intensified inequalities, climate stresses, and health and energy emergencies. Post-neoliberalism does not imply the end of neoliberalism, but it certainly captures its fragility. As Davies and Gane (2021: 4–5) argue, post-neoliberalism represents 'a set of emergent rationalities, critiques, movements and reforms that take root in neoliberal societies and begin to weaken or transform key tenets of neoliberal reason and politics'.

As a form of post-neoliberal rationality, the digital order breaks from the strategies of neoliberal hegemony in three ways. First, it breaks away from the previously dominant system of ordoliberalism, which Foucault defined as the 'general regulation of society by the market' (Foucault 2008: 145) – a system in which nothing but the market is seen to be sacred (133). Against the brutality and determination of neoliberal order in the form of ordoliberalism, we see a new order, which emerges as a result of widespread pressures to recognize the sacredness of life (as reflected in US cities' responses to George Floyd's murder or in Polish cities' responses to the abortion ban) and the value of society (as reflected in the surprisingly widespread economic support that citizens received from neoliberal governments at the peak of the pandemic, for example through furlough schemes). Second, the digital order integrates instability into stability through the promotion of unpredictability, openness, and diversity as optimal ways to live in the city. This is seen, for example, in the pop-up economy, where shopping and eating take place in temporary shops that consumers only get to know through social media. Thus the digital order is reinforced as both achievable and desirable, even when the multiple systemic crises could make it look impossible to attain (Wrong 1994). The example of the pop-up economy captures this contradiction, through which order is being reinforced: the systemic and large-scale breakdown of small businesses across cities leaves many shops empty, but this crisis becomes opaque, as celebrations of the pop-up economy across social media hide the collapse of so many small- to medium-size urban businesses. Consequently, the symbolic constitution of the digital order takes neoliberal libertarianism to a new level: its fundamental dogma of unregulated markets and assertive individualism expressed through deregulation extends to all elements of urban life. Now we see hegemonic discourses of deregulated economies and unregulated urban lives expanding into ideologies of how lives should be lived on networks and platforms: on platforms urban humans are promised freedom, through networks they are assured of new opportunities to build humane cities, but at the same time the elements of control, surveillance, and exclusion from this vision are fully obscured, rendered opaque. Third, the digital order is ideologically messy and morally malleable as a result. This shows in its adoption of a contradictory set of values – an amalgam of liberal, neoliberal, and anti-neoliberal ideals. The many public–private partnerships that invest in smart technologies to promote green cities are a good example. These partnerships are highly publicized and celebrated as progressive, but in many cases the investment in smart green technologies mainly conceals polluting activities for which the participating corporations are responsible.

The digital order, then, creates peculiar discursive synergies between progressive feminist, anti-racist, and environmentalist values and reinvented versions of individualism and entrepreneurship, which now appear as less aggressive, market-driven forms of urban living. The digital city, for example, is frequently imagined in media discourse through green technologies and digital campaigns that celebrate female and ethnic minority executives, with little mention of the market or Big Tech as driving forces of 'positive change'. Thus the city looks inclusive of all its different urban actors, whose trajectories converge around a digitally mediated openness: an openness celebrated by digital corporations, the media, and the state, and also an openness that digital users embrace through hashtag activism and ethical consumption across cafés, restaurants, and shops. It becomes apparent, then, that this order's appeal resides in its ability to avoid *othering* difference: it not merely integrates it into aesthetic and non-political forms of representation and practice but, more boldly still, suggests that difference drives digital order. For example, it is now commonplace for the image of a start-up's Black female executive (or of the model who poses as one) to be circulated on social media campaigns as the leading face of change. The graffitied and ever-so-slightly seedy street is more often than not chosen for trendy, shared workspaces, implying the dependence of innovation upon urban difference. Even direct symbols of urban dissent, such as those associated with Black power, are regularly integrated into cutting-edge designer urban fashion; and activists of urban movements are invited to gallery openings and urban government events, to be loudly celebrated as leading figures in these institutions' hashtag activism.

Cities emerge as privileged, albeit not exclusive, sites for researching the digital order. As the hegemonic discourse of planned and applied digitization emphasizes 'the common good', and as the demotic practice of urban humans invests in technological solutions to many urban crises and collective vulnerabilities, it is the values of human betterment that appear to drive the relationship between urban humanity and innovation. Gone is the technodeterministic capitalist future; the urban future is now human. So we are repeatedly told.

These trajectories reveal the rehumanizing promise and the dehumanizing implications of the digital order. In fact, the urban human becomes an ambivalent figure of change, discursively and performatively implicated in reconfigurations of already existing inequalities in the city. Specifically, racial, class, gender, and spatial inequalities come to be obscured as the technological promise of progress recentres the politics of social change *outside and beyond* structures of inequality, and *within* imaginaries of technologically capable, agentive, and progressive individuals who can change the world. As I will discuss later in the book, such discursive tropes reveal the rehumanization–dehumanization continuum upon which the digital order lies. As the digital order functions through urban humans, it has never been more urgent to understand what this means for controlled cities and lives.

Why do I privilege the category of the human – and, consequently, of rehumanization and dehumanization – in understanding the digital order? First, as the digital order is not just digital but also urban, it needs to be understood through its rootedness in the sociocultural life of the city – the lived, human experience and its entanglement in meaning-making. This is a key point in my analysis. Somehow this approach challenges core arguments on digital urbanism and its emphasis, on the one hand, on data- and platform-driven spatiality and, on the other, on social connection now being prescribed by digital and data rationalities. I want to insist on bringing the analysis of connection back into everyday life, in the messy multimodal space of friendship, love, family, and work. Everyday life, I argue, both shapes and is shaped by the communicative and economic dimensions of the digital order. I also feel strongly about bringing debates on digitization back into the lived experience of the city and of the urban street, in their digital and material incarnations and interactions. In fact, thinking of sociality in and through the city can function as one of the most conspicuous reminders of the situatedness of digital lives in their embodied, affective, and emotional as well as cognitive and rational constitution, through which the digital order is formed and contested. When lovers exchange messages on WhatsApp and when migrant mothers conduct long-distant parenting on Messenger, we are reminded that digital lives are not merely situated on platforms, with human freedoms prescribed by datafication, but lived on and through platforms and networks of new and old connections and disconnections; they are conditioned by new and old forms of profiling, assorting, and profiteering and subjected to values that debate humanity's present and future.

Second, the constitution of the situated couplet Self/Other reveals how humanity is produced *with* order, not *after* order. This means that conceptions of the human and of urban economies and societies are mutually constituted. For example, the digitally savvy subject is now produced as a desired human, within economies that compulsively generate and sell objects and technologies that supposedly serve this kind of human best. As digitally savvy subjects then depend on innovation to enhance the opportunities for work and play, an order is affirmed where both the digital economy's prominence and specific humans' privileges appear as inevitable, natural. At the same time, as no element of the economy and governance can be imagined without high technological 'solutions', knowledge-rich individuals are produced as desirable citizens and workers, against failing and undesirable ones, who are knowledge-poor. The co-constitution of order and humanity starkly reminds us of how narrow the assumptions of the universalizing figure of the individual digital user can be; and these assumptions are often reproduced even in critical research – the kind that develops theories on the basis of limited research, which generalizes the middle-class experience and western whiteness (Noble 2018). Challenging our conventions about the isolated ontologies of 'the individual user', cities make us aware of humans' intersectional positionalities. Within them, the self, individual and collective, as well as the many Others are produced through complex urban histories, through intersections and trajectories of colonialism, capitalism, and patriarchy, but also of revolt. Thus, recentring the human in digital urbanism means understanding the digital order neither as a machine-generated and -controlled social order nor as a story of fragmented experiences among autonomous individuals. Instead, this is an invitation to consider ongoing, multimodal, and conflicting processes of meaning-making and life-making in the city at the juncture of technological promises and the still social and collective experience, which is grounded in solidarities and communities and in their associated boundedness.

Third, an analysis situated in the urban life of the digital order is, literally, a realization of digitization's embodiment. The digital order is a biopolitical order. In the city, urban humans are human bodies (even if changing ones). The body is experiencing the city through the inequalities of its enjoyment, as it unevenly navigates and consumes its resources, but also through the affective inequalities and threats of sexual violence, police brutality, and systemic processes of state and corporate assortments of gendered, classed, and racialized bodies. The digitally connected body seeks embodied pleasures and finds discipline through connectivity – especially through smart, haptic technologies; it also seeks to secure physical safety by being guided and warned by data and tracking technologies about urban risks and opportunities. These same technologies are mobilized by the state and the market to track and datafy the movement of bodies in the city, to classify desired and undesired subjects, to catalogue humans as consumers or (potential) lawbreakers. Countering or exacerbating exposure to urban risks, the embodied constitution of the digital order reminds us what is at stake: the prospect of cities where humans move as data that are always traceable, or where they are equitably supported to live safe and fulfilling lives among and with others. This challenge requires a critical humanist analysis that locates the human within systems and hierarchies, attached to privileges and rights that matter when cities become imagined, planned, and lived as digital cities.

If indeed *the human* – as a category of analysis and as an actor of change – is being mobilized to normalize ordered, corporatized, and controlled cities, we need analytical and ethical responses that *see* and *hear* the human within the historical and future trajectories of order and its discontent. Such critical approaches need to recognize the human as an autonomous but not independent actor, as an agentive but not individualized subject, as narratable self, not as statistical data – a maker of the digital city within sociotechnical systems, but also within sociocultural and moral systems of being and becoming (Hall 1997). These conditions require a critical humanist analysis: one that does not dispute infrastructural power but at the same time recognizes the discursive and performative significance of being and making claims to becoming human in the city. Thus in this book I examine through a critical humanist lens why and how the incorporation of the human into the project of digital cities becomes both a threat and a hope for contesting controlled, segregated, and unequal cities and lives. This is the analytical approach of this book as well as its normative stance, best reflected in Mbembe's (2021: 229) statement that humanity is not a given formation but is 'pulled up and created over the course of struggle': even as it is under attack from racial and data capitalism, this humanity bears the responsibility for creating 'a great universal future equitably open to all peoples, all nations, and all species' (229).

Aims and structure of this book

The present book examines the (re)configuration of order in digital cities at a time of permanent crisis and heightened mistrust of the state, the market, and Big Tech. It analyses the urban and transurban trajectories of a fragile order – the digital order, which aims to maintain controlled and commodified cities through the human – and reflects on this order's instability and discontent. As analysis unfolds while we turn the pages of the book, we will see how urban humanity – as a performed, imagined, and always contested category – has returned to the core of powerful but competing claims to humane, sustainable and open cities. Technology per se is not the target of this book's critique. Technology is not discussed here either as a distinct 'thing' or as a deterministic independent variable. Instead, it is always looked at in its embeddedness in social, cultural, and economic systems and in relation to *what it does* rather than *what it is* (Seaver 2017). Thus this book offers a cultural reading of technology, examining meanings of digital change and order in the city as they are situated in the materiality and performativity of urban life and as they embroil experience, affect, and agency into the technologies and rationalities of networks, platforms, and machines.

This approach reveals how the human is discursively and performatively mobilized to mediate power and order in unequal and diverse digital cities. The mobilization of the human as a category for enhancing control and as an agent for advancing change shows how much is at stake: sovereignty over cities (Sadowski 2021), but also sovereignty over life. The high stakes around the competing claims to the human are discussed in Chapter 2 through a detailed analysis of the digital city's competing humanisms: popular humanism, demotic humanism, and critical humanism. As will be shown, these coexisting humanisms and their competing values reveal core ideological contentions, but also struggles around the control of urban territories, resources, and life.

Popular humanism, I will discuss in more detail in Chapter 2, is mobilized by the city's powerful actors – corporations, the state, and the media – to support consensus in cities torn by various crises. Popular humanism incorporates and updates established liberal and Eurocentric values of a universal humanity in order to promise cities rehumanized through technological innovations; in this way it elevates certain humans – those who work and play on platforms and networks – to the status of legitimate and celebrated owners of the city, while pushing still further the dehumanization of those who cannot or do not want to consent to the digital order. I refer to this ideological frame as popular humanism, since I understand it to be a discursive system that aims to *manage people* – not unlike how, in ancient Roman law, the people (*populus*) was conceived of as needing to be managed if ordered societies were to be achieved.

The chapter then introduces the notion of demotic humanism – the contradictory and messy space of everyday life, where urban humans experience, negotiate, and contest the digital order. Demotic humanism represents a reflexive space but also one of practice, where those who live the city create meanings with the technologies that mediate work and pleasure, private and public life. These technologies promise a lot, control even more, and in the process shape desires and fears of what the city and life within it is and should be. This is the space of the *dēmos* – of 'the common people' (in classical Greek) – where the promises of technological betterment are experienced, negotiated, and contested through the vernacular and the visceral city.

The chapter concludes with a discussion of critical humanism as an analytical and normative framework through which activists and academics can (and do) understand and resist the incorporation of humanity and of its claims to freedom into projects of controlled and corporatized digital cities.

Chapter 3 unravels the empirical grounding of popular humanism. Through its focus on urban sociotechnical imaginaries of the digital city, it shows how state and corporate strategies, as well as media representations, elevate urban humans to the position of prime actors responsible for the sustainability and legitimacy of the ordered and prosperous city. The powerful discourses of popular humanism, it will be shown, obscure the incremental and unequal subjection of urban humans to divisive and often cruel urban inequalities. Dominating the sociotechnical imaginaries of digital cities, the promise of humane futures, it will be argued in this chapter, effectively rehumanizes certain humans *within* and *through* digital knowledge, while dehumanizing others. Those who fail or refuse to perform the city within that framework of individualized and marketized, technologically driven life become more and more invisible in the imaginaries of digital cities. The analysis that unfolds in Chapter 3 is situated in the unequal geography of digital cities and of the differential forms of othering and ordering that constitute them.

Chapter 4 moves from popular humanism and its discursive constitution of the digital order to the complex and contradictory entanglement of its discourse and practice in the context of urban everyday life: demotic humanism. By engaging with empirical data that illustrate urban humans' experiential, affective, and agentive everyday lives, the chapter shows how the digital order produces liminal subjects, precariously balanced between processes of rehumanization – which are associated with their integration into digital economies and sociotechnical 'pervasive human–computer culture' (Lamola 2021: 138) – and dehumanization – which result from profiling and separating those who matter from those who don't, especially on the basis of digital skills, buying power, and the desire (or lack thereof) to invest a personal and collective future into the digital promise.

Chapter 5 returns to critical humanism as a politics and as an ethics formulated and enacted in urban activism as much as in critical scholarship. It starts by analysing the empirical evidence for its many different incarnations across cities, then moves to a reflexive conclusion on what we learn about power, technology, and humanity by adopting a critical humanist perspective. Identifying the blind spots in dominant perspectives of digital urbanism that marginalize or ignore transformative humanist responses to the technologization of political, economic, and cultural urban life, the chapter concludes by setting out a normative thesis: one that proposes a politics and an ethics that respect and defend the right to life and freedom of all those who live in the city, and do so on, through but also off platforms and networked communication. The critical humanism that Chapter 5 sets forward is radical, environmental, dewesternizing, and hopeful.

2
The Competing Humanisms of the Digital City

The realization of the digital order through the human is more than an empirical observation; it is more than a discursive trope developed by policy makers, the media, advertisers; it is more than the enactment of a neoliberal system of control. At the heart of this book is the thesis that the digital order reflects the revived and contradictory mobilization of humanist values across different quarters of the city – but only for opposing purposes. These are values that, through their contradictions, are gaining renewed currency by imagining and planning relationships between humans and data, humans and machines, humans and humans, humans and non-human life. For example, 'smart camera' networks expand in the name of sustainable urbanism and are used for managing 'the complex urban metabolism', as suggested by D'Amico et al. (2020), who adopt the language of living organisms ('metabolism') to describe the seemingly convergent needs of the city and its people. A corporate–academic–local governance network, TmplTalks, is concerned with urban populations' loneliness, setting as its goal 'to use technology to enhance life in the city and decrease the negative effects of always being connected' (Collier 2019). And the United Nations now identifies Internet connectivity and information and communication technology (ICT) infrastructures as 'digital public goods' – these being considered fundamental to fighting the social inequalities (United Nations 2022b) that impoverish so many and destabilize several societies.

Fundamentally, the mobilization of humanist values for order (and sometimes against it) reflects the discursive and performative struggles for the city: on the one hand, these values rally to obscure the cruelty of urban inequalities by relocating hope for change within technology; on the other, when integrated into oppositional political imaginaries, the same values appear as a call for imagining different ways of 'being human in a connected planet' (Plummer 2021). Alongside Chernilo (2017), I am wary of the revived currency of humanism, especially as it is historically tied to a Eurocentric humanist episteme and the contemporary reproduction of specific conceptions of humanity and its values – not least because these reproduce 'racist claims of Enlightenment rationality in the West/North as well as the equally racist claims laid by elite postcolonial theories that see universal values as unique to the Western project' (Dutta and Pal 2020: 350). But, like many scholars of critical humanism, from Fanon to Mbembe and from Chernilo to Plummer and Gilroy, I, too, am aware that what is at stake in the revival of humanist values surpasses their hasty dismissal. As humanist values in fact drive many humanisms rather than just one, they reveal struggles between power and resistance and between opposing promises about the urban world and statements about what it should be like. These dynamics are reflected in the coexisting but competing humanisms that emerge for, within, and against the digital order: popular humanism, demotic humanism, and critical humanism. In what follows I will discuss them one by one.

The ideology of the digital order: Popular humanism

If humanism was to be understood merely as an old discursive property of colonialism and racial capitalism, the advance of the digital order in the name of the human good could be simply read as a marketing trope of corporate, media, and state actors. Digital practices centred on the individual or collective self could be simply read as performative enactment of datafied lives. This book questions this reading. It challenges conceptions of the performative and discursive manifestation of digitization as mere effects of an order determined in Big Tech's headquarters, laboratories, and factories. Instead, it identifies the rhetorics and performances of the digital order as core elements of deep and wide processes of change in the relational constitution of cities, technology, and power. The more I have observed practices and studied discourses of digital transformation, the more it became apparent that the rhetorics and performances privileging progressive values against patriarchal and racial capitalist domination are not an add-on to the digital order. In fact, when we think of established or aspiring technologized cities, we cannot understand their current constitution outside these rhetorics and performances of greener, more equitable and diverse urbanism, what I understand as the popular humanism of the digital order. This proliferation of the popular humanist rhetoric is the first manifestation of ideas and practices showing how the digital order cannot be normalized and legitimized through infrastructural and market priorities alone. The digital order also needs a cultural justification, a promise for better human futures.

What does this mean? The digital order, as it emerges in the contexts of deepening systemic crises and growing public mistrust, works not as a technocentric but as a humancentric project. Popular humanism elevates the human who consumes, works, and socializes digitally to the condition of agent who makes and changes cities – a new, digitally constituted, but also progressive and ethical entrepreneur of the self and of the city. This humancentrism is not interchangeable with anthropocentrism – which is the elevation of (certain) humans' interests above all forms of life, with catastrophic effects for the planet (Plummer 2021). Rather anthropocentrism, as we will see in what follows, is hidden behind popular humanism's contradictory narratives, which range from individual well-being to sustainable cities.

In the rehumanizing discourse of popular humanism, we are being repeatedly told, technology is not the endpoint. It is instead the means for achieving better lives, sustainability, and freedom. Investment in digital infrastructures advances equitable, green, and sustainable cities (Mayor of London 2018a), reliable connectivity, and sustainable relationships (Collier 2019) among humans and between humans and non-humans, while smart technologies are fundamental to ensuring political accountability and transparency (World Bank 2023). Anti-racism, feminism, and environmentalism are at the heart of the rehumanizing rhetoric of popular humanism. This is seen, for example, in a corporate campaign of France Digitale for humane technological futures, and in Big Data for Humans (2017), a start-up declaring that it programs data and platform applications to listen and speak to users as humans, and not the other way around.

'The popular' in popular humanism speaks to Raymond Williams' (1958) and Stuart Hall's (1981) influential definition of popular culture as a site of power. The concept of popular humanism works in tandem with that of demotic humanism, as will be shown later. The former mobilizes a technological populism to take possession of everyday life by promising progress through digitization, while the latter reveals how culture, as an ordinary presence, remains a site of negotiation, struggle, and resistance (Williams 1958) at a time when these conditions are being rearticulated in tech cities. The concept of popular humanism also draws on current conversations around the manifestations of the popular as a site of struggle within digital cultures – important conversations, which have been a source of inspiration for this book. Most notably, Banet-Weiser (2018) speaks of popular feminism as a normative realm where claims for gender equality are mediated through the lens of a consumer- and screen-friendly positive change within, and never against, the heteronormative whiteness of the capitalist and corporate order. Popular humanism is situated on the same terrain of technological, visual, and discursive economy that in this case normalizes digital change as a necessary and unique pathway to progress, sustainability, and freedom in the city.

The digital order's popular humanism needs to be situated within the political and moral ecosystem, where the concept of humanity seems to gain new relevance as a political and moral category. Even now, at a time of fierce critique of the Anthropocene – the disastrous domination of humanity over nature – or perhaps precisely because of this critique, many claims are being made on behalf of humanity (Cielemęcka and Daigle 2019). The rise of new social movements most powerfully expresses the recentring, in crucial matters, of a decentred and pluriversal humanity: Black Lives Matter puts the value of living in safety and dignity back at the core of its activism, #MeToo reclaims care, solidarity, and respect for women in its campaigning, while Extinction Rebellion contests environmental catastrophe's threat to all life and well-being on the planet. Resulting from many urban citizens' shattered trust in the state, the market, and technology, these claims have been anchored in cities and amplified through decentred networks of communication. They are claims to pluriversality and justice that often originate at the social margins and can in principle destabilize order. While their oppositional politics may and sometimes does still achieve that, as we will discuss in Chapter 5, what we often also see is their incorporation into market-based discourses that celebrate difference and digital solutionist responses to inequalities.

In the context of the now perpetual crises that hit cities hard, urban humanity has become a site of radical claims to freedom and justice on the one hand, to counter-claims for a humane capitalism through technology, on the other. The former are represented by performative statements, made on the digital and on the material street, against structures that divide humanity on the basis of race, gender, sexuality, ability, and geography. The latter are discursively constituted by corporate, media, and state declarations that seemingly adopt progressive values, such as promises of reliable and free connectivity and digital opportunities for work and sociality for all. As we will see in the next chapter, the rhetoric of order adopted by these powerful actors noticeably moves away from talk of growth, individualism, and global marketization, leaning instead towards humanist values of freedom, diversity, and inclusion. This happens while in the city, where inequalities make full consent impossible, the digital order comes to compensate for the failings of other structures of order. Unlike at the national level, where consensus is achieved through the myth of cultural homogeneity, rising nationalism, and social peace, in the city consensus is promoted through the myth of freedom and self-realization that digitization and urban economies and cultures promise.

Thus what appears to be a counterintuitive claim – that popular humanism drives digital order – is actually very predictable: popular humanism reflects elite strategies in the city that are designed to incorporate trust and human capabilities into planned and controlled digital transformations of urban life for profit and order. At city level, the corporations' and the state's appreciation for (certain) capabilities demonstrated by humans to engage with digitization in diverse and sometimes subversive ways is quite obvious. Unlike national or global research, where such processes may remain opaque, popular humanism becomes visible when one looks closely at it and into urban life, from sustainable cafés and shared working spaces (the hyperlocal level) through governance and investment in digital infrastructures for tackling digital inequalities (the local level) and all the way to corporations' celebrated choices of diverse neighbourhoods for their digital hubs (the global level).

Popular humanism becomes spectacular, yet familiar through the media, which amalgamate liberal, neoliberal, and post-neoliberal values such as individual freedom, entrepreneurship, multiculturalism, environmentalism, and feminism. As Banet-Weiser (2018) notes about popular feminism, this involves practices and discourses associated with progressive politics such as hashtag activism and conscious consuming, but excludes any systematic critique of and action against deep-seated systemic divides, or any committed confrontation of the racist, anti-environmental, and patriarchal structures of capitalism. Like popular feminism, popular humanism becomes a way to validate 'an economic subject and an economic context' (Banet-Weiser, Gill, and Rottenberg 2020: 10) by rhetorically and practically promoting progressive values through digital applications (e.g. green technologies), but without challenging the racial, gender, and environmental inequalities that caused the contemporary crises in the first place.

The state's and the corporations' strategic promise of progress depends on the machine – a symbol of progress repeatedly projected as a solution to human problems through the long history of Eurocentric humanism. In fact, the digital order depends on this rationality, as it frames the believability of the promise that computational logic and AI predictions can effectively respond to human questions and needs. That core narrative connects what makes us human with machine thinking and learning; it aims to strengthen the belief that one is rallying rationality for the individual and common good. Glorifying the ability of machines to give rational responses to individual and societal problems may appear as a commitment to humanity, when it comes to its manifestations in popular humanism; but in fact, as Mhlambi (2020: 5) argues, this is a logic that reproduces 'the perceived infallibility and supremacy of rationality' and disguises its dehumanizing effect. This logic, Mhlambi continues, has been summoned throughout modernity to dehumanize 'those in society whose exclusion has been rationalized or found "productive"'.

Thus popular humanism does a lot for the digital order. Through its selective application of the values of freedom, equality, and rationality, it produces the rehumanization–dehumanization dialectic of a hierarchical urban humanity, organized around the normativity of technologically mediated recognition. Popular humanism normalizes the digital order's set of rationalities by gradually transforming the city – which is in fact an anthropocentric yet dehumanizing city, and at the same time an unequal but rehumanizing city: in other words, a city of two paradoxes. This means that certain humans are worth seeing and hearing, as long as they are integrated into digital economies and cultures, as we will see in the next two chapters. Those outside, or at the margin of, those economies and cultures become irrelevant, both as producers and as consumers of the digital city. As popular humanism recognizes only subjects who are digitally savvy and always connected (or who desperately want to be both), the humans of the digital order become a cultural construct beyond and outside inequalities. For urban humans are recognized as agents of change only when they can perform progressive openness through digital connectivity, 'empowerment', and 'resilience'. The media-friendly spiel of popular humanism makes the digital order difficult to perceive, the inhumane conditions of datafied and securitized lives opaque, and the wholehearted assignment of humanity's hope to technology hypervisible.

Producing a seemingly innate, albeit ordered, urban humanity, popular humanism discursively acknowledges racial, class, and gender divisions, but effectively ignores their deep, production and reproduction, historical and systemic. Instead, through an innovative, anti-hierarchical yet commercialized communication of notions of inclusive urban humanity, it strengthens Eurocentric, colonial imaginaries that dehumanize so many. For this is a set of norms that recognize a progressive and essentially tolerant urban humanity: keen owners of electric cars, consumers of 'ethical clothing', advocates of equality and diversity when performing the self across platforms. These norms leave little space for oppositional subjects – those who contest the normativity of the free market and the controlling governmentality of a class, racial, and patriarchal social order.

The humans whom popular humanism sees, communicates, and identifies are thus self-governed and adaptable individuals (Butler 2006) whose cognitive and affective capabilities cannot be understood outside their dependence on non-humans – the platforms on which they live and play, the data that distribute them into market-relevant categories. But the appeal of the digital order resides in recognizing humans as more than data; humans are not merely consumers but moral agents. They are invested in digitally ordered societies; they are workers and consumers of digital economies, not of changing societies. The shift in the mutual constitution of humanity and order in the post-neoliberal city is such that cities can no longer depend on obedient humans who believe in the rewarding effects of individualistic and self-governed entrepreneurial and competitive subjectivities (Foucault 1982). In cities shaken by so many crises and by the consequent mistrust of those in power, popular humanism comes to guarantee stability by giving recognition to individuals who are seen – and see themselves – as progressive agents of change and as digitally equipped survivors of instability. This happens because the digital order cannot be sustained without humans who believe that they have some power to shape their world – and have a stake in it as well. These are humans who can imagine change in the form of becoming a 'smartphone-equipped crowd of independent contractors' (Sundararajan 2017: 7), who are promised recognition as long as they display buying power and particular market behaviours (Benjamin 2019a; Eubanks 2018), and who can make profit-generating contributions to urban cultures of diversity through viral videos and shareable commodities that celebrate difference. Their vision of cities led by electric cars, organic food, ethical fashion, and effective digital communication for remote working is a vision of progress as much as of new and exacerbated exclusions.

The digital order in many ways produces teleological subjects through its narrow and contained humanism of privileging a normative whiteness and market-friendly 'cultural otherness' (Dutta and Pal 2020), subjects whose cognitive abilities and affects are mobilized for ordered cities and market economies, never against the systemic order of things (Foucault 1970). Thus urban humans become rehumanized subjects with a cause – which is to sustain the order, the status quo, by digitally enacting its humancentric promise. In reality, of course, this teleology does not work linearly. Instead, as we will see in Chapter 4 and in the practices of demotic humanism, initially introduced in what follows, humanism also produces liminal subjectivities, precariously balanced between the digital order's rehumanization (when individuals are seen and heard through their digital engagement and successful integration into computational networks of work and consumption) and its dehumanization (when others who do not conform to the digital norms are denied access to the city's resources).

The contradictions of the digital order: Demotic humanism

Popular humanism becomes a cultural exercise of power, as it promises a recognizable, inclusive humanity, seemingly spoken to through technology indiscriminately, while in fact it displaces people and practices that do not comply with the rationalities of ordered digital societies – namely of a post-neoliberal amalgam of humans defined through digital competence, self-reliance, and buying power. Popular humanism matters because it is more than discourse; it actually maps onto the performative, embodied constitution of technologized ordered cities. Thus, alongside its analysis as hegemonic discourse, I ground this research in urban experience, affect, and agency – in what makes up the lived space where the digital order is enacted, negotiated, and contested. Popular humanism, even with its own contradictions, systematically incorporates into urban imaginaries the interests of elites and their desire for order, as we will see in the next chapter. Yet the hegemonic discourse does not pre-empt the practices, imagination, and values of the many who occupy the city.

Now as always, lived experience (de Certeau 1984; Lefebvre 1991; Marcuse et al. 2021) reveals the city as a complex and agonistic space: a space where the digital order is incorporated and contested, not least through embodied and creative practices (Moores 2017; Markham 2020; Mattern 2021). Like others, I have observed, through my research, how the boundaries between incorporation and contestation have become permeable and unstable, and more so through the wide circulation of revamped and malleable humanist values. While discursively driving the digital order, humanist values also have a resonance, even an urgency, for many urban humans. The city's powerful actors may promise digital answers to dehumanizing inequalities; many of its marginalized actors really need those answers. Do the two converge? Seeking answers to this question, I introduce demotic humanism alongside popular humanism, as I understand the former to represent the experiential, affective, and agentive ways in which urban humans imagine and live the city through everyday practices and uses of digital technologies.

Throughout my research I have seen how urban humans engage with material (phones, watches, computers) and immaterial digital infrastructures (networks, data) ordinarily, but not only habitually. Urban humans' digital lives unfold in everyday work and play. They are so much more than a mere reflection of human subjection to data and racial capitalism; they reveal individual and collective desires for self-realization and belonging to a world that many know is fragile, deeply unequal, and in perpetual crisis. The smartphone, for example, has become a personal manager of identity: carried everywhere in the city, it is now a virtual stage for performing and archiving the self as reflexive subject (Giddens 1990; Georgiou and Leurs 2022), for knowing what happens close by and at a distance (Papacharissi 2021), for placemaking and for teaching others who and what is 'instaworthy' (Gupta and Ray 2022). As the smartphone draws the boundaries of the city, of the self and the other, it becomes a technological site for mediating individual and collective morality – how the city is and should be lived, and by whom.

These observations demand a phenomenological sensibility, which examines humanism as more than a top-down exercise of power. Demotic humanism offers precisely that. It is an insight into the ordinary, dynamic, and contradictory engagement of urban humans with humanist values, especially as these emerge from the spatiality of the city and from the dilemmas it presents – most notably, how to be and become *with* others, human and non-human alike. Learning from Merleau-Ponty's phenomenology, I understand demotic humanism as a humanism grounded in practice that 'considers indivisible the awareness of human values and ... the infrastructure that gives them existence' (Merleau-Ponty, as quoted in Simonsen 2013: 21). These infrastructures are increasingly digital, and the values they give rise to are not only narrated but also practised, specifically through urban experience, affect, and agency. I, in turn, will discuss the constitution of demotic humanism through experience, affect, and agency.

The city is an experiential space. Popular humanism emerges as a discursive construct at the heart of state and corporate strategies and media's fascination with its potential for digital transformation. But the city is not merely a discursive construct. It is also a site where knowledge is produced through experience; this is where meanings 'become sedimented, performed in habit and inertia, and interwoven with power and obfuscation' (Simonsen 2013: 23). We cannot understand the appeal of humanist values unless we situate them in the city of experience, in the vernacular (Gilroy 2004; Georgiou 2017) and the visceral (Doughty 2019; Nava 2007). Creative capabilities, which for humanism are at the heart of what makes humans (Plummer 2021), are rooted in urban experience: 'We, humans, *make* urban information by various means: through sensory experience, through long-term exposure to a place, and, yes, by systematically filtering data' (Mattern 2017). For example, as urban humans use smartphones for tracking fitness, entertainment options, and job opportunities, digital technologies of tracking the self and the Other become ordinary. Technologies of tracking are not random events, they become ways of governing everyday life through the ordinary '"coding" of public/private behavior' (van der Graaf and Ballon 2019: 364). As they situate experience within a geography of digitization, fundamentals of urban life – bodies that converge, differences that collide – become more and more digitally mediated. It is now customary to use a smartphone to find one's way into an unfamiliar part of the city, to meet a stranger on a dating site, to witness police violence digitally (but also to block all these possibilities, of course). While technologies of blocking are becoming sophisticated, technological affordances that enhance knowing about difference map upon both the urban experience and the rising popular humanist discourse of openness. The digital city is thus a site both of order and of 'potential new modes of co-existence' (Simonsen 2013: 23).

The city is an affective space. Urban humans position themselves and others inside or outside the frame of the urban world through 'affective performances of place' (Halegoua 2019: 170). These affective performances include, for example, emotional narrations of self-making in an urban world, as seen in selfies that strategically situate a happy or sad subject in front of loved or hated locations respectively. They also include the search for happiness and self-realization through apps that mediate contact with strangers, but also with certain kinds of strangers; and they even involve playful experimentations with the self as well as with the city, through engagement with 'secret cinemas' and 'authentic' underground clubs, all of course discoverable on social media. Urban humans also digitally remake the city when they assign and reassign roles to people and places on social media, making them desired or undesired and contributing at the same time to visual cultural economies where what's 'different' has high value. The city becomes an affective space, as digital mediations of the unfamiliar difference and diversity take place on the screen, but also on the street. With a smartphone at hand, one can see and feel the city's difference – with orientations of bodies and minds towards (or against) others (Ahmed 2007; Moores 2017) encountered on screens, at farmers' markets, or in protests.

As urban humans become acculturated to the pedagogy of urban coexistence with different actors, histories, and voices, digital orientations become both affective and tangible. But they are not teleological in their effects; encouraged by platform sociality as a way out of the already familiar and banal, digital orientations may open spaces of responsibility for others, but also spaces where the other can be merely consumed, which is not unlike what popular humanism often promotes through its celebratory but inconsequential embracement of difference.

The city is an agentive space, and this can be most powerfully, though not exclusively, understood when we approach it from its margins. Marginality makes the city in ways that are rarely recognized and often silenced. But those occupying the urban margins are the ones who most acutely endure an order that rarely recognizes them as rightful owners of the city – both in the established capitalist order, which socially and racially marginalizes many, and in its current digital incarnation, which promises recognition and voice only to the exceptionally digitally savvy and talented among the marginalized subjects. When we study the city looking from the margins inwards rather than the other way around, the digital order reveals itself to us in its violence, but also in its fragility. Speaking from, and living, the position of the Other involves suspicion, discontent, and dissent from the vision it carries. Suspicion comes as those at the racial and social margins are more likely to experience excessive surveillance and pressing inequalities, especially when these conditions are enhanced through data profiling and the sorting of certain people as less than human, an undesirable surplus – on account of their location, origin, or ill health and assumed unemployability, for example (see Eubanks 2018). Dissatisfaction with the digital promise of diversity, sustainability, and freedom comes from being constantly reminded that voices from the margins do not usually matter. This is 'a sound nobody wants to hear' (hooks 1989: 16). Estrangement from the mainstream vision of the city alienates many of those at the margin from the project of the digital order, especially those who cannot identify with the sleek, beautified, and commodified representations of urban difference. But estrangement also produces political agency (Scoville 2016). The margins, hooks reminds us, are not only a site of deprivation but also 'the site of radical possibility, a space of resistance' (hooks 1989: 20), a site where embodied and creative practices have historically given rise to struggles for the right to the city (Lefebvre 1991) and now for 'the right to the smart city' (Kitchin et al. 2019). We will see in Chapter 4 how agentive capabilities – 'reflexivity, interrogation, improvisation and transformation' (Simonsen 2013: 23) – are mobilized to contest digitally generated and enhanced violence towards social and racial marginality. We will particularly look at how witnessing, sociality, and voice from the margins contest the digital order by generating humanist discourses and practices that expose popular humanism's systemic incorporation of progressive values in order to affirm rather than contest the order of things (Foucault 1970).

In conclusion, demotic humanism, in its experiential, affective, and agentive performativities, reminds us that the meanings and consequences of order are played out in the ordinary, but this is done unevenly. While it is important to record ordinary voices and experiences, this is not enough. The inequalities and hierarchies of humanity, revamped as they are through the digital order, also call for normative, political, and ethical enquiries, most notably into whether and under what conditions individual and collective freedoms are surrendered or fostered in technologized cities. Can the revival and reconfiguration of humanism be more than an observation of hegemonic and demotic imaginaries and practices? Can humanism revive a politics of hope, as Mbembe and Posel (2005) suggest?

Against the digital order: Critical humanism

Popular humanism might have become an order of discourse (Foucault 1970) across many cities, that is, a normative cultural frame that legitimizes the digital order, but it does not preclude alternative imaginaries and actions. Popular humanism's depoliticized, or rather repoliticized, claims to technology as a force for the common human good may well promise progress *beyond* structural inequalities. However, experiences of deepening inequalities sealed in predictive AI and corroborative data technologies of class and racial stratification make these claims extraneous, if not harmful, especially for those at the urban margins. As argued briefly earlier and as will be discussed in more detail in Chapter 4, demotic humanism reminds us that the city has always been, and remains, an agonistic space of competing claims to rights and resources. In its contradictions, demotic humanism, as an assemblage of experiential, affective, and agentive claims to *being* and *becoming human* in the city, reveals the impossibility of a fully consensual order. Even if order is understood as 'the higher-dimensional "settlement" that enables a minimal level of stability' (Couldry and Hepp 2017: 191), it is an unstable construct during a period of multiple crises of neoliberalism such as we experience today.

My observations about competing humanisms in the city reveal the workings of power and consequently raise the following question: if popular humanism discursively normalizes order, if demotic humanism reveals its contradictory manifestations in urban life, what are the conceptual and ethico-political implications of these competing humanisms? Observing the workings of power is important, but it is not enough. Addressing the ethico-political challenges they present is as necessary as the conceptual untangling of the digital order. I engage with these challenges in this third and final part of the current chapter, which outlines critical humanism as an analytical, theoretical, and normative compass for the book. In the present section I prioritize the epistemological, conceptual, and methodological configurations of critical humanism. I return to its ethico-political implications – its normative outlook – more systematically in the last chapter, to raise questions and reflect on what we can learn from a critical humanist perspective about the kinds of cities and the kinds of life that contain, supress, and advance prospects for freedom and justice.

Critical humanism, introduced in this section, contests the containment of humans and humanist values in the order of the market, the nation, and their datafied racial and patriarchal hierarchies. Critical humanism is not a belief or conviction – that is, it does not represent or result from the elevation of an imagined unified Human (with capital 'H') to the status of a universal symbol of progress and morality, or of a form of life superior to others (Plummer 2021; Sartre 1961). Neither is it a discursive celebration of technologically generated freedom, equality, and sustainability, like popular humanism. It is not even a reflection of the messy and contradictory claims to resources and rights in the city, like demotic humanism. Critical humanism recognizes and critiques the subject conceived of as a singularity and enforced through the knowledge and violence of the classic European Enlightenment ideal of the 'universal human', as this 'human' is conceptualized on the one hand through a normative rational white masculinity and, on the other, as a fully formed and singular Other (Chernilo 2017; Fanon 2004; Mbembe 2021; Mhlambi 2020; Noonan 2012).

The humanism I propose here learns from critical scholarly enquiries into values and meanings associated with the human as much as from my own observations and from participants' stories of experiences in the city, of being and becoming, and of doing things together with others, human and non-human, and with respect to all forms of life – in other words, from those ordinary acts and voices that reveal everyday politics and an 'ethics of compassion, equity, relationality' (Mhlambi 2020: 7). Thinking through critical humanism is a necessary intellectual exercise, I argue, because research *without* or *after* the human neglects two important dimensions of digital urbanism: how (contingently recognized) humans make a comeback as a valuable symbolic resource for securing order during neoliberalism's multiple crises; but also how humans can, and sometimes do, mobilize creative capabilities to generate human and non-human assemblages of life and hope outside or against corporatized and controlled cities. These struggles around power, around controlling the city and its humanity, have important implications. 'What is at stake here is the human expectation of sovereignty over one's own life and authorship of one's own experience', writes Zuboff (2019: 521). The urgency is this, she continues: 'Let there be a digital future, but let it be a human future first' (522).

With Simonsen, I argue for a humanism that records and recognizes 'an interrogative orientation as integral to modes of both co-existence and critical intellectual engagement' (Simonsen 2013: 24) and for a critical and sometimes frail political and conceptual response that directly challenges the mobilization of rationalities and techniques of computational knowledge and AI towards selectively rehumanizing some urban humans while sealing the dehumanization of many more. In practice, this means adopting research perspectives that make us hear and see how humans construct a sense of self, of a collective self, and of responsibilities towards proximate and distant others, human and non-human, through – and sometimes in spite of – technologies of connectivity and computational knowledge production. These concerns come from my observations about the clashing ways of engaging or 'conscripting' humanist moralities that can now be seen in the digital order. This order, I noticed, selectively adjusts human freedoms and visions and incorporates them into new invisibilities of dehumanized humanities and into the hypervisibilities of a rehumanized but exclusive connected humanity.

In response to the observations and voices of the digital city, I refuse to dismiss humanism altogether, either as irrelevant or merely as a source of oppression. With Benjamin (2019b: 32), I contest technocentric and posthuman conceptions of digitization and endorse her powerful critique: 'posthumanist visions assume that we have all had the chance to be human'. In fact, being and becoming human remains an unresolved and incomplete affair, situated between the multimodality of mediated systems of power and intersubjective claims to the city's resources, rights, and freedom. Critical humanism provides a normative and heuristic frame for understanding the manifestations and consequences of being and becoming in the digital city.

While critical humanism has only recently become a distinct philosophical enquiry – as most notably seen in Plummer's (2021) *Critical Humanism: A Manifesto for the 21st Century*, in Mbembe and Posel's (2005) rhetorical provocation, and in the works of Chernilo (2017), Noonan (2012), and a few others – critical enquiries into the meanings of 'the human' and 'humanity' are not new. Effectively, questions about what it means to be and become human and why this matters have been asked for many centuries throughout the world. While the point of origin of humanism is often assumed to be the European Renaissance, humanist philosophies have been generated in different parts of the world. Ubuntu, often referred to as African humanism, promotes values of compassion and a relational humanity, in which being human is possible only through responsibility to others (Gordon 2014). Confucianism is considered by some as an East Asian humanism that speaks to our inner awareness of values as much as to a social ethics with responsibilities (Huang 2010). Historically, the Black humanism of W. E. B. Du Bois and Frederick Douglass emerged both from and in opposition to Eurocentric humanism, to contest the degrading of Black humanity and to demand universal access to rights and recognition for all. Such alternatives to the humanism of the Enlightenment have contested the claim that the human has developed along just one historical and cultural trajectory; and their contestations have become even more urgent in digital times. Specifically, with the advance of automation, networked communication, non-human intelligence, and algorithmic decision-making, critical questions of who the human is and why this matters have been re-energized. How much, if at all, do we need the human, in order to understand urban digital change? Two main critical approaches – posthumanism and critical data studies – have driven most of the responses to this question.

Posthumanism has influenced a substantial body of research on digital urbanism, especially through science and technology studies (STS). Posthumanism offers a systematic, though diverse critique of capitalist modernity and its selective recognition of certain voices and certain kinds of life that matter, unlike others (Latour 1993). It has tackled the violence that modernity's exclusionary and western-centric ideology has reproduced (Deleuze and Guattari 2013), especially by exalting a very specific idea of humanity into an exceptional and superior form of life. Specifically, scholars like Latour (1993), Braidotti (2013), and Haraway (1991) have questioned fundamental assumptions of humanism, such as humans' autonomy and their exclusive ability to create meaning on their own, outside relations and networks. These ideas are most influentially articulated in actor–network theory (ANT). Central to posthumanism is the notion that non-humans – especially networks, machines, and data, but also other living forms, such as animals (Haraway 1991) – have agency and the ability to create meanings with or beyond human action. Haraway's arguments on species coming together into new formations, most famously cyborgs, have challenged conceptions not only of human autonomy but also of the universality of one kind of human. 'We may really have become human no more', Whitehead and Wesch (2012: 6) claim, as they argue that growing possibilities of experiencing life online make it difficult to draw distinctions between human, bestial, and mechanical forms. Posthumanism's challenge to the unique 'Human' has also advanced radical responses to the patriarchal and Eurocentric assumptions of human superiority over non-human actors. Most influentially, Braidotti (2013), also drawing on Deleuze and Guattari (2013), has argued for an intersectional approach that recognizes the agency of actors that humanism has historically marginalized and silenced and the end of distinct borders between species, identities, and geographies.

Alongside posthumanism, critical data studies, through its concern with technological transformations and their consequences for power and life, has also influenced digital urbanism. But, unlike posthumanism, which is preoccupied with the meanings of the posthuman, the altered human, the antihuman, and the non-human, critical data studies has primarily focused on the exploitative capitalist transformations that come with Big Tech's power. 'Capitalism has turned to data as one way to maintain economic growth and vitality' Srnicek (2017: 6) argues, identifying (among other things) how cultures of connection have advanced extractivist economies of domination and violence by using human experience as raw material for profit (Zuboff 2019) and have effectively produced a new kind of colonialism: data colonialism, in the words of Couldry and Mejias (2019). The economy and architecture of platforms and data are at the heart of this critical trajectory, which discusses humanity primarily through experiences of exploitation produced and reproduced within platform and algorithmic order. Some critical data studies scholars have paid particular attention to the exacerbation of class, race, and gender inequalities (see Benjamin 2019a; Eubanks 2018), emphasizing how digital capitalism has enhanced patriarchal and Eurocentric ideologies through the reproduction of normative conceptions of class, gender, and race on platforms and networks that further marginalize those who already experience multiple forms of discrimination – especially the racialized minorities and the urban poor.

Interestingly, in both these approaches humans appear on the receiving side of digital change, even if in opposing ways. With a primary focus on the growing power of Big Tech and its aggressive colonization of everyday life, critical data studies often privileges debates on datafication's and platformization's domination *over* humans; it engages less systematically with humans as agents (including as participants and co-creators of research and new knowledge) or as ideological representations upon which the digital order relies. Since human voices and experiences appear inconsistently in this literature, human capabilities have also become marginalized as a subject of study: inevitably, they seem to

The Competing Humanisms of the Digital City 61

be largely absorbed by technology and its economies. On the other hand, posthumanism recognizes the symbolic value of the category of the 'Human' in reproducing order throughout Eurocentric, patriarchal, and colonial modernity, yet its preoccupation with histories of oppression in the name of a selective humanity sometimes ends up marginalizing the agentive capabilities of humans that in the past have defended rights, freedoms, and equitable futures for all forms of life – and continue to do so in the present. For posthumanists, who are captivated by the possibility of *a different kind* of (post)human emerging from and as a result of technological change, human capabilities for change become almost immobilized: they remain subjected to the powerful and transformative agency of the machine.

Yet challenging 'the death of the human' and humans' overpowering subjection to datafication is necessary, if we want to understand not only the technological footing of the digital order but also, importantly, the normative sociotechnical frames that legitimize it and the experiential grounding that both normalizes and contests it. Once again in history, (selective) humanity is being rallied to affirm an unequal urban and global order, but our fixation with the machine makes this mobilization difficult to see.

The moralization and politicization of the digital order requires a critical humanist perspective, not a posthumanist, data-driven analysis. Thus this book draws from, but also hopes to contribute to, debates developed through critical race, queer, and feminist theorizations of the human, through critical data studies on datafication's oppressive force (Benjamin 2019b; Couldry and Mejias 2019; Noble 2018), and through posthumanism's critique of the essential 'Human' (Braidotti 2013; Shaw 2018). The book requires a critical perspective on the digital city – a perspective that recognizes (1) the hegemonic popular humanism and its dangerous incorporation of humanist values into corporate and state projects that aim to contain rights and freedoms; (2) the contradictory nature of demotic humanism, in which humanist values are differentially played out, from hashtag sensibilities to digital literacies against exclusion; and (3) the potential of a radical and reconfigured humanism that defends life (human and non-human), dignity, freedom, and equality, as demonstrated for example in movements such as BLM, #MeToo, and Extinction Rebellion and as expressed in critical humanist literature and critical data studies.

Throughout the book I remain committed to understanding urban humans not as a stable, unitary category but as one relationally constituted through human and non-human assemblages (Qiu 2022), and as producers and products of changing racial, gendered, and class positionalities, rooted in and routed through the histories and trajectories of technologies and urbanisms that – partly (but increasingly) through computation – regulate AI and networks, access to resources, rights, and forms of recognition. Critical humanism offers epistemological, theoretical, and methodological possibilities of developing this approach. These I outline in what follows.

A critical humanist epistemology

Epistemologically, I understand humans' relational constitution through discourse and practice of cognitive and creative capabilities. These are capabilities sometimes recognized, sometimes manipulated, and sometimes dismissed in planning, imagining, and living the digital city. Humans are situated within systems of history and power (Chernilo 2017; Mhlambi 2020; Noonan 2012; Fanon 2004) and, in Hall's (1997: 232) words, they are 'a matter of "becoming" as well as "being"', belonging as much to the past as to the present. In Arendtian terms, they are constituted as pluralized subjects and at the same time as unique individuals, as members of collectivities, and as a species with shared abilities to engage in 'practices of freedom [that] prevent this subject' from ever being fully docile (Foucault 1970: 13; see Arendt 1958). This is an epistemological stand that recognizes that the making of the human is always political and always subjected to 'the realm of transpersonal values, mercenary, and mundane interests, and dominant ideologies' (Jackson

2013: 15), which now include interests and ideologies routed – but also constituted – through the digital economy (Couldry and Mejias 2019; Srnicek 2017).

Thus the epistemological perspective I subscribe to does not merely de-universalize a Eurocentric universalism of humanity by identifying both 'us' and 'them' as members of a common humanity (as liberal humanism does). Through the lens of the city, it deconstructs holistic categories of us–them, of people whose (digital) lives are worth attention or not. Such dualities are sealed in systems of knowledge production that, historically, have in the first place justified drawing boundaries between those seen as people who matter and those seen as people who don't. Critical humanism recognizes the many ways of being, becoming, and being denied being human – within as well as across the social and cultural systems associated with geographies and histories of class, race, gender, sexuality, and ability classifications that have themselves produced knowledge and subjects. Thus my call for recentring urban humanity in digital urbanism is a call for recognizing the *devolved human* against the universalizing Eurocentric and patriarchal figure of the 'Human' and against any bounded, pigeonholed, and stable conceptions of otherness. Within this framework, urban humans are always plural and the urban world is pluriversal (Escobar 2020), as much and as long as life on the material and digital urban streets contests delimited, commodified, and bounded digital promises of progress and diversity. A critical humanist epistemology recognizes ontological plurality (associated with human capabilities) and structural plurality (different histories and systems of structural exclusions); it is also open to observing and understanding humans' diverse engagement with technologized cities and, further, defends the right of urban humans to this pluriversality.

A critical humanist theory

Prioritizing the human does not represent a naïve claim of humancentrism, a revival of the dangers of anthropocentric arrogance, but is a call for the renewal of a humanism that understands the shifting but critical positions that subjects take or are expected to take as citizens and as consumers. A critical humanism, next to and partly in opposition to posthumanist and critical data studies scholarship, grounds any question about the future of the urban world in the structures that regulate the city and its gradually shifting but not entirely novel norms for connections, connectivities, and participations. None of these norms turns humans into a unique force, elevates them to the role of unchallenged owners of the city against other forms of life, or subordinates them fully to the corporate rules and algorithmic control of digitization. Instead, all these norms recognize urban humans as discursively and performatively constituted: circulated in media representations as subjects who emerge through the digital pedagogies of rational and individualized personhood, cultivated, normalized, and circulated widely on digital networks and platforms and through the mobile infrastructures of connectivity that 'carry the city' everywhere all the time, on smartphones and smart watches.

These digital pedagogies reflect the ideological marketplace of the Internet, which precariously combines neoliberal values with the post-neoliberal discontent they engender. In practice, this means that urban humans, rehumanized through social media performances and dehumanized through data profiling, acculturate themselves to networks and platforms that condition personhood to mediated and machine-driven rationalities and promote one kind of humanity only: a humanity constituted by individuals who deal with neoliberalism's deep crises not by contesting them but by seeking solutions in a post-neoliberal digital promise of better, more sustainable, and more diverse urban worlds. Against this conception of rational but seemingly humane societies, Mhlambi, alongside many postcolonial scholars (see also Escobar 2020: 7), speaks of a relational conception of humanity according to which self-making happens through an 'ethical maturity' that recognizes social duties and responsibilities towards others, who themselves challenge the mechanical rationality of digitization.

Finally, critical humanism opens conceptual spaces for a critical but normative theorization of the city: it recognizes humans' capabilities to use technologies for advancing freedom and social justice (Noonan 2012) and critiques the sociotechnical threats to justice when these demarcate the recognition of one kind of human alone – the subject who is or is becoming digitally savvy, the urban dweller and consumer who is progressive but settled within existing structures of inequality. A critical humanist response to the containment of humans within technologically mediated and controlled cities of unequal order challenges the analytical limits that privilege data, platforms, and their political economy as deterministic forces in the constitution of cities and people.

Against the prospect of a contingently recognized humanity, I subscribe to Escobar's (2020: 30) 'theoretico-political principles' of pluriversality, that is, of urban humans' right 'to weave multiple paths toward a world of many worlds, countering the power of the current model of a single globalized world and the capitalist hydra that anchors it'. Importantly, then, this perspective also allows us to understand and recognize what the digital order does not account for: disorder as dissent and disobedience or, put another way, the human capabilities for political agency and collective action. As will be discussed later in this book, the organic disorder of the city, the collective opposition to pressing inequalities and suspicion of surveillance technologies can never be fully contained and controlled (Mooney 2000; Sennett 1970). Thus, while the digital order is obscure and seductive, it remains unfinished and uncertain.

A critical humanist methodology

From a critical humanist perspective, we can indeed fully see how neither cities nor humans represent homogeneous, singular, or predetermined categories of analysis. Instead, when it comes to research design and practice, both need to be studied relationally, as shaped through the interconnection of people, places, and systems – technological and sociocultural.

I propose that methodological operationalizations of critical humanist epistemology and theory are best reflected in three methodological choices. First, through preference for multimethod approaches, we can best record and analyse how the human is constituted through discourse and practice in the context of governance and representation, but also in the context of everyday experience. This means that big data and algorithmic analyses are treated as reflexively and critically as any other data, in order to avoid conceiving of human activities as mere statistical patterns and generalizations about what technology and its economies *do to* people. Second, by seeking transurban and comparative approaches to digital cities, we develop a research outlook that decentres and pluralizes the city as a complex and contradictory space of technology, power, and life. This approach contests technocentric and normative western models of analysis that approach cities as laboratories for Big Tech. As the digital order is conceived of, operationalized, and contested differently across the world but also within different quarters of the same city, the calls for dewesternizing knowledge are yet more important and our assumptions about who, where, and how to engage with the actors of change are part of this interrogation. Third, through commitment to a reflexive and participatory ethical research practice, we need to challenge the boundaries of Eurocentric methodological imagination and to commit to an ethics of engagement rather than mere reproduction of established frames that speak for and on behalf of people and places we already know. Thus we need to expand the methods of research practice, not least through co-creative and participatory approaches that engage with the city's many and different actors – those in the centre and those in the margin, those who occupy different locations in the intertwined transurban geographies of the global North and the global South, those given visibility (and thus recognized as humans) and those silenced (and thus made invisible as worthy humans). When we carry out research on digital change, we need to reflect on the habitual reproduction of privilege by primarily engaging with recognizable and digitally literate subjects – those more likely to enjoy class, gender, and racial order privileges. We need to move beyond the norms of familiar practice that often stereotype or silence those at the margins either by representing migrants, refugees, working-class, and minoritized groups more generally as fully disempowered or by paying attention only to the exceptionally successful individuals, selectively recognizing their attempts to subvert power, for instance as hackers or influencers.

By referring to a critical humanist methodology, I want to highlight particular sensibilities in the study of digital change through the human: not the pre-existing and familiar subject or research, but the subject being and becoming in the digital city. Together with Ingvarsson (2020) and Alinejad et al. (2018), I contest research practice that focuses merely on digital objects, networks, and systems, because digitization matters both infrastructurally and as it takes its meanings discursively and performatively within specific historical and cultural contexts. In line with this methodological orientation, the book draws on a three-dimensional approach to research, as applied in studies conducted over the period of seven years (2015–22) across transurban settings. In particular, it draws first on a multimethod methodological approach to the digital city that covers (1) a discourse analysis of media texts, policy, corporate documentation, social media narratives, and strategic communication from across eight cities that identify as digital cities, even if this label is differentially understood among them; (2) interviews (semi-structured, unstructured, and group) taken within the broader frame of ethnographic research, conducted with more than 100 urban humans across these eight cities; and (3) co-creative and participatory methods, including asset mapping and digital storytelling, deployed in online and face-to-face environments where urban humans co-led the production of narratives on the digital city. Second, the research behind the book adopted a transurban and cross-border comparative approach, with primary empirical research across eight cities (Athens, Berlin, London, Los Angeles, New York, Seoul, Songdo, and Havana) and a systematic qualitative analysis of documents on planning and applications of 'smartcitization' across all continents. This transurban approach, which examines the discourse and practice of the digital city in different parts of the world, challenges assumptions about a stable and bounded global North that leads and a distantly situated global South that follows in digital change (Punathambekar and Mohan 2019); instead the book speaks to the networked but asymmetrical transurban geographies of digital urbanism. Third, as is reflected by the book's analytical lens, the research behind it is committed to the integration of human experiences and voices from the centre but also from the margins of the city; it aims to go beyond the presumed top-down construction of technologized cities that privilege the agency of the machine, of technologists, and corporate and state actors. In practice, the methodological choices of the project of engaging systematically with urban humans promote welcoming open-ended creative and participant-led approaches sensitive to the voices of urban actors, who were invited to speak to their own conceptions of digital assets and obstacles to good, open, and safe cities.

Adopting this approach, I aligned with the methodological approaches of critical postcolonial, feminist, and cultural studies (Datta 2020; Degen and Rose 2022; Komarraju et al. 2021; Simonsen 2013): all are driven by an imagination and an ethics of research that recentre the human as a category of analysis but devolve it as a concept, especially by paying attention to the plurality of human engagements with the symbolic and the material culture (Law and Singleton 2013) and with technologies' materially situated and imagined affordances (Komarraju et al. 2021). This ambition and this ethical commitment do not resolve inequalities in conducting research but show how important it is to be aware of them and confront them, when possible, through research praxis.

Critical humanist methodologies thus recognize that co-creative, participatory, and transnational methodologies do not represent pure and fully equalitarian approaches, as they themselves involve power relations and conceptions of knowledge production rooted in academic authority and in western ways of knowing (Signona 2016). Yet, as they aim to reflexively engage with urban humans, these methodological approaches become more accountable to them. The more humans are recognized as co-creators of knowledge, the more they become engaged in questioning predetermined interpretations of urban digital life and the more likely they are to challenge the reduction of life and agency to statistics and algorithms.

Engaging with these epistemological, theoretical, and methodological principles, I delve into an empirically informed and inductively produced analysis of the digital order. In the next three chapters I discuss, analyse, and reflect on the workings and ideologies of popular humanism, demotic humanism, and critical humanism.

3
Popular Humanism
The Sociotechnical Imaginaries of the Digital Order

A digital cities index, developed by Economist Impact in 2022, identifies four key pillars – 'digital connectivity, services, culture and sustainability in order to assess the extent and impact of digitisation in 30 global cities' (Economist Impact 2022). The report refers to a 'suite of "frontier capabilities", including AI, 5G connectivity, and other innovations as necessary to 'make cities smarter, safer, cleaner and more inclusive' (ibid.). And, in building the narrative of successful digital cities, *The Economist*'s research and policy branch, Economist Impact, emphasizes that these capabilities need to move beyond the 'top-down and technology-driven' model of smart cities; instead, cities need to bring humans to the heart of their project – 'engage citizens and stakeholders from design to delivery'. Digital cities, we are now told, need their humans.

This chapter starts unscrambling the digital order's concerted blocks. The first stop is popular humanism and its discursive normalization of the digital order. Through an empirical exploration of popular humanist discourse, the chapter will show how the digital order's workings become opaque and dominant frames for imagining urban digital futures. Specifically, by studying corporate, media, and governmental discursive constructions of digital cities across the world, this chapter reveals the shift towards a promise of rehumanizing urbanism through technological innovations and infrastructural expansions. In different but assertive ways, these discursive constructs, it will be shown, reimagine digital cities not as technological projects but as ethical projects that promote – or should promote – progressive, inclusive, and open urban societies. The technocentric and technocratic vision of controlled, corporatized smart cities, we are now told, is a thing of the past.

I deliberately start this empirical exploration from discourse rather than infrastructures, so as to illustrate how digital cities have become a canon for imagining urban, but also more broadly human futures. From billboards to policy bills and from mass media imagery to social media influencers' narrations of the urban self, we repeatedly notice an assertive exercise of power through the reproduction of the discourse of digital progress as a normative one. As the many empirical examples that follow will illustrate, the human-centric discourse of popular humanism establishes a system of knowing what is right for the city and its people – an order of discourse (Foucault 1970). In Foucault's terms, this discourse is 'controlled, selected, organised and redistributed by a certain number of procedures whose role is to ward off its powers and dangers' (1970: 52). In our case, we will see how hegemonic discourse embellishes the digital order and excludes the possibilities of imagining and living the city outside this order.

Popular humanism's discourse that assertively promotes digital pathways to urban and human betterment has become a hegemonic force of transurban appeal, shaping sociotechnical imaginaries across established, new, and aspiring digital cities. In its differential and unequal expressions, we will see how popular humanism reconfigures sociotechnical imaginaries away from technocentric, technocratic, neoliberal versions of digital urbanism and reorients them instead towards imaginings of technologically mediated open, diverse, and sustainable cities. Such powerful discourse for reimagining digital cities is the spine of popular humanism

– an instrument through which the digital order is legitimized and normalized. The adoption and adaptation of progressive values in hegemonic discourse, a phenomenon that the empirical evidence adduced in this chapter will exemplify, reflects the urgency with which the elites try to sustain order and to control the many crises of the now mistrusted neoliberalism.

At the heart of this chapter, then, is the discursive hegemony of popular humanism that displaces old imaginaries of the racial, patriarchal, and Eurocentric neoliberalism and revamps them as new, progressive responses to humanity's pressing problems. This is more than an urban affair, of course. The shift in urban sociotechnical imaginaries reveals a key struggle of our times: the struggle between the city and the nation. At the level of the nation, as many current examples from around the world show, we see how authoritarian governments and hostile 'anti-woke' and anti-antiracist mobilizations (Cammaerts 2021; Meadway 2020; Titley 2020) project a regressive post-neoliberalism. At the level of the city, another post-neoliberal trajectory seems to become discursively powerful (though it is not unchallenged by right-wing populism): we find, on the urban street, political claims to social, racial, gender, and environmental justice that cannot be ignored by the cities' media or by policy and corporate actors. As the *dēmos* calls for fundamental changes in a social order of inequalities that are unsustainable and often catastrophic to many communities and the environment, the elites seem to respond with technological solutions. Thus we will see how imaginaries of technology have become mediators of instability and diffusers of eminent threats to social order. As the existing mechanisms of social order – institutions such as the police, the government, and corporations – come to be mistrusted, imaginaries of the digital order offer a fresh, seemingly democratic alternative to injustice and inequality. Discourses of the always promising progressive technology appear as a post-neoliberal alternative to the ideological bankruptcy of neoliberalism. The question, of course, remains: how much is the neoliberal order shaken and how much do these discourses mutate rather than challenge 'previous forms of liberalism and neoliberalism' (Davies and Gane 2021: 10)?

The paradoxical systemic promise – which is at the heart of this chapter – of a digital rehumanization of dehumanizing, unequal cities needs to be understood in the context of wider struggles for urban and human futures. As I argue here, it is the symbolic power of technology rather than its fundamentally transformative potential for urban life that explains its puzzling but rising appeal. The technodeterministic promise of a digital transformation has already collapsed as a normative frame. Across the world, a first and a second generation of smart cities have already shuttered the pledge of urban optimization through datafied services and predictive automation. The first-generation smart city of Songdo in Korea has attracted more attention on account of failing to become a vibrant destination for people – and also for capital – than on account of being 'smart' (Lara et al. 2016). The Google-led Quayside Toronto came into disrepute because of its corporate unaccountability, which prompted the discredited withdrawal of Google's subsidiary, Sidewalk Labs, from the project (Jacobs 2022). And New York's Hudson Yards, for all its promise to use data to predict and respond to human needs, has become no more than a luxury destination and a vanity project for the super-rich. These examples are only the tip of the iceberg in a series of uneven successes and many failures in the technological transformation of cities – what some call the 'techlash' (Weiss-Blat 2021) and the end of the 'tech arms race' (McLean, Rachal, and Zukowski 2021).

Yet, paradoxically, the project of the digital city as a better city remains a favourite brainchild among corporate, media, and state actors, against other models for making cities more profitable, or even more sustainable and equitable. How does this paradox remain justifiable? The states' and the corporations' determination to invest and promote fully networked cities and integrated urban AI systems is unshaken, with smart city projects being expected to reach a market value of

US$1.03 trillion by 2028 (Polaris 2021). This ongoing faith in cities' technological transformation cannot be explained by looking at it under a technocratic or political economic lens alone. As we will see, the digital city is now in fact a core but reconfigured project when it comes to mustering the collective imagination for the twenty-first-century city. And popular humanism has become the discursive vehicle for what it seemingly represents.

The rising force of popular humanist imaginaries

Popular humanist discourse is now a fundamental symbolic resource for framing urban sociotechnical imaginaries, even if in contradictory ways, as we will see shortly. Sociotechnical imaginaries are often understood as the 'collectively held, institutionally stabilized, and publicly performed visions of desirable futures, animated by shared understandings of forms of social life and social order attainable through, and supportive of, advances in science and technology' (Jasanoff 2015: 4). In Chapter 4 we will see how publics – urban humans – perform or reject those visions. Here we focus more closely on their production from the top of urban hierarchies. We examine the widely shared stories that now shape what it is that makes the allegedly desired and optimal city rest on promises of digital infrastructures that democratize public services, of data that enhance equitable access to education and health, and of networks that safeguard well-being and public safety. These stories come to replace the unpersuasive and discredited neoliberal discourses of the city dominated by the figure of the entrepreneurial individual (usually white, male, middle-class) and by the thriving market. For decades of aggressive neoliberalism, discourses of growth, wealth, exploitation of natural resources, and normative whiteness have been promoted via media, corporate, and governmental campaigns, framing imaginaries of what the modern, smart, and successful city looks like. Yet the 2008 financial collapse, the rise of populist governments, the growing suspicion of

Big Tech's enormous and exploitative power, and the consequent urban and transurban protest movements have shaken both the existing economic order and its symbolic viability. This is precisely the context of systemic crises in which popular humanism emerges. The imaginaries of the city are now revamped; against crisis, the city becomes a space of possibility and hope.

Urban imaginaries, of course, have been mediated throughout modernity (Bender and Cinar 2007; McQuire 2008). Cinema and the mass media have played a key role in constructing images and ideas of desired and feared cities. Now the mediation of urban imaginaries is no longer fully contained in the representational space of cinematic and televisual screens and print media. Instead, it expands across the diversified spaces of mass media and social media, the converged spaces of advertising and policy campaigns, and the association of numerous and diverse institutional and non-institutional actors with the production and circulation of visual and textual representations of the city. From news makers to social media influencers and from policy documents to TikTok videos produced by corporate, state, and individual actors alike, the notion of urban subjects who live, love, work, and consume through their smartphones, computers, and haptic devices has now become a staple of the process of imagining cities. Consequently I argue, following Taylor (2004), that the constant circulation of discourse that normalizes and idealizes technologized urban life plays a key role in advancing social consensus around what is deemed appropriate, desired, and also just for society. Urban imaginaries are thus constituted within systems of knowledge that make the ethical value and use of technology hypervisible and its political and economic dangers invisible. These systems of knowledge become hegemonic, yet not uncontested, as we will see in Chapter 4.

This chapter moves on to illustrate, through its three main empirical sections, how discourses of popular humanism become hegemonic – an order of discourse (Foucault 1970) that dominates urban sociotechnical imaginaries. As will be shown here, popular humanism is constituted through specific social significations of discourse (Taylor 2004), in three ways: first, through the discursive intertwinement of innovation, humane cities, and the market, as it emerges in corporate and media imaginaries; second, through the mobilization of the language of rights and diversity in order to justify what seems to be digital pathways to their achievement, as revealed in urban, transurban, and transnational institutions' strategic communication; and, third, through state, corporate, and media constructions of specific imaginings of urban humans – humans who accept the digital order as appropriate, natural, and just (Boltanski and Chiapello 2005; Castoriadis 1987). It is precisely this entanglement of digital change with a reconfigured, consenting humanity that affirms the digital order and frames what rehumanized cities are and how this rehumanization is, inevitably, technologically mediated.

Empirically, the discussion that follows analyses the workings of the digital order, as these are discursively generated by its powerful institutional actors – corporations, media, urban and transurban–transnational government. It analyses media headlines and shiny brochures, as well as regeneration plans and strategic corporate and state communication within and across cities. On the basis of this broad analysis, I take the intended audiences of this vision to include government and corporate actors but also urban humans. This vision actually reveals how those in power strategically use communication to turn corporate and governmental plans into collective imaginaries.

Initiating the book's analysis from the top of urban hierarchies is deliberate. It reveals how power structures are embedded and reproduced through spatial and historical trajectories of urban order, even when this order discursively appears as horizontally organized through networks and platforms with opaque hierarchical structures. In the following three sections we will see how the frames of a digital order that benefits people, cities, and the environment are discursively constituted, first by the media and by corporate strategic communication and then by state actors;

then we will finally move to the discursive constitution of an imagined urban humanity produced by all these actors.

Mediating imaginaries of humancentric digital urbanism: Media and corporate discourses

'Delete Technology, Add Humans', reads a line in a 2019 article in the influential business-oriented *Forbes* magazine – a publication of appeal and authority among transnational corporate elites (Ladouceur 2019). The author of the article announces there the end of the smart city; the smart city, he argues, is now replaced by 'the new normal' of the digital city, which is more interested in people; and this contrasts with earlier preoccupations with 'smartness'. And Ladouceur goes on to argue that AI-based digital cities work when they invisibly enhance quality of life. This discursive signification of a reimagined order is quite precise in its conception and definition. The digital city, we read, is 'built with a focus on the citizen, small business, enterprise and consumers, everyone wins'. By recognizing a range of urban actors while ignoring others through the generic reference to 'everyone', the author articulates a contradictory post-neoliberal amalgam of imaginings of the digital city: on the one hand, as a good city that is entrepreneurial and business-led; on the other, as a city driven by (certain) urban humans' interests and desires – especially those who are part of the urban entrepreneurial ecology.

While Ladouceur (2019) draws out the vision of the digital city, another impressive example reflects the promised realization of that vision. This is the case of Toronto's waterfront regeneration in the post-Google era. After the collapse of a partnership between the city and Google that was destined to build a fully networked (and largely datafied) waterfront city within the city, the relationship between city, technology, and humanity was fully reimagined by those who are now in charge. Yung Wu, CEO of MaRS, the largest innovation hub in North America, and now one of the key figures in Toronto's waterfront project, says: 'What is the vision that inspires people to want to live here, to work here, to raise their families and children and grandchildren here? What is it that inspires that? It's not a smart city. It's a city that's smart' (Jacobs 2022).

These words capture and dismiss the discredited conception of the smart city as a technocentric and technocratic project. The rejection of the smart city model, however, does not dismiss the core role of technology in producing seemingly better cities. On the contrary, technology is still at the heart of Toronto's waterfront's regeneration. This is confirmed for example by Wu's leading role. So technology is not downgraded; technocentrism is, since now we are told that better cities are technologized cities, where 'families and children and grandchildren' feel they belong.

The case of Waterfront Toronto is particularly interesting if we wish to understand the reimaginings of digital cities through the human. This is not only because it empirically proves how digital urbanism led by Big Tech is now discredited, but also because it vividly illustrates the significant synergies that support similar projects. For example, we see how the media 'learn' from this case to construct their own revamped imaginaries of digital cities. In an article published in the *Guardian* and titled 'Toronto swaps Google-backed, not-so-smart plans for people-centred vision', Leyland Cecco (2021) has praised Toronto's shift away from the Sidewalk Labs-planned smart city. Suspicion of Big Tech's conception and realization of digital cities is now anything but uncommon in the media. Even more assertively than Cecco, an anonymous author in the conservative British newspaper the *Telegraph* expands on the urgency of rethinking technodeterministic urbanism in an article headlined 'Of the people, by the people, for the people'. In the subheading we are told what technologized cities should be about – not about technology but about people: 'Smart cities don't have to be urban vanity projects, but instead they should focus on putting people's needs at the forefront' (*Telegraph* 2019). The convergence of media frames from the left and from the right is revealing of the circulation of popular humanist narratives of the digital city: there seems to be an ideological consensus around reaffirmed faith that technological innovation is by definition good for cities, yet this innovation needs now to be subjected to a new morality.

Reimagining how digital cities work through technology – and thus how they become ordered sites of life and economy – unfolds across all different kinds of media. Most visibly, the redefinition of cities that work best digitally is laid out in more detail in social media and digital business media. While reimagining digital cities in niche media spaces may often escape the attention of wider publics, corporate narratives influence policy and business imaginaries, and often in substantial ways. For example, the business information hub Smart Cities Dive (smartcitiesdive.com), a branch of an online corporate news portal, Industry Dive, vividly illustrates the reimagining of technologized cities as progressive projects. 'How cities have stepped back from a "tech arms race"' (McLean, Rachal, and Zukowski 2021), reads the title of an article. The article discusses conceptions of technologized cities and their aims through the words of local authority actors interviewed all over the United States. Most interviewees eagerly distance themselves from established conceptions of the smart city, which, as they are repeatedly quoted saying, ignored citizens and instead privileged corporations and flashy technologies. One interviewee, Kevin Martin, Portland's Smart City PDX manager, is quoted saying that smart cities 'focused on technology that was oversold and that communities weren't asking for'. The article recognizes the shift towards the digital city as a model developed around 'unsexy' technologies that nevertheless promote citizen-centred systems with an 'equity perspective', inclusion, and accountability in mind. Jeanne Holm, Deputy Mayor of Budget and Innovation for the city of Los Angeles, speaks along similar lines: 'The pandemic changed the way Los Angeles provisioned its services and heightened its focus towards equity, especially surrounding issues of Internet access and connectivity and digital literacy.' Protecting personal data and rebuilding trust are values fundamental to new smart city visions, as the article emphasizes throughout. This imaginary is confirmed by Martin's additional reflections: 'Digital justice demands more transparency, accountability, and access to resources, literacy, information and decision-making in technology and information.'

Issues of mistrust and privacy concerns among citizens seem equally impossible to ignore in contemporary efforts to plan digital cities. Policy actors like those quoted in the Smart Cities Dive article (McLean et al. 2021) clearly feel the pressures from civil society and citizens to recognize the voices and the agency of urban humans as they shape their digital strategies. The humans who now appear to be central to official discourse are, of course, those assumed to want technology and to place it at the core of their lives and cities, those imagined to benefit from 'technology for good'.

Similar shifts on narrations of optimal digital cities appear across the corporate sector – a fine balance between profitable, ordered, and humane cities. A business publication article on the digital marketing Propmodo digital hub bears the title 'How privacy concerns can derail a smart city' (Pipitone 2021). The article reviews plans for the construction of National Landing, a new smart city promised in Arlington County, Virginia, as a project designed to accompany the vast development of Amazon's new headquarters in that region. National Landing is planned as a city built from scratch, through investment, by major corporate actors, especially Amazon, AT&T, and JBG Smith, but also by state actors. The article contextualizes this still new utopian city, which is 'fully smart' but could have the same fate as other projects, now failed – not least the Google-led Quayside in Toronto. Voicing scepticism about the intention to reproduce a vision – now discredited – of cities built 'from the Internet up', as a Google executive once described the Toronto project, Pipitone (2021) quotes an Amnesty International 2019 report according to which the 'introduction of fully integrated, data-centered technologies in city infrastructures and management presents serious threats to human rights'. It is indeed interesting to witness the incorporation of an oppositional discourse against surveilled and datafied cities into some of the corporate narratives and market-led imaginaries of digital cities. Propmodo, which represents real estate (or realtor) interests, is one of the many business-led projects that raise concerns about privacy. Against the background of digitally controlled cities, we see how public mistrust of the tech industry is widening. This discourse, incorporated into but seemingy oppositional to surveilled and datafied cities, emerges as some corporations are increasingly concerned that their own interests are threatened by the aggressive promotion of an outdated vision of technologized cities. Propmodo, for example, speaks of the importance of prioritizing humans – presumably the humans whom realtors depend upon for their trade. Landmark cases such as Google's loss of profits in Toronto, or many corporations' failed investments in Songdo, have alerted a wider corporate sector to the risks of privileging technological innovation at any cost. As Pipitone's concluding remarks show, scepticism of a model that has already failed elsewhere is spreading: 'All the connectivity and amazing uses of technology in National Landing won't matter much if residents there find it intrusive' (ibid.).

The reconfigured conceptions of an order that is desirable and believable on account of its potential to succeed show that the neoliberal aggression of profit-driven technologization is not sustainable any more. The corporate sector behind the project of smartcitization seems aware of the need to reinvent itself. For example Dell, a major corporate player leading infrastructural change in the urban governance of many cities across the world, assertively sets the tone of its popular humanist discourse. Targeting primarily large organizations and local government, Dell (2018) presents infrastructural products in its publicity (which includes strategic communication campaigns, not just advertisements). These products include cloud solutions and applications for governance and security that promise 'optimized, data analytics-driven, people-centric solutions to the digital cities of tomorrow'. The imaginary of 'people-centrism', 'sustainability', 'social responsibility', and also 'tremendous economic value by improving the efficiency of citizenship services and fostering entrepreneurship' is unfolding across Dell's promotional material, as in so many other corporate actors' strategic communication. In fact the framing of this tech company's offerings could not capture more powerfully the narrative components of the digital order. These narratives speak more and more of collective rights and responsibilities in cities, offering people what they need – inclusion, sustainability, openness – but, of course, they promise to do so through more of their products and innovations that are pushed as essential for urban governance.

Such corporate-led imaginaries are also adopted by cross-sector alliances that amplify their appeal through collaborative and lobbying initiatives, perhaps in an attempt to sustain their fragile appeal to city governments that are growing more cautious about their digital investments. For example, City Possible™, a network of corporate, urban, and academic actors 'pioneered by Mastercard', promotes in its discourse these same humanist values when explaining its agenda: 'City Possible™ is a new model for urban innovation in which a global network of cities, businesses, academics and communities work together to make the world's cities more inclusive and sustainable', and 'City Possible™ aims to build a path towards a sustainable urban future focused on the needs and dreams of people'. (City Possible 2021). It is striking how corporate networks like this one (which even add the trademark symbol ™ to their name) absorb the discourse of progressive urbanism into their clearly commercial interests. Just by itself, that discursive articulation of what these corporations claim to represent is a stark reminder of how the city becomes a troubled site – a site where the neoliberal advance and its order are anything but taken for granted.

Importantly, the articulation of a humanist digital order into corporate discourse is not limited to cities of the global North. In fact popular humanism circulates on networks that link corporations' headquarters (and their interests) in cities of the global North with hubs in different places that aspire to become technologized transcontinental cities. Innovation is projected as the prime force of rehumanization and democratization in postcolonial cities from Delhi to Kigali, as part of a discourse through which transnational corporations aim to displace systemic inequalities and colonial power. This discourse spills beyond Big Tech's promotion of digital change, across a range of transnational corporate actors that have pushed digital innovation in the name of development and progress. Often focused on the tech industry alone, scholarship has paid less attention to other corporate players with high stakes in the project of transurban digital transformation. The giant consultancy firm McKinsey & Company, for example, may well have its headquarters in London, but it sets the agenda for digital urbanism across continents. 'Imagining the cities of the future' is how it headlines its projects in this area (McKinsey & Company 2018b), promoting 'digital solutions for a liveable future' (McKinsey & Company 2019).

McKinsey & Company is involved in numerous multimillion digital city projects around the world. Through its synergies and influence on governments and international organizations and its incorporation of discourses on the regional development of autonomous and prosperous cities, it aggressively pushes the vision of smart city orthodoxy across the global South. Like other transnational corporations, McKinsey & Company – along with its own branches, for instance the McKinsey Global Institute – promotes digital responses against threats to humanity. 'Leaders must tackle increasingly complex economic, social, and environmental challenges to ensure cities stay competitive. Harnessing new technologies can help', reads a report that proposes measures to revive digitally post-pandemic cities (McKinsey & Company 2021). In its report on South Asian smart cities, McKinsey & Company proposes digital solutions to most problems of urban humanity, fully decontextualizing technological innovations from structural inequalities and making its promise of transformation attractive to corporate and state actors. '[S]mart cities could have a substantial impact' across South Asia, the report claims:

> Smart solutions could: eliminate up to some 270,000 kilotons of greenhouse-gas emissions annually. Some 5,000 lives lost each year to traffic accidents, fires, and homicides could be saved through mobility solutions, crime prevention, and better emergency response. Intelligent traffic and transit solutions could save up to eight million man-years in annual commuting time. Deploying smart healthcare solutions for the urban population could reduce the region's disease burden by 12 million disability-adjusted life years. (McKinsey & Company 2018a)

As the likes of McKinsey & Company establish the credibility of the idea that the digital order is a success story – and they often do so in collaboration with governments that promote their own agendas through such initiatives, like the Modi government in India – projects that promise to improve lives, save the environment, and tackle poverty have become a new staple of national and regional development. For major western corporations, of course, such projects become lucrative opportunities to sell strategies and digital infrastructures across the world. The vision of better cities is packaged, resold, and adapted to the different spatio-political frames of digital urbanism.

Baraka (2021) identifies the problem with the selective humanist promises of the digital order: 'Eko Atlantic City in Nigeria, HOPE City in Ghana, an Ethiopian city styled as the "real Wakanda" after the film *Black Panther*, Kigali Innovation City in Rwanda, and Senegal's Akon City – all promis[e] to solve the problems of poverty and economic stagnation in their respective countries through innovative tech.' The delivery of the many promises of digital cities is of course yet to come, and projects such as Konza Technopolis in Kenya already move into decline before they are even completed. With vast public investment and private profiteering already in place, Konza's promise – 'to develop a sustainable smart city and an innovation ecosystem, contributing to Kenya's knowledge-based economy' (Konza Technopolis Development Authority 2021) – remains incomplete and doubtful as to its realization. While most of the other projects mentioned here are still in the early stages of development, their promise to deliver better cities and sustainable urban lives remains fragile – perhaps a promise destined to be fulfilled only in their glossy brochures. Realizable or not, what these projects achieve is the transnationalization of a discourse that mainstreams the co-dependence of technological transformation and conceptions of democracy, equity, and freedom, while it further distances those values from discourses of colonialism, exploitation, and borders.

From growth to rights and diversity: Policy imaginaries for the digital city

The progressive language of a human-led digital urbanism converges not only in corporate and media discourse but also in the agendas for technological urban change, as set out by urban, transurban, and transnational state actors. In fact we now see systematic, determined, and strategically planned (trans)urban policies that call for an urgent reorientation of the digital vision in order to tackle pressing social and environmental problems. Assertively, UNESCO and Netexplo Observatory (2019: 20) directly target dehumanized cities by speaking of 'a *global utopia*, supported by a combination of three strong feelings: disgust with unliveable megacities, humanist idealism, and gaining markets'. UNESCO expands the progressive vision of the functioning and ordered cities, which it understands as being about technological solutions 'with humanist ideals ... to promote socio-economic development while enhancing quality of life ... their "smartness" must adopt a humanistic approach and leave no one behind' (UNESCO 2019). The reference to humanist values here is direct and uninhibited. Alongside the adoption of humanist discourses in the communication of digital strategies, we also witness an advance in the language of rights. 'Building people-centered smart cities from the ground up' is how UN Habitat frames its digital strategy, explaining that this strategy is realized through a 'rights-preserving approach to digital technologies for inclusion and sustainable urban development' (UN Habitat 2020).

Popular humanist ideals are anything but hidden in these examples. Popular humanism is clearly expressed here as UN Habitat and UNESCO promote converging visions of urbanism across centres of power, corporate and state alike, and geographies of a shared humanity. This significant shift in the centre of gravity of the hegemonic discourse of the digital order is most apparent in a UNESCO-sponsored book tellingly titled *A Journey through Smart Cities: Between Datapolis and Participolis* (Pisani 2015). The book counterposed its humanism ('participolis') with the corporate limited understanding of 'the inherent complexity of human settlements … the fact that the most powerful urban movements play out in somewhat informal spaces that are more often difficult to classify'. The author emphasizes that 'a major [corporate] tendency [is] to ignore the involvement of citizens when designing the spaces in which they live and work' (131). What is consequently proposed is a reconciliation of corporate and democratic visions of the city through 'participolis' – 'the city in which citizens participate in the design and management of the space in which they live' (132). Pisani concludes by identifying the tension of the digital order:

> But we can't just rely on the data (the dominant trend today). The other key dimension of ICT is that it allows horizontal communication, and therefore participation or even collaboration. The big companies promoting smart cities are putting their money on the first aspect. We need to push the second. (Pisani 2015: 129)

While UNESCO has historically challenged western corporate hegemony, its current critique of surveillant and unequal capitalism has become less exceptional within transnational governance, for example by comparison with older UNESCO campaigns against media imperialism that stood out against the dominant conservativism of international governance institutions.

Transnational governance itself is now diversifying; a whole range of players beyond the nation-state claim a stake in the debate for urban futures. Among them is the corporate-driven City Possible™ introduced earlier, but also new formations of progressive governance. These various urban and transurban players show an ethical commitment to promoting 'digital inclusion'. Agendas with digital inclusion on the list are on the rise; they tend to be the most prominent social policy agendas that progressive city governments promote. The Smart Cities World (2021), a network that brings together city authorities from all over the world, describes its priorities as building 'stronger communities', 'creating opportunities for all', and tackling social exclusion through digital inclusivity training programmes. The concept of a technology that responds to human needs is at the heart of its vision.

These contradictions become most apparent if we zoom in from the transurban to the urban level. Urban governments' discursive attempt to balance neoliberal economics and post-neoliberal mistrust of the market is expressed in their situated embrace of popular humanism. For example, Berlin's plan for infrastructural transformation promises innovations related to 'benefiting citizens, climate protection, resource conservation and sustainability' – a plan that the strategy Smart City Berlin ties to 'international competitiveness ... climate neutrality of Berlin by 2050, and creating a pilot market for innovative applications' (quotations from http://okosvaros.lechnerkozpont.hu/en/node/494; see also Berlin Partner 2020). As in Berlin, in many other cities, too, progressive local governments that are now associated with the rise of municipalism (Janoschka and Mota 2021; Russell 2019) centre their digital strategies on tackling urban problems such as inequality, segregation, and pollution, while they still avoid challenging systematically the power of corporate actors. This contradiction is also visible in London's digital strategy Smarter London Together. The strategy critiques previous models of smart cities that were 'integrating new digital technologies, without understanding citizens' needs first' (Mayor of London 2021a) and, beside 'smartness', prioritizes 'togetherness' in diversity (Mayor of London 2021b).

London's digital strategy (Mayor of London 2021b), not unlike New York's (New York City Office of Technology & Innovation 2022) and Amsterdam's (Amsterdam Smart City 2021), projects technologies as social equalizers – technologies that bring together government, citizens, and start-ups, in entrepreneurial projects of innovation that support better cities. The assumed connection between the different actors is mediated through the language of entrepreneurship. In Smarter London Together, for example, the principle of 'respecting diversity' comes as an ethical commitment: 'human rights principles should be incorporated by design into digital platforms which serve our city' (Mayor of London 2021c). This ethics combines with a declared commitment to the market, as well as with a call to the market to join the vision. In addressing the corporate sector, the strategy calls for 'user-designed services ... free from bias ... understanding how your users think, how they behave and ultimately what they need' (Mayor of London 2018a). These narratives combine digital solutionism – in fact they regularly use the concept of technological and technical 'solutions' (e.g. in all the examples mentioned here) – with a continuing commitment to a market economy and a governmental pledge to advance equitable and diverse cities. In the assumption that the two are compatible we find a truly post-neoliberal vision – one that does not abandon the market's priorities, but rehumanizes them.

The concept of togetherness – which London's progressive government puts forward to emphasize the pathway to digital innovation through the recognition of the city's diversity – travels widely: it is to be integrated also in

Singapore's digital city campaigns. The 2020–1 campaign #SmartNationTogether requires the state to grant citizens better connectivity for access to all services. The concept of togetherness runs across all digital governance campaigns – such as the compulsory TraceTogether Token, a monitoring technology to be used by everyone while moving in the city. This token was devised for Covid-19-tracing purposes and justifies tracking by appeal to a collective commitment to the common good. Citizen-led imaginings and enactments of the digital city are assertively established through public narratives of togetherness, citizenry, and uninterrupted connectivity. An initiative named LifeSG expands digital connectivity between the state and its citizens, focusing on the young and on seniors. Assertively promoting uninterrupted connectivity, Smart Nation Singapore develops infrastructures 'anticipating citizens' needs and providing meaningful solutions' (Smart Nation 2021). The language of the project is intent on emphasizing collective responsibility and benefit with great ideological firmness.

State discourse on the digital order illustrates a shift in governmentality as far as urban lives and infrastructures are concerned. Pressures from the top (expressed in an urgent need to manage systemic crises, from the 2008 financial crisis to the pandemic and the climate crisis of the 2020s) as well as from the bottom (expressed in the rise of social movements for racial, gender, class, and digital justice in the city) turned state actors into major players that not only mediate the neoliberal order but also take responsibility for managing social peace. While at the peak of neoliberalism the state generated, through deregulation, policies in the service of the market, now it 'acts with explicit cultural, ethnic and economic biases. In that sense, the exit from neoliberalism is authentic' (Davies and Gane 2021: 19). What the examples adduced here reveal is of dual importance. First, the rhetorical entanglement of digital progress and the common good (expressed in narratives of responsibility towards humanity and nature across different forms of strategic communication and media representations) draws the parameters of a desirable order, which is both humane and inevitably digitally mediated. Second, concepts of humanity, humanism, diversity, and togetherness, mobilized as urban and transurban linguistic tropes, seal a normative frame of a recognizable humanity on the basis of perceived common interests and benefits, shared through innovation and digital investment.

Specifically, in this section I presented several examples (a few in a very large group) to illustrate the transurban rise of discursive frames that gradually replace technocentrism with humancentrism in urban planning. In these frames, market economies become entangled in urban humans' progress, well-being, and wider inclusion. As the popular humanist discourse adopts the language of privacy, environmental emergency, and social exclusions, the digital order appears by definition as a humanist project – progressive, commonsense, and liberating. The promise of democratic, prosperous, and liveable cities can then be imagined only through digital change. But now the discourse of progress is carefully and strategically shifting from the machine to the human. Through the various illustrations given here of the popular humanist frames of digital transformation, we can see how such frames become a normative and a moral compass for urban life; putting humans first is the ethical and right way to think about technology and about urbanism. The transnational currency of popular humanism does not erase local particularities from its discursive applications. What it does reveal, though, is the symbolic power of digital transformation promised by urban elites as a way out of the many crises of our time.

Imagining the human: The order of discourse of the digital city

The popular humanist discourse does not produce only imagined cities; it also produces urban humanity. Humans have designated, specific identities, roles, and responsibilities; and their complacency about the digital order promises recognition and a good life for individuals and communities. Interestingly, while these designations are adapted to the specificities of urban economic and political contexts – for example, they are differentially articulated in the archetypally neoliberal city of London, in paternalistic Singapore, or in postcolonial Kigali – we can see in them a transnational circulation of particular attributes that constitute, or should constitute, a desirable, digitally constructed urban humanity.

The exceptionality of individuals and their talent for benefiting from the digital economy, or even excelling at it, is perhaps the most prominent component in the discursive constitution of the imagined urban human, circulated as it is across continents, in its different forms. This is manifest, for example, in the Digital Talent Programme launched by the mayor of London in 2018. Through this programme, the city's digital strategy converges with its widening participation agenda, the aim being to 'inspire and train more young women and BAME Londoners to enter digital, technology and creative job roles' (Mayor of London 2018b). Here the digital economy is celebrated as a sector of major promise, able to lift minorities and women out of marginality, poverty, and invisibility – as long as the talent is there.

The celebratory discourse of digital talent and exceptional potential becomes transnationalized, not least as major corporations build and promote ideological frames that enhance their neocolonial expansion into the global South. The figure of the agentive and digitally savvy subject is geographically and culturally reconfigured as transnational corporations seek to expand their digital markets. African cities are identified now as some of the most promising markets of the kind, for example as is recognized by the UK-based research hub Tomorrow's Cities. Their major strength and potential, we are told, is their urban humans.

In a white paper titled 'Africa is ready to leapfrog the competition through smart city technologies', Deloitte, a major consulting corporation with headquarters in London, builds a discourse of African human agency as the driving force behind positive change:

> Anyone who has travelled to Africa will notice her people's 'Can Do' attitude. Africans operate within an environment where anything and everything is possible. This, from the homeless person standing at the motorway intersection accepting rubbish from passing traffic for a small donation to the street-side vendor (hawker) who sets up a makeshift hair salon in the shade of a leafy tree, with nothing but a battery powered electric shaver and a cardboard box on which to sit. If there is an opportunity to generate business, the opportunity is generally welcomed with both hands. (Deloitte 2015)

There is no irony in the enthusiastic reference to homeless people's 'entrepreneurship', but rather a determination of western corporations such as Deloitte to ignore the deep-seated colonial, structural, and dehumanizing conditions of inequality and to promise instead rehumanization through innovation. Deloitte, like other western corporations with huge interests in the development of technologized cities, pushes further its popular humanist discourse. 'The key stakeholders in the city are its citizens', although of course the citizens those corporations engage with are not the homeless and the impoverished working class just mentioned. The recognized stakeholders have substantial economic capital: 'One could argue that the biggest driver launching the African continent into the twenty-first century is the rise of the African middle class. Africans are also aspirational, with African consumers wanting the same things as other consumers across the world: choice of food and housing; entertainment and interconnectivity; and access to the latest fashion trends' (ibid.). The humans of the digital city described here are a particular breed of humans: already familiar to transnational corporations, having economic capital, they are assumed to be able to surpass 'their racialized exclusion from the dreamscapes of indentured consumerism' (Gilroy 2011: 21). These are the humans who are considered as agentive enough to consume and willing enough to embrace the many projects of African smart cities, where the economic stakes remain hidden behind discourses of the middle classes' seemingly respected needs and desires.

The recognizable humans of the digital city are not just individual self-made entrepreneurs – the archetypal neoliberal subjects. At a time of multiple crises, the media, the state, and the corporations speak to individuals who are becoming more aware of the collective needs of societies. For example, we see humans invited to maximize their engagement with digital technologies in order to meet their responsibilities towards the community in the best way. In Singapore's digital Covid-19 campaign, this message was communicated clearly: 'Together, we will emerge stronger. Let's care, appreciate and support one another!' (Singapore Together 2021). In this state-generated top-down campaign, citizens are recognized as having (or needing to have) multiple digital capabilities, which the community requires in order to control the pandemic. The digitally savvy citizens, whom this campaign takes to represent the norm or the majority, are called to support those with low digital skills (or none). The elderly and migrant workers are targeted in this campaign, as limited digital skills, we are told, incapacitate them and prevent them from reaping the benefits of collective initiatives to control Covid-19.

The normative discursive frame through which the digitally savvy are imagined as benefiting from the digital order is anything but exceptional. In its different versions, it circulates widely across the world, as many examples in this chapter show. However, the example of the Singapore Together campaign highlights a chilling necropolitical (Mbembe 2019) dimension of the digital order: individuals who disconnect themselves from the networks of information and opt out of databases and tracing technologies may end up alone in the face of illness, even death. As a result of Singapore's interventionist and paternalistic policies, this campaign renders even more visible the often hidden symbolic violence of the digital order: this is an order that demands from urban humans to let themselves be integrated into the digital economy and the surveillant state, or else suffer the consequences.

For many urban humans, the conditions of life depend more and more on their compliance with the digital order

– even when this is not a matter of life and death, as perhaps in the case of the 'disconnected'. Compliance or the lack of it makes the difference between succeeding or failing as professionals, between having access to rights or being denied them. For example, for many refugees whom I met during my spell of research in Berlin, finding employment was often conditional on the ability to develop digital skills. Significant amounts of public and private money were directed to the city's digital integration projects after the 2015 'migration crisis'. These projects promised newcomers that, if they were to become 'digital refugees', they could find employment and eventually earn the right to settle. While such policies have been beneficial for some, they also intensified many others' exclusion, as we will see in more detail in Chapter 4. As funds poured into producing humans who could be swiftly absorbed by the digital economy, only few resources were dedicated to supporting refugees in need of fundamental education, health support, and family care. For many, the lack of digital skills became yet another failing, as they were pushed further into deprivation, marginality, and invisibility (Georgiou 2019).

What kind of humans does popular humanism construct? First, urban humans are rehumanized. Shifting away from the invisibility of humans beyond consumerism – the core narrative of the neoliberal city – popular humanism gradually transforms the previously dominant neoliberal figure of self-responsibilized individuals – of those who make themselves responsible for their individual fate – into that of post-neoliberal agents whose digital capabilities can contribute to tackling inequalities and urban crises – environmental, economic, epidemiological. Now urban humans have rights to privacy and individual freedoms, which they can claim through digital citizenship and work, as they cannot expect – or even trust – old structures of order such as the state, police, or the market to deliver them fully. These humans are liberal, idealized, agentive subjects: they speak and act, they make smart decisions alongside the corporate and the state sectors. These humans are consumers, but also moral subjects who have to commit to digital change, as this is now part of their social responsibility.

Second, urban humans are represented in their cultural diversity and geographical situatedness; but they are not recognized as subjects made through their different biographies, histories, and locations. In the popular humanist discourse, individuals' distinctiveness comes with a rhetorical celebration of diversity, which nevertheless remains blind to historical, class, race, gender, and age inequalities. Digital capabilities, we are told, can overcome those divides. Within such an imaginary, those who struggle to overcome inequalities become invisible: the Afghan refugee woman I met in Berlin who cares for the elderly and the young and has no time to develop digital skills, or the working-class young man I met in London who works two shifts a day and can use his phone only for brief respites of escapism – people such as these are absent from the sociotechnical imaginary of the digital city. As Rose (2020) writes, the elderly are recognized as participants in digital cities only when they access the data (with little understanding of or interest in what they do with it). Thus a fundamental element of the digital city is the selective and contingent recognition of humanity, with old and new divides sealing its order.

Conclusion: A progressive discourse, a humanism without responsibilities

This chapter started by revealing how the hegemonic discourse of the digital order assertively ties technological promises to humanistic values of equality, respect for difference, and sustainability, displacing in this way the significance of privilege and marginality in shaping cities. The analysis reveals instead how urban imaginaries – hegemonic, negotiated, and oppositional – come to be implicated in the legitimization of the digital order; and this discussion continues in Chapter 4. Popular humanism, we saw, displaces the visibility of power and of urban antagonisms by projecting an infinite potential for the digitally mediated betterment of people and cities. The order of discourse asserted through corporate, media, and state narratives about desirable and just cities leaves little room for truly capturing the contradictions of the digital order: the persistent and extreme inequalities in the conditions of ownership and data control, or the limited benefits of shifting employment, educational, and health inequalities through digital literacies.

This order of discourse is fundamental to recentring urban imaginaries within a systematic, persuasive, and seductive humancentric technologization of all elements of urban life – that is, giving the good life in the city a political (Castoriadis 1987) and moral orientation (Taylor 2004) that privileges technology. As we saw through examples from different cities, a technologized digital future that is human-led – and not merely *user*-led – reveals a three-dimensional rhetorical strategy of affirming the digital order.

First, digital transformation is represented as an unquestioned human desire and need, precisely because it is assumed to serve at the same time the needs of citizens (for access to resources such as work and education) and the needs of the market (for investment and profit). It is this ideological frame of technological betterment that is presented as an unquestioned fact across corporate, governmental, and media narratives. More often than not we see these narratives represented as just and neutral, as merely recognizing needs and desires of the different urban actors, and offering solutions to what looks like an inevitability: the intensification and expansion of technological solutions. The fetishization of technology against the opacity of economic and political interests ties conceptions of cities and fulfilled humans to a teleological digital future of privatized and controlled urbanism and promotes the ideological myth of consensus and convergence of citizens', consumers', corporations', and governments' interests. As Benjamin (2019b: 82) puts it, 'this feel-good grammar also makes it difficult to recognize, much less intervene in, the deadly status quo'.

Second, the discursive constitution of converging interests does not represent marketeers' merely linguistic tropes; they signify a realization, among the elites, that the neoliberal and technocentric imaginaries of controlled and divided cities have become ideologically bankrupt. What we consequently see is a revamped moral vision, which points to potentially democratizing processes that recognize and address urban injustices and demands for a right to the city. But we can also observe, in popular humanism, a strategic attempt to contain these opportunities within solutions that do not challenge structural divides. The visibility of inequalities in popular humanism is visibility without responsibility.

Third, the humancentric narrations of the digital city carefully disguise the workings of what powerful actors sell: they disguise them as digital transformation, through euphemisms like 'optimization' (IBM 2023), 'smartness' (McKinsey & Company 2021), 'data-rich and people-centric' (Dell 2018) cities. In their commercial manifestations, these narratives carefully manage the expanded surveillance of public space and private data extraction for profit, for governance, and for health. But now they do all this not by ignoring concerns about datafication, surveillance, and control but by offering new promises, yet again technologically generated, of individualized solutions. In this context, the city becomes a universalizing space for gratification and fulfilment if you have the right tools – smartphones, fast connection, security cameras. People have to join as decision makers lead the way, themselves jumping on 'a run-away train, with law-makers, regulators and governments forced into an endless game of catch-up' (Trauth-Goik 2021: 64). Consequently, in the converging lines of rightful technological change for better and sustainable human cities, the digital order emerges as a moral order, an appropriate and just organizational system for our times (Boltanski and Chiapello 2005).

The next chapter moves from the current focus on the hegemony of popular humanism to the complex space where urban humanity is enacted and imagined, in compliance and negotiation with and opposition to the digital order. Chapter 4 will examine how urban humans live the digital city and how they perform and reflect upon their networked lives, bodies, and neighbourhoods. It will thus explore how everyday life becomes a site where popular humanism is decoded and where fears, hopes, and claims related to urban futures are performed through the contradictory, incomplete, and dynamic practices and discourses of demotic humanism.

4
Demotic Humanism
The Liminal Subject of the Digital Order

A flustered and embarrassed friend, arriving late at a dinner party, explains the reason: walking on a busy street, she tripped and fell as she was finalizing a purchase on her phone. In the midst of sympathetic laughter, others admitted to similar experiences. Most guests remained unimpressed, as this experience sounded more like the ordinary than the exceptional. Day in, day out, urban humans ordinarily perform similar acts, using media that have moved from being new to being habitual (Chun 2016): scrolling through platforms, posing for selfies and posting them, and recording it all on smartphones that have now become personal pocketsize archives. The obvious and banal commonality of conducting digital lives reveals the city as being the site of digital capitalism's success par excellence. *The digital* – its infrastructures, artefacts, and platforms – unites us as consumers.

Only a few days later, I came across another very urban and very digital story. An 18-year-old Syrian refugee in London shared his frustration and despair. His predicament is written all over his data profile: as he turned 18, the state withdrew all his welfare benefits, demanding that he finds employment to cover his expenses and to prove that he will eventually have the right to citizenship. His data profile is held at the jobcentre; the jobcentre passes it back to the Home Office, which monitors his migration status; and the jobcentre also has links to transnational databases, where his international data profile is composed. To the young man's urgent need for paid employment, the jobcentre responds with 'an opportunity for volunteering', that is, unpaid work for a thrift shop chain. The jobcentre's employee explains, to the young man's disappointment, that 'volunteering' will apparently boost his data profile, improving his chances of eventual employment and citizenship rights. 'What should I do?', he asks. This story reminds those of us without such dilemmas that the digital divides us as citizens.

What these stories reveal, like so many others, is that urban life is now digital life – for many people. But, while urban humans share the feature of living digitally connected lives, at least in most cities the meanings and consequences of connectivity break this shared feature apart, and, in the process, they also split practices and values related to what it means to be and become human. If we try to understand what's going on in digital cities, as we often do, by starting from the core of the digital order, we can see how connectivity unites urban humans as consumers. But if we follow hooks (1989) and start from the margins, we can see more clearly how the digital divides them as citizens – and does so with the same tools and through the same processes that unite them as consumers. Between the first and the second story presented at the beginning of this chapter we capture two different but coexisting conditions that make up digital cities' urban humanity. We see in that in-between space how urban humanity is constituted at the demotic, ordinary level – namely as a common but hierarchical humanity of digitally enhanced possibilities and asymmetrically distributed freedoms. While the commonalities of the digital lives described in the first story are familiar to most consumers, the particularities that split them through data profiling, predictive policing, and the dividing rules of Industry 4.0 (Bai et al. 2020) are apparent to those at the urban margins but opaque to those at the centre. It is in the city, in the intensity of its experiences and divisions as well as in its advanced digital infrastructures, that we can most vividly see what it means to be and become human, always differentially but together, in the digital era.

The ethnographic imagination and praxis that drive my research could not ignore the ordinary registers of a humanism that emerges through uses of technologies and cities – affectively, experientially, and agentively rather than merely discursively. Thus this chapter develops an empirically grounded approach to demotic humanism, as this is understood to be the performative space of the ordinary, a place where city dwellers imagine and enact humanity. The chapter reveals how the digital order dominates – but does not fully control – everyday life through a paradoxical enactment of power: by regularly uniting and dividing urban humanity, all at the same time. The imaginaries of a shared urban humanity, which are necessary for sustaining social order in the city, have increasingly become mediated by the digital. The fact that it is now almost impossible for teenagers to socialize off platforms across many cities or for senior citizens to access services offline goes to show that the digital order performatively enacts commonality through connectivity. As moral systems, such as religion, and social visions, such as shared prosperity, cannot convincingly assure societal cohesion any more, the promise of betterment through a common digital present and future becomes seductive and believable. We see a manifestation of this belief, for example, in the substantial investment in the digitization of most public services, from school enrolment to voting. This shift rests upon the assumption that everyone is connected. Enacting digitally so much of what it means to be human (e.g. learning) and to be urban (e.g. voting) becomes a norm that surpasses mere convenience. What living conditions does the city of multiple connectivities and advanced digital infrastructures actually present?

We saw in the previous chapter that popular humanism represents the discursive spine of the digital order. By promising that the intensification of investment and the diffusion of technologies in the city are driven by human values, especially those of progress, sustainability, and freedom, popular humanism maintains the digital order's legitimacy, believability, and desirability. Popular humanism, we saw, normalizes the digitally ordered city from the top down. In the present chapter, which is the second block in this book's analysis of the competing humanisms, we will see how the digital order's top-down exercise of power is circulated, negotiated, and challenged from the bottom up. Specifically, the discussion moves from the site of authority to the site of ordinary practice. By examining how urban humans – those who constitute the *dēmos* – perform consumer and citizen identities as digital users, within and against the digital order, the chapter does not merely describe how order is established (and occasionally challenged). It also unveils the city as an unstable site of order, a liminal space for being and becoming human.

In line with the book's critical humanist epistemology, as introduced in Chapter 2, this chapter's discussion is built around the voices and experiences of urban humans with whom I engaged over a period of seven years: people who inhabit the core, but also the periphery of different digital cities. Adopting an ethnographic lens and a commitment to a politics of justice, I draw inspiration from hooks' (1989) epistemological incentive to start understanding the world from the margins rather than from the core of order. As hooks reminds us, the margins uncover the otherwise opaque exercise of power, but also of agency. This approach drives the project's intended contribution, as the experiences and rights (or lack thereof) of those pushed outside the centre of social life underscore the stakes of asking what it means to be human in the digital era. I deliberately privilege experiences and voices from the margins in my analysis: hence those less often heard will be at the heart of the discussion on digital cities. These are not voices out of the ordinary but the many voices often silenced. Of course, voices and experiences of the urban cannot be contained in a few pages – or, for that matter, in the discourse I produce as their reader and interpreter. Since I am aware of these limitations, my discussion and analysis are driven by an ethics of creative and discursive knowledge production, best put in the words of Chris Killip, a British photographer who dedicated his career to working-class visualities: 'These people will not appear in history books because ordinary people don't. History is done *to them*. It is not acknowledged that they make history' (Killip, quoted in O'Hagan 2020; my emphasis). I, like many readers, have often seen how ordered visibilities, voices, and silences are reproduced in hegemonic and sometimes critical perspectives on cities and technologies. I am thus aware of the responsibility to recognize and respect (Honneth 2007) the intersubjective multitude of urban humans and the differential and intersectional constitution of actors (Nash 2008). Urban humans do not merely perform *already existing* roles prescribed by Big Tech and the infrastructures of platform urbanism but are cultural and political agents of change.

The critical epistemology of demotic humanism

The approach developed in this chapter is at the heart of the book's critical humanist epistemology, as it centres urban humans in the always incomplete struggle between control and openness and between freedom and unfreedom. As practice theory establishes, these competing forces of change can be fully understood only by paying close attention to human action (Bourdieu 1977; Couldry 2004). The concept of demotic humanism responds to this epistemological call in three ways. First, it recognizes that the people are being and becoming actors of the digital city within always incomplete systems of power and history (Hall 1997); Hall's poststructuralism, against some science and technology studies (STS) and posthumanist perspectives, reminds us that the human never pre-existed technologies of power and knowledge, be it in the past or in the present. This approach also recognizes humans, always and constantly, as actors in the making of cities and technologies, not only as their product. Second, demotic humanism identifies 'the ordinary' as a productive discursive and affective space for meaning-making – a space where rationality and affect are most visible, in a continuum rather than in opposition, as forces of oppression and as forces of resistance. As the ordinary is now produced on the street as much as on platforms, it is also important to understand how user-generated content reproduces and challenges authority (Turner 2009). Third, if we are to understand how and with what consequences the digital order is established or challenged in everyday life, we need to engage with the horizontal viewpoint of the *dēmos* rather than only with the perpendicular gaze of institutions. This approach reveals the power, but also the fragility of the digital order. We will see how the digital economy, with its Industry 4.0 (Bai et al. 2020), which promises progress and inclusion, rewards those who comply with it, and especially those who embrace it, by promising them a technologically induced rehumanization. We will also see how this same economy punishes those who fail or refuse to comply, consequently dehumanizing other humanities – the urban poor, the racialized minorities, and the permanently or temporarily disobedient. As this is a post-neoliberal order, that is, an order that enmeshes progressive with neoliberal values, it is also unpredictable – as we will see, the digital order's exercise of power produces lives of suspension and uncertainty, but also of possibility.

The discussion that follows is organized in three main sections. The first section offers a conceptual challenge to understand the urban everyday as a space of liminality. Drawing on Turner's (1969) influential definition of liminality, this section maps out the ambivalent, uneven, and open-ended possibilities produced in the context of ordinary life, where sociotechnical imaginaries of technologically induced rehumanization clash with the dehumanizing inequalities of a city divided and torn by crises. The second section engages with empirical evidence that shows how urban humans, as users, produce an individual and a collective self in this space of liminality. This section is organized across the subthemes of experience, affect, and agency, which were initially introduced in Chapter 2. By focusing on urban humans' experiential, affective, and agentive performativities of self-making as users of technologies and cities, I examine the workings and the limits of the digital order. This order is a project that promises but only selectively delivers rehumanization against the unjust distribution of resources and capitalism's aggression towards humans, non-humans, and the environment. The final, concluding section highlights how the digital order and its contradictory moral compass inevitably produce liminal subjectivities that are precariously situated along a rehumanization–dehumanization continuum. These subjectivities legitimize but also challenge, if only ephemerally, the digital order's command over the city.

Liminality: The transitionality of the digital order

Against the backdrop of urban inequalities, which are becoming starker and increasingly multidimensional (Nijman and Wei 2020), the demotic space of the city is where so many seek ways to be and become human. The digital order's regimes of truth (Foucault 1978) circulated in media, corporate, and state narratives constantly preach that it is through advanced digital infrastructures and sophisticated systems of AI and data production and extraction that well-being, happiness, and freedom can be advanced. Performative successes among YouTubers and music celebrities who, against all odds, escape poverty, and social media campaigns for green smart cities that bring together environmentally conscious citizens provide popular evidence that it is possible to challenge the dehumanizing, unequal city. At the same time, in the demotic turn (Turner 2009), where 'ordinary people' speak as authorities and against authority, social media celebrate agency and offer connection, friendship, and love against loneliness and alienation. The hypervisibility of those narratives not only exaggerates their techno-utopian optimism but also blocks out any questions about the city's growing saturation with material and immaterial digital commodities. From fibre-optic cables to 5G towers and from CCTV to wearable technologies, the city is a site of substantial investment and consumption of new and often experimental technologies. All of them, we are repeatedly told, offer enormous opportunities to fulfil human needs and desires. As these practices and discourses become standard, the digital order appears more and more as a natural order and less as a system of control. Even after the aggressive enhancement of OpenAI in 2023, which generated anxiety in universities as well as among city authorities, popular media swiftly moved to normalizing the use of artificial intelligence as inevitable to learning, working, and managing services. Marr (2023) describes how to get the best of ChatGPT by making it 'enhance your productivity and learning'. It is in the ordinariness of its workings that we can see how the digital order is diffused. The digital order is more appealing than many other forms of order, including that of the market economy; it is in the believability of its promise of rehumanization against the dehumanizing cities of pollution, inequality, and alienation that we see its power. The only condition for rehumanization is: all change.

In the digital city, the promise of good cities and a good life is fundamentally anchored in the imaginary of an infinite potential for positive change for individuals and communities through technology. But the site of ambivalence is practice: how much do these imaginaries match users' practices, expectations, values? The core rule that governs the digital city is that huge progress comes with new skills, the diffusion of innovation, adaptability, and a willingness to embrace the infinite potential of data, AI, and the Internet of Things. In all its operations, from getting access to cutting-edge research and supporting career development goals to writing new songs, Marr (2023) writes, OpenAI is not to be feared but to be embraced. This is a discourse that builds upon existing urban neoliberal narratives of individual entrepreneurship (Altan-Olcay 2014; McRobbie 2016), newer narratives of technologically enabled optimization (Powell 2021), and their convergence into a post-neoliberal discursive amalgam that responds to the cities' many crises. We hear and read that people armed with the right technologies generate individual, but also collective solutions against systemic obstacles, historical inequalities, and even authoritarianism.

The digital city becomes a place of transition as promises of technologically induced progress, happiness, and betterment are constantly in dialogue with ordinary practice. A digital future of *better anything* is written all over the ordinary – from communications with loved ones to work. The 'everybody should change' logic turns the city into a liminal space where the rules of old divisions are presumably suspended but the rules of the new, better city are still not in place, although they are constantly imagined as coming. In conditions of liminality, a lot of what urban humans took for granted is suspended, too: old identities lose their legitimacy and subjects 'slip through the network of classifications', as Turner (1969: 359) has influentially explained. In smart city projects, for example, we often see categories of class, race, gender, sexuality, and ability becoming suspended as significant classifications of inequality; technological solutions are projected instead as having the potential to overturn structural urban divides, to unite urban humans through a common digital present and future, and even to make them successful and visible. Campaigns for carbon offsetting, for preloved fashion, for food and clothes donations, or even for feminist causes trend on Instagram and TikTok and, as the website best-hashtags.com reminds social media users, the right social cause hashtags help personal social media accounts grow. Digital pathways that promise to tackle inequalities, climate change, and also loneliness and alienation are as much about performing individual identity as they are about shaping collective visions of a common future.

In conditions of liminality, where the expectation of something new is always present, subjects occupy a state of suspension, Turner (1969) also argues. In the digital city – the current incarnation of capitalist urban development in many locations – we can see the many consequences of this suspension. From insecurity to creativity, from experimentations to protest, the digital city is both a space of openness and one of uncertainty, submission to 'general authority', or 'intense comradeship and egalitarianism' (Turner 1969: 360). Liminality, the discussion shows, effectively manifests itself in practices that further divide but do not fully enclose order in the city. For many, this is about hovering between the deep human desire to find ontological security by grounding the self through stable connections and discovery of new ways to become urban in cities that always change. For some, liminality is expressed by imagining digital work as a compensation for the existing dehumanizing conditions of marginalization. For others, being liminal is the only way to be – suspended between the ephemerality of connections, which can be enjoyable (though consumption) or political (through fleeting acts of citizenship). In what follows we will see what values liminality aggregates as an intermediary but unending state of transition (Kelly and McAdam 2022; Thomassen 2012; Turner 1969). The empirically driven analysis shows how digital practices are embedded in the experiential, affective, and agentive making of urban humans.

Becoming human in the digital city

Becoming human is about being (as much as about becoming), *with* others, an intersubjective affair of human and non-human assemblages (Ahmed 2007; Bottero 2010; Braidotti 2013). Becoming human in the city is about finding experiential, affective, and agentive ways to do just this, within uneven urban geographies of intersubjectivity. Becoming human in the digital city is about reflecting, speaking, and acting for or against shared values and the 'infrastructure that gives them existence' (Merleau-Ponty, quoted in Simonsen and Koefoed 2020: 21) in these uneven geographies. Thus a humanism grounded in practice demands a phenomenological sensibility and a multiperspectival insight into how the *dēmos* turns into a hierarchical but unstable urban humanity through digitally mediated experience, affect, and agency. While experience, affect, and agency are all integrated processes of being and becoming, here I examine them separately, in order to operationalize a multiperspectival analysis of demotic humanism.

Experience

Walking the streets of Havana, it's hard to miss four- or five-star hotels. It's not the opulent constructions that give them away – at least not at first. In a city where beautifully restored mansions host foreigners and abandoned wreckages house many locals, it is not just the built environment that exposes the intense juxtapositions of global inequalities. Even before identifying the hotel buildings, an observant walker can spot dozens of people congregating around luxury hotels' gates. What for? To get access to the otherwise scarce and overpriced Internet connection in a city that, like so many others, has the ambition to become a smart city (Portal del Ciudadano de la Habana 2022). Hotels' Wi-Fi is available to their clientele – the affluent westerners who can afford overpriced rooms and, in return, enjoy scarce resources, free Internet among them. When I visited Havana in 2019, the image of the crowded gates around hotels presented an ordinary yet stark reminder of the division between haves and have-nots.

Like so many other cities, Havana already is, arguably, a digital city: both those inside and those outside the gates have a smartphone at hand. At this point of shared connectivity, rigid class and racial divides restricting the right to the city and to communication become blurred: against the firm infrastructures of walls and gates, the infrastructures of communication become standard, normal, ordinary – at least momentarily. Young people take selfies that they post on social media. What makes a good selfie is known to all, on both sides of the gates. Others are having transnational conversations with loved ones, thousands of miles away, and turn the phone camera around to record the urban surroundings – evidence of their groundedness in a specific place, and also of their desire to share it with others in a transnational space of love, be it as tourists or as members of diasporic families. Observing these different people one can see the performative enactment of a common urban humanity, united through the production of the self within social media's visual and narrative grammar of consumption.

In a city suffering from extreme levels of deprivation and having an urban economy that depends on foreign currency, it doesn't take long to see the fragility of this commonality, as those who take pictures of the luxurious swimming pool through the gates, unlike those who sit on its loungers, are soon to be stopped by the hotel security guards. CCTV on the gates alerts security of intrusion into the symbolic, albeit not the physical, space of privilege. The sharp division is hypervisible again, as the materiality of the class-based and racialized city mediates the potentiality of the symbolic representation. Those inside the gates, this episode reminds us, can be citizens of the world, possessing passports and capital that allow them to move freely across borders and to consume the 'authenticity' of touristy Havana. Their humanity – privacy, happiness, freedom – is protected by the material, digital, and embodied interventions of gates, cameras, and guards against the intrusive approach of those who do not have the same access to citizen and civic rights. Around these gates, as on so many occasions, the digital order is enacted as biopolitical power: the bodies of consumers are tolerated, but those of the citizens who want to get access at least symbolically to their city's resources are banished, dehumanized.

I started this section from the margins of the digital cities' global order and will continue to privilege the margins, local and global, in the discussion of demotic humanism. I do so in order to challenge the centre of gravity of debates preoccupied with the oppressive force of datafication and platformization, since these debates often silence the subaltern and underestimate the long histories of oppression and resistance. As the experience of those pushed out to the periphery of both the city and knowledge production reminds us, surveillance and extractive technologies have long histories of sophisticated applications associated with urban material and symbolic divisions. Thus, if we are to understand how humans become in the digital city at an intersubjective level, we have to situate this process within experiential, material, and symbolic assemblages relationally constituted in time and space and through human and non-human encounters and embodiments of order and disorder.

If we bear these ideas in mind, the snapshots from Havana discussed here cannot capture the full complexity of life in the city. However, within the limits of my narration, the digital city emerges as a product of human and non-human, symbolic and material encounters. Havana becomes a digital city, not through its sophisticated infrastructures but through its ambience: it is a city where almost everyone moves with a smartphone in hand. Its rhythms (Lefebvre 2013) are felt in the filtered encounters, separated by walls, between the haves and have-nots as much as in the smartphone mediations that negotiate the firmness of material divides. The digital city Havana is felt, sensed, and seen everywhere, through norms that have become ordinary, common. For example, the visual grammar of the selfie or the transnational connectivity that supports cross-border love relations is just one of the many banal reminders of identities performed through the digital. While digital mediations of identity are ubiquitous, felt and seen everywhere, the ambience of the digital city is also one of ever-present inequality. I heard how access and speed of connection vary enormously and how infrastructures of connections do as well, since locals often rely on hand-me-down smartphones from relatives in the United States – reminders of digital and global power asymmetries. But I also found out that those asymmetries are always unstable. Some of the middle-class Habaneros/as I engaged with displayed their deep knowledge of global affairs and their views on the latest Hollywood and Bollywood blockbusters. El Paquete, the terabyte hard drive circulated weekly in the underground markets of the city, provides access to enormous amounts of entertainment and news material – material that neither the slow and scarce Internet connection nor state censorship would allow, but that the urban underground economy and its transnational connectivities enable.

Havana's transnationalisms and digital cultures – those of the rich tourists on the one hand, those of the locals on the other – reveal an urban humanity, always relationally constituted through connections with various places, economies, and actors – human and non-human. This is a humanity always incomplete, as both the privileged tourists and the underprivileged locals become human relationally, through encounters that mediate their situatedness in time and space. Within broader structures and cultures of asymmetrical co-dependence between rich and poor, what digital connectivity does in particular is to enhance a sense of performative commonality: the desire to connect feels almost universal in the city. Another thing it does is to remind people constantly – those with privilege, and especially those without – that this universalism has little depth. As many Habaneros/as know, the cost of data, the slow connectivity, the filtered information – all these mean that, even when they want to be on the platforms and networks that extract data, do surveillance, and commodify connection, they cannot fully do so. In a digital economy where connectivity is necessary for the performance of individual identities, Habaneros/as join the rehumanizing project of the Internet when they are momentarily hypervisible on social media. But, in this same economy that requires stable and fast connectivity and expensive infrastructure, they also become dehumanized, since they cannot regularly perform the self online; they always remain at the periphery of the platform economy of individualized omnipresence and constant visibility.

The rhythms of Havana, both embodied and social (Lefebvre 2013), reveal the city's order and disorder at the current conjuncture, which brings together global and local power asymmetries, imperialist politics, and the advance of digital communications. These rhythms are different from those of other places, situated elsewhere in the global urban order. Yet, as I hope to demonstrate in this chapter, the asymmetrical distribution of economic and technological power does not determine how humans enact values and identities; humans create conditions through which certain values and identities become possible or impossible. Thus, by exploring global and urban margins and centres, we can observe how urban humanity is digitally imagined and performed – differentially and in ways that enhance, asymmetrically and contextually, the experiences of rehumanization and dehumanization.

Experiencing the city, and so much of it now digitally, is about becoming (or being denied to be) human, as much as it is about being and learning to be urban. While for many people digital tools such as GPS technologies are ordinary – tools to navigate with and to own as consumers – their significance for the process of becoming urban (effectively, an urban human) is most obvious when we observe their mobilization from the margins.

During seven years of research with migrants across cities of the global North, from Athens to Los Angeles, I have come to realize what is at stake in researching the many claims to become human and urban in the digital city. My research with migrants revealed two paradoxes that inform the discussion to follow. First, migrants' experiences present rehumanization–dehumanization as a continuum rather than as a blunt opposition. This is because digital technologies enable meaningful connections and claims, even as they aggravate the element of surveillance and control over all aspects of life. Second, if we pay attention to migrants' experiences, it becomes apparent that the global South is ever present in cities of the global North, as migrant biographies, transnational connectivities, and economic interdependences constantly connect the 'here' and the 'there' and the colonial and postcolonial past and present. Thus it is from the vantage point of the margins that what happens across urban societies becomes visible – not exceptionally, but most evidently: how urban humanity is imagined and enacted within the complex assemblages of infrastructures of control, support, and freedom.

The rehumanization-dehumanization continuum of the digital order became apparent in research I conducted with colleagues in Athens and London with more than sixty teenage refugees. This research was done in the context of a European project on young people's digital lives[1] (all the first-hand participant quotations that follow in this section are from these interviews). In the course of this work, we repeatedly witnessed sentiments of enthusiasm and relief when participants were talking about what is now one of the most basic urban technologies: Google Maps. 'Google Maps helped me a lot to learn the city and its mysteries', a 14-year-old Syrian boy in London told us, full of excitement; and a 15-year-old Syrian in Athens explained with similar enthusiasm how he visited the Acropolis and many of the city's museums, all under the guidance of Google Maps. Becoming urban is not only about learning but also about being an autonomous subject – at least in navigating the city. A 17-year-old new Londoner from Mali spoke positively about this mediated autonomy: 'Google Maps is very, very important for me because, when I want to go somewhere, I don't have to ask a lot from people, just [need] the postcode and address. I don't have to ask what time the train comes and goes. I just go on Google Maps on my phone and I see everything. I use it a lot like this, every day.' Variations on this theme came, again and again, from many teenage and adult migrants whom I interviewed across cities in Europe and the United States. Autonomous mobility in the city is hugely important to being urban, and a conception of self-governed knowledge is fundamental to constructing one's identity in a new and often hostile environment.

Migrants' stories of daily experiences that link the city, migration, and technology uncover their acute awareness that building autonomy protects them from certain experiences of dehumanization. This autonomy is often mediated through the smartphone. A city like Athens, which is itself at the margins of Europe but acts as its territorial and symbolic border (Chouliaraki and Georgiou 2022), is a site of ambivalence within the complex geographies of transnational mobility. In the context of a research project on cities of refuge,[2] I heard from an Afghan woman settled in Athens how she was ridiculed by passengers on a bus when she asked, in broken English, for help to get somewhere. Another young refugee who lived in Athens, a 14-year-old Iraqi boy, told me clearly and sharply that he would never ask for help again but only turns to his phone now – implying that he has experienced racism in the city before.

The stories of the new Athenians are not uniquely situated in the regional geographies of the Mediterranean border: but some of them belong in the transurban geographies of migration. Within those geographies, cities play a dual and contradictory role. On the one hand, they function as a perpetual border, with digital and embodied policing and racism that divide 'us' from 'them'; on the other, they constitute a new home, offering opportunities for employment, education, community life.

Conducting research in East Los Angeles, a part of the city with long histories of Latinx migration but also of intense policing that is now enacted through material and digital systems of control, I heard many stories of how those vulnerable to police violence and deportation seek to develop ordinary communicative autonomy to reduce their risks. Avoiding encounters with strangers builds walls, but also shields against vulnerability, as the stories of undocumented migrants testify. In a creative workshop at a local church, a young man mapped out his family's sophisticated network of local assets that includes material and symbolic resources, for example the church and the neighbourhood, but also smartphones and social media. Such assemblages of diverse resources, I soon came to realize, support a sense of belonging in the area but also provide invaluable infrastructures against vulnerability and threats of deportation. The same young man described how he taught his undocumented grandfather to use a smartphone so as to get transport information, and also how to reduce the risk of deportation by getting alerts, through social media, about neighbourhood raids of the immigration police, US Immigration and Customs Enforcement (ICE). For many occupying the urban margins, smartphones and apps now represent social assets for building capacities against the politics and policies of surveillance, racism, and fear. These capacities are about more than navigating and consuming the city. They are about striving to be recognized as human and about living the city with autonomy and dignity.

While these are striking examples of the value of everyday technologies for those excluded from so many other spaces of representation and claim-making, it is the nuanced use of those same technologies that reveals how collective freedoms can be systematically degraded even as individual autonomy is being advanced. GPS technologies of urban navigation constitute one of the most powerful examples of surrendering collective freedom and citizen privacy as a collective right. Geotagging has become 'an open secret of journeys', Shaw (2018: 17) argues, as individuals' ordinary shares of location produce massive amounts of data on the purposeful movement of urban humans for the consumption of spaces and things. Young middle-class Londoners participating in one of the focus groups I conducted with young people of different backgrounds enthusiastically told me that 'the secret city' is to be discovered, and effectively consumed, through their smartphone. They are well aware that knowledge of 'the secret city' is power. But what kind of power is this?

The secret city, of course, only exists within a sociotechnical imaginary that names certain places as 'hidden', while such naming always implies that they have been 'revealed' to the consuming gaze of individual smartphone users. The secret city' comes to be imagined as a site of consumption. Thus it is actually not secret at all. As social media and navigation technologies promise infinite revelations of a not-so-secret city for consumers, they simultaneously push the digital city of the margins further away, into hiding. In London, 28 per cent of the population lives in poverty (compared to 22 per cent in the United Kingdom), according to the Trust for London (2023), while in New York City almost 14 per cent of the population lives in poverty, exceeding the national average for eight years in a row, according to Thomas diNapoli (see New York State Comptroller 2023). A 17-year-old Black man who participated in one of my focus groups felt – unlike his white middle-class peers, who expressed enthusiasm for discovering 'the secret city' via social media – that this is the kind of city that makes him unwelcome: although he was born and brought up in London, it was clear that there was no prospect for him in this exciting city. London is full of consuming opportunities but is completely inaccessible to him:

> [Living in London] is extortionary. So, like, I'm guessing they only need a certain type of person or people in London in the next, let's say, ten, or fifteen years and I might not even be here myself. So, I don't know if I'm really a Londoner or not. I don't really know the rules.

These words reveal how acute the experience of exclusion is for many urban humans and how reflectively aware they can become of the digital city's violent continuum of (selective) rehumanization–dehumanization. With a smartphone at hand, everyone can navigate the city. But not everyone can own it. Those who can navigate and consume it can also enjoy new experiences and freedoms; others, who may be able to navigate it but not to consume it, are denied being in the city, as they become undesirable, their right to the city cruelly withdrawn.

The ordinary experience of digital navigation contributes to the unequal sociocultural geographies of the city that make certain kinds of humans and places worthy and unmake others. But technologies of navigation, like other technologies that extract citizens' and non-citizens' data day in and day out, represent more than a spatially bounded affair of rehumanization–dehumanization. The digital city is not self-contained; it is a node in transnational networks of governance. I have often heard that navigation technologies bring convenience; these are harmless technologies, with nothing political about them. However, in the political economy of the digital order it is precisely in acts of the ordinary that political and economic power are affirmed. This is the digital order of the everyday.

The banalization of navigation technologies through wide use is just one of many examples of a demotic legitimization of Big Tech's right to hold and monetize knowledge about every corner of the city. After all, corporate narratives emphasize that digitally mapping the city works only to serve its humans better, and in this way it makes the city more accessible; their city is now *a city of their own*. As Google explains in its Google Maps About page, it all exists to 'Make your plans happen by connecting with the places you're interested in … Navigate the world around you … Control your data with confidence', reassuring users: 'You're in control' (Google 2023). Of course, these maps of convenience are the same data-rich live archives of space and life that not only individual users have access to but also corporations and the state. What is more, when urban humans use these apps, they produce data that Big Tech and the state can use to optimize military and surveillance technologies (Tucker 2015). The humans dehumanized in the process may live not always in the digital city, but somewhere far away: migrants trying to cross borders to safety, families trying to protect themselves from drone attacks in warzones.

What this section has shown is that the ordinariness of connection performatively produces values and identities. This is the space of demotic humanism, where connectivity as a right is assumed to be shared, but where the divides that the same connectivity produces and reproduces remain opaque to those who enjoy the digital city's securities and joys while they are most apparent to those who seek these securities and joys and are denied them.

Affect

During my research across different cities that attempt to be smart, from the archetypal Songdo to the aspirational

Havana, urban humans are promised prescriptive and predictive happiness and security, guaranteed through effective networks of information, communication, and order. However, as research on the streets and neighbourhoods of these cities has shown, each city represents a complex sociotechnical and cultural environment, where embodied experiences and reflexive narratives intersubjectively shape people's imagination, fears, desires. Across these cities, I heard and observed how urban humans make sense of the promises and accomplishments of digital change and of their own position in the sociotechnical order. They do so not by thinking and talking about technologies but by imagining and feeling relationships: among humans, between humans and non-humans, between humans and the urban environment.

While, across different historical and spatial contexts, every city and its human residents are shaped by institutional structures as much as by the subjective and intersubjective emotional world of the everyday, digital cities converge, even if differentially, in their affective trajectories. As discussed in the previous chapter (and we will be reminded of it through the case of #LondonIsOpen), digital cites are now paradigmatic examples of post-neoliberal cities. The post-neoliberal orientations of these cities are expressed by the variegated ways in which they bring together neoliberal values of individualism, entrepreneurialism, and profit-driven digital urbanism on the one hand and, on the other, progressive values of openness, diversity, and sustainability. The ambivalent values at the heart of the digital city's sociotechnical imaginaries also mean that urban humans constantly find themselves in an affective condition of liminal anxiety (Kelly and McAdam 2022). On the one hand, they are permanently exposed to the digital city's mainstreaming of celebratory openness and 'happy' diversity (Ahmed 2007); on the other, many of them become aware of the cruelty of this optimism (Berlant 2011), as they see and feel how unevenly those promises are delivered across the digital and the material street.

One of the most powerful cases of the post-neoliberal paradox I came across in my research was London's intensely emotional response to the results of the Brexit referendum. After this event, both on social media and in offline conversations, urban authorities and Londoners became enmeshed in passionate conversations around the values of urban openness, diversity, and freedom. Through my audiovisual analysis of the social media campaign #LondonIsOpen and a series of focus groups with young people who discussed the campaign, I had the opportunity to see and hear how the meanings of these values are generated intersubjectively and emotionally.

The Brexit result was, for many Londoners, a traumatic event. Against the nationalist Leave vote of sealed borders that won in the country with a majority of 51.9 per cent, London voted Remain with 59.9 per cent of the vote – and more than 70 per cent in some areas (BBC 2016). In a post-Brexit London that realized the void between the nation and the city, values of urban openness and diversity became more prominent than ever. The campaign #LondonIsOpen is the most striking example. The campaign was initiated by the Mayor of London and was primarily organized through a series of short video spots produced to be circulated on social media. The video spots represented an attempt to rehumanize discursively the many Londoners, especially from racialized, minoritized populations, whom Brexit dehumanized. In the refined post-neoliberal aesthetics of #LondonIsOpen, we saw representations of minoritized populations being hypervisible side by side with celebrities and London corporate and state actors who projected a positive and celebratory story of the city's diversity.

The affective cultural economy of #LondonIsOpen visually celebrates an inclusive and diverse urban humanity through the imagery of happy faces of people who represent different communities of the city and through the symbolism of doors open to welcome everyone. Openness and diversity are conspicuously present in the spots. So is the visual grammar of freedom – freedom to be and look different, freedom to move in and across the city, freedom to be happy in community and diversity. More than anything, the videos represent a festival of humanism against the dehumanization of nationalism. These representations, of course, are situated within the familiar visual grammar of social media and of the corporatized digital city. Rehumanization is visually subjected to their conditions: celebrities take centre-stage, while the faces of ordinary citizens who parade through almost cinematic representations made for social media are strategically situated in the cultural economy of a joyful urban humanism: they all look different and are affiliated with the urban creative and consumption economies – standing on doorsteps of shops and businesses that serve those who can afford them, or performing on the stage of a London theatre. Faces are interchanged and interchangeable via fast edits, while individual Londoners appear on the screen to represent typologies – beautiful, colourful, happy, aesthetically pleasing – rather than agentive subjects in an open city – which should be 'a bottom-up place' because it 'belongs to the people' (Sennett 2013: 14). The urban humans of #LondonIsOpen are subjected to the feel-good factor of recognizable and consumable openness.

The audience responses I recorded reflect the contradictions of the post-neoliberal affective cultural economy of #LondonIsOpen. Some of those impassionate responses were generated on social media and in focus groups when a number of people felt like responding to a literary line that appeared in one of the social media videos of the campaign: 'When a man, or a woman, is tired of London, then they are tired of life.' Two comments on the Mayor of London's Facebook page (https://www.facebook.com/MayorofLondon) were most striking:

> I used to think when I was tired of London I'd be tired of life. Now I'm just tired. As a single working mother not on benefits almost all of my income goes to rent and childcare and all of my time working or commuting. The city is becoming less and less for the average family and certainly [not] for the average single parent.

Mr Sadiq Khan, need your attention. Yesterday it happened. A very awful incident with a woman she was in hijab. Someone tried to remove from her in yours city London. Kindly make freedom well known for every one specially for women.

In these quotations the humanist values of freedom and equality are contrasted with the affective economy of celebratory diversity and urban openness. In the focus groups, too, I observed a stark contrast between young people who reported how emotional they felt when they saw this and the other video spots, which made them proud to be Londoners, and young people who felt alienated from the aesthetics and ethics of the same videos. It was in fact a few working-class and ethnic minority youths who were most vocal in expressing indignation at the values of a consumer-driven diversity and spoke to citizen-led openness. A 17-year-old Alevi woman said, in one of my interviews: 'You know, showing the world that London's a very, very nice place, but that's all it's [i.e. the video spot] saying. There are so many problems that people, citizens, that citizens themselves see … Go out on the street at night and you see tonnes of people are homeless.' And this scepticism is echoed in the words of a young man who is also Alevi:

> He [i.e. the mayor] tried to bring a lot of celebrities to it, because the celebrity culture's big, obviously. So [he] tried to pass on a message through celebrities but for me it just, the celebrity influence is nothing to me. Who knows? London is open, Central London is open, but everywhere is dying from poverty.

These responses to #LondonIsOpen show how those at the margins are being reminded of their precarity through the cruel optimism that promises unachievable fantasies of freedom through a digitally imagined openness (Berlant 2011). This promise – the promise of a 'good life', as Berlant would call it, 'is for so many a bad life that wears out the subjects who nonetheless, and at the same time, find their conditions of possibility within it' (27). It is in fact those conditions of possibility and their limits that I heard so many young people at the urban margins being aware of. Some were reminded that they do not belong, others, like the two young Alevis quoted here, turned instead to collective action against the affective economy of consumption and London's deepening divisions; and, on occasion, social media became spaces for advancing claims, as in the examples from the Mayor of London's Facebook page.

The affective making of humans takes place in the city that is imagined but also surveilled, vertically and horizontally. One of the main ways in which emotions of security and insecurity are unequally distributed is through systems of surveillance. Zuboff (2019) defined surveillance capitalism as the new economic order that claims human experience as raw material for profit. We have seen above how the use of extractive technologies such as GPS navigation in effect expropriates everyday experience. The examples of expropriation of experience and emotions are endless. They spread across all the elements of ordinary life, from technologies of well-being such as fitness apps, which constantly monetize data that promise happiness, to AI technologies that endlessly try to predict emotions and to respond to them. These are technologies that do not just generate profit; they allocate urban life to a culture that turns places, things, and even people into consumables, and they appropriate cities by turning them into testing grounds for technologies of control, including for the advancement of the necropolitics of borders and warfare (Mbembe 2019).

Turning experiences into profitable data is fundamental to digital capitalism; turning affects into expropriated data is essential to its order. As the digital order depends on the credibility of the proposition that technologized cities are better for humans, its affective successes, such as the cases of supporting the good life through relations of love and care discussed above, secure its legitimacy. But those 'affective successes' also hide the digital order's failings, expressed through mental violence and psychological abuse. These are mostly caused by technologies of surveillance, which turn the city into a space of unaccounted vulnerabilities.

In this part of the discussion I want to speak precisely to those vulnerabilities and their biopolitics. Across the cities I navigated during my research journeys, I have seen and heard about the many dehumanizing effects of digital surveillance and control; these have been stories of suffering, which ranges from anxiety and fear to full-blown trauma, usually caused by the denial of dignity and autonomy. Surveillance is vertical – routed through sophisticated data and AI systems of state and corporate control – and it is horizontal – largely expressed in the mobilization of digital technologies to advance patriarchal and racial violence in the city. This discussion moves beyond the general discussion on surveillance capitalism and looks more specifically at the detrimental mental and emotional effects of particular technologies of surveillance that target urban populations already exposed to the discriminating politics and economics of dehumanization. Hopefully this particular angle on surveillance will also provide a useful reminder that surveillance capitalism (Zuboff 2019) is always gendered, is racial and spatial, and is vertical as well as horizontal.

Vertical surveillance is generated through the corporatization of the digital city. Critical data studies (Benjamin 2019a, 2023; Couldry and Mejias 2019; Eubanks 2018; Zuboff 2019) has systematically studied the expropriation of human experience and rights within the current order of capitalism. The predictive profiling of the urban poor and racialized minorities further push these people to the margins, creating 'different genres of humanity' (Benjamin 2019b: 17), as many are now ordinarily denied access to health, employment, and housing on the basis of their data profiles. This most brutal side of the digital order does not just marginalize economically those classified as high risk but denies their humanity its due recognition, which is a process of dehumanization with deep psychological as well as social consequences. Alongside the dehumanizing effects of surveillance capitalism, occasions of rehumanization emerge through these same systems. For example, Big Tech companies such as Microsoft and Facebook became enthusiastic sponsors of refugee digital skill development in Athens and Berlin in the aftermath of the 2015 'migration crisis', enhancing opportunities for migrant employment in the digital economy. Projects such as hackathons and schools of digital integration have benefited from these sponsorships and in fact succeeded in supporting a number of people at the urban margins to integrate into the city and its urban digital economy. However, the rehumanization offered through these initiatives remained contingent. Driven by the rationality of entrepreneurial securitization (Chouliaraki and Georgiou 2022), these initiatives offered rehumanization under two conditions: first, individuals were welcomed to participate as long as they were recognized by the surveillance system as having refugee status or as being asylum seekers; and, second, their success was made dependent on their *performative refugeeness* (Georgiou 2019), that is, their ability to demonstrate to the surveilling eye of corporations and states that they are self-reliant entrepreneurs who can make it, no matter the obstacles. In practice, as I have observed, these conditions sustained rather than challenged the order, so that most people who attended these skill-building opportunities in the end slipped through the net of impossibilities and the violence of the border, rather than benefiting from the possibilities of conditional rehumanization.

Vertical surveillance also implicates the state. Critical data studies has primarily focused on Big Tech and the political economy of platformization and datafication. Hence it has paid much less attention to the role of the state in surveilling citizens, a process with detrimental consequences for their sense of ontological security and even for their life, especially in the case of those at the margins. Automated policing is regularly used in racialized neighbourhoods and in the necropolitical racial governance of cities. Chris Kaba, a Black Londoner, was killed while driving a car, because an 'automated number plate recognition (ANPR) camera alerted police that the vehicle was linked to a previous "firearms incident"' (Ferris 2022). The police killed Kaba with a single shot through the windscreen, while he was still in the driver's seat. Alongside such incidents, which reveal the extreme violence of predictive policing, a mundane form of symbolic violence is regularly applied across the city. For example, data profiles kept on migrants are often used in order to deny them access not only to national citizenship but also to urban citizenship, along with the right to housing, work, and health (Yuval-Davis, Wemyss, and Cassidy 2019).

Many migrants living in cities across Europe are acutely aware that they are constantly monitored. The young Syrian introduced at the beginning of the chapter explained how aware he was that he needed to be constantly on his best behaviour, work hard, and keep his head down, as he wanted to show that refugees are not a menace to the state or the city. He was well aware that the jobcentre databases produce classifications of deserving and undeserving migrants. A middle-aged Afghan woman in Berlin was almost in tears when she explained that her low literacy skills would most likely disqualify her from permanent residency, as her data profile would put her on the wrong side of the divide between desired or undesired migrants. And most of the young migrant men whom I met in Athens, Berlin, and London had resigned themselves to the fact that their data profiles as male, Arab, and Muslim already categorized them as risky and that they had to develop strategies to manage conditions of possibility within the technologies of surveillance and racial capitalism by separating their digital affective lives from their citizen lives. Many of them spoke of their different social media profiles, which were divided into profiles built to speak to loved ones and profiles built to speak politically (profiles in this category were almost always used under aliases).

Surveillance is also horizontal, as its technologies are not only racial but also class- and gender-based (Devadas 2022). Technologies that can turn from communication to control, such as the smartphone, mediate relationships of desire, but also of fear. In Berlin, through the participatory method of urban walk storytelling, our research team had the chance to hear how horizontal digital surveillance plays on the lives of young migrants and on their sense of always being in-between. Direct questions were avoided, so we moved away from a testimonial method that so often migrants encounter and we made room instead for participants to lead their own narrative and introduce their humanity. Walking with us across spaces that define their relationship with the city, from the multicultural neighbourhood of Neukölln to the shores of the river Spree and the decommissioned airport and now refugee shelter of Tempelhof, some participants spoke about managing flirting and love on social media, many with joy, others with concern about their digital exposure to the gaze of people they know and people they don't. One of the repeated narratives was about their wariness of always being watched, while spaces for recovery and freedom were shrinking as a result. Here are the words of a transgender Syrian refugee from our fieldwork:

> I am 28 years old and I have already seen all those things. I'm strong, it's true, but also I feel like nobody sees me, nobody touches me. And this is when you start to feel like all this is for nothing. I'm asked for so many things here. Integration, fine, I'll do that. I learnt German on my own, I didn't go to school. My language is not perfect but I managed all my papers on my own without a translator. But just give us some space, that's all. We are coming from war.

The oppressive force of horizontal surveillance – or, put otherwise, of the culture of interveillance (Christensen and Jansson 2015) – is symbolically and materially normalized through narratives of desired humanity reproduced on digital media and about digital media. Exhausted by the constant monitoring of the lives of Syrian refugees by the media and the public, a Syrian young man in Berlin told us during fieldwork: 'These people think, "they need to speak like me, eat like me, listen to the same music I listen to". They probably also think, "he should look like me too". Maybe they want us to dye our hair blonde!'. A friend of his also explained how monitoring takes place not only through digital infrastructures but also in relation to infrastructures and artefacts. Asking who is the legitimate owner of smart technologies, for example, becomes a pathway to pathologizing certain humans. In his own words,

> There is also this expectation that you should not own nice things because you are a refugee. If people see you with a new iPhone or nice clothes they automatically think you are using government money to spend on leisure items. I am working seven days a week, 10 hours most days, and I get to spend my money the way I want. I pay my taxes!

Tufekci (2012) speaks of 'grassroots surveillance', the constant monitoring of ordinary enactments of the self on social media updates, which in fact makes it more difficult to perform identities differently because, being watched all the time, individuals are called out if they divert too much from what is expected. The interplay of technology and identity is always ambivalent – it creates space for visibility and at the same time for identity control. For some, the risks of horizontal surveillance are produced with and through the same technologies that present conditions of possibility to become rehumanized in new environments. For example, in a refugee women's centre in East Berlin, participants speak of this ambivalence – being monitored while also being able to connect with others as young women, as mothers, as lovers. They are liminal subjects torn between the productive possibilities of representing and speaking for themselves and the risk of being exposed and punished for their voices and presentation of the self. For many women, this liminality is a way to be, a risk they take every day. But in some cases this risk generates intense fear. We were reminded of the transurban intersectional power of technologies that surveil and control gendered bodies not only in Berlin but across many cities. A Syrian woman in Athens told us that she was tormented by the thought that her former husband would use tracking technologies to find her whereabouts.

She moved to a women's shelter at an undisclosed location after years of abuse, but her phone could always expose her, she thought. Her dependence on her smartphone to sustain familial relations terrified her, as she felt that those same technologies of love can at any time turn into technologies of violence. The anxiety tearing her everyday life apart was not unlike the affective state of distress that a 15-year-old girl in London described to us. For over a year, she had been haunted online and offline by a controlling uncle who stalked her. Neither a restraining order nor police intervention would reassure her that her ordeal was over; the fear that her phone and use of social media might revive acts of stalking and harassment remained omnipresent.

The affective making of urban humans comes with the ambivalence of converging anxieties and joys, of the possibilities and impossibilities of rehumanization within the dehumanizing conditions of forced migration. This is an embodied and affective ambivalence, tied to the ambiguity of the digital order: its promises exaggerate the potential that digital technologies open – a potential for living positively and for imagining openness, diversity, and freedom – but they underplay the dehumanizing workings of the very same technologies. Consequently those who really need the values of openness, diversity, and freedom to achieve ontological security are instead exposed to more precarity, anxiety, and uncertainty, as the discourse of 'cruel optimism' on the one hand and the material risks of surveillance on the other constantly remind them that those values remain a privilege associated with a certain kind of humanity.

Agency

For many residents of East LA, the system of notifying one another about ICE raids is simple but effective. It is all about sharing messages fast across social media and making sure that everyone knows how to send and receive those vital notifications. At a local church in East LA many talked about 'how to' share tools and educate everyone in the use of social media for protection – a collective act of citizenship against the individualized use for consumption. In Berlin I observed how grassroots groups developed tactics to support undocumented migrants under the radar, while avoiding publicity around these activities. Networks of media publicity were being carefully separated from the social media networks of solidarity, where vital support not desired by the state has organized. Mobilizing the same discourse and technologies, similar acts of solidarity emerged in London. I observed how a food justice programme's communication popped up across local social media networks, inviting neighbours who mostly congregate online rather than in the street to buy a fruit and vegetable box, so that another box may be donated for free to a family that cannot afford it. This hyperlocal initiative in North London was but one of the many successful projects that I recorded through my transurban observations. From Athens to Los Angeles, the cases are many: collective agency comes to life when the human and non-human agency of networks shapes imaginaries and performativities of solidarity.

The city may be a site of order – more and more, the site of a digital order normalized through data and platforms' symbolic and material technologies of control. But the digital city is also agentive – that is, a site where humans intersubjectively, reflectively, and creatively develop capabilities to seek freedoms that enable them to meet their needs and fulfil their desire for a healthy, enjoyable, and moral life (Mansell 2012; Nussbaum 2011; Sen 1999; Simonsen 2013). At the peak of neoliberalism, these capabilities have emerged as values fulfilled through individual 'utility maximization' (Fukuda-Parr 2003: 304). During its crisis, which is expressed in the ambivalent regime of post-neoliberalism, such values become a site of struggle – between the popular humanism of sociotechnical imaginaries of happy diversity (Ahmed 2007) and 'woke capitalism' (Kanai and Gill 2020) on the one hand and, on the other, the collective agency of demotic humanism and its contradictions, expressed in everyday uses of technologies and their integral acts of solidarity.

Demotic Humanism

This section draws on the many sightings of collective agency that I have witnessed across cities. More specifically, I refer to collective agency here as a way in which urban humans imagine and enact togetherness in order to advance the perceived or material conditions of the common good. I understand agency, according to Giddens' definition, as 'the stream of actual or contemplated causal interventions of corporeal beings in the ongoing process of events-in-the-world' (Giddens 1976: 75). Yet here I move away from his and others' focus on individual agency, as I adopt a Marxian understanding of agency as a historically situated and collectively perceived capacity to think and act freely. My focus on collective agency in fact represents a conceptual response to observations I made across cities that are socially divided and digitally connected. It is my observations that generated the interest to understand collective agency alongside and in dialogue with individual agency. In many of the cities where my research was conducted, I saw how urban humans, together, mobilize their own capabilities to manage their environment and its dehumanizing effects, especially in times of crisis. Those capabilities – capacities to reflect and act in response to the dehumanization of individuals and groups – are often generated collectively, since social media connectivities enable or even force urban humans to imagine the city as shared – at least momentarily.

Digital cities are much more than controlled, surveilled, and datafied spaces, neatly divided between the privileges of individualistic rehumanization and the reprimand of extractive dehumanization. Researching cities and their neighbourhoods has unravelled enormous richness in difference; but it has also shown how, across difference, being and becoming human always involves performative enactments of subjectivity within, but also against, order. In this last section I want to focus precisely on this ambivalent space, the space of urban humans' agentive making of the individual and collective self, and at the same time of the city. Collective agency reflects most intensely a human sense of responsibility and desire for freedom, autonomy, and dignity. These are values that, as we have seen, urban humans try to fulfil through connections with other humans and with non-humans – hence values that need to be understood intersubjectively (Lockie 2016; Pelenc, Bazile, and Ceruti 2015). This focus also enables me to speak more systematically of *the social* as a defining dimension of the digital city. Critical data studies often focuses on platformization's and datafication's attack on individual agency, as if the social either doesn't exist or has been so corrupted by platforms that it is irrelevant. The city and the horizontal viewpoint of a demotic analysis empirically reveal how short-sighted such assumptions are: the social remains important both as a site of consumption and as a site of citizenship, both as a site of power and as a site of resistance.

Solidarity, in its ambivalence and contradictions, is par excellence a site for analysing how agency is enacted collectively, being made by and making the social. Across material and digital streets, urban humans figure out and experiment with solidarity – together, though not all together. Especially at times of intensified and hypermediated anxiety around successive crises (such as from the pandemic to immigration and racial injustice), urban humans reconfigure solidarities and experiment with boundaries between those who deserve solidarity and those who do not, between online and offline manifestations of solidarity (Cammaerts 2021; Chouliaraki and Georgiou 2022; Koch and Miles 2021). Driven by these empirical observations, my discussion is also inspired, on the conceptual side, on the one hand by de Certeau's (1988) provocative invitation to write histories that recognize ordinary practices and disruptions and, on the other, by the political incentive launched by hooks (1989) to listen attentively to voices and to see acts at the urban margins – a space that she recognizes as one of radical openness. Eloquently put by Ahearne, this invitation could be articulated thus: 'through the insinuation of anomalous historical and cultural fragments; by exposing writing to other "voices" and fables; through an attention to the forms of other peoples' practices; by setting up encounters with the itinerant stories which circulate through "metaphorical" towns or which lie dormant in archival recesses' (Ahearne 2007: 192).

Historically, urban acts of solidarity have been performed either at the organic but small-scale level of the neighbourhood or through the methodical and large-scale mobilization of political parties, labour unions, and community and religious associations. In the digital city and at times of crisis, acts of solidarity have become a multiscalar amalgam of the ordinary, the political, and the commodified. The Covid-19 pandemic of 2020–22 exemplified the moment when social media networks, generally used for mundane interpersonal communication, came to signal a transformation, at least ephemeral: after mediating ordinary urban experiences, WhatsApp, Facebook, and other social media such as Nextdoor became mediators and themselves actors in networks of urban solidarities. That moment of acute crisis is a moment of temporal particularity, but also of wider political significance: the crisis became a productive moment in which the radical possibility of digitally generating collective agency became achievable. In the neighbourhood and in the city, urban humanity was reimagined, at least momentarily.

The case of mutual aid groups in British cities is a striking case. Within a few days into the strict 2020 lockdowns, hundreds of self-styled mutual aid groups mushroomed across the country. The vast majority of them appeared in densely urban neighbourhoods – not on their physical streets but on their digital streets. There is no doubt that, during that period of acute isolation, social media emerged as the most precious networks of connection. Overnight, thousands of urban humans turned into activists. At that moment of crisis, activism became popular, hyperlocal, and granular – as citizens organized on social media networks to support neighbours in need and in isolation. Observing how many of these networks emerged and how they evolved, I noted that the crisis became a reflexive moment for imagining a shared urban humanity outside consumption (Frosh and Georgiou 2022): inequalities of access to food and care became a topic of shared concern, digital exclusions also grew into issues of thoughtful conversation and action, and the new activists made sure that there were other ways to connect to the network apart from social media.

Reflecting on the unequal digital city, the new activists of the hyperlocal mutual aid groups shared phone numbers, visited impoverished council estates, produced real-life posters and flyers for those who were not (or not constantly) online. The language of mutual aid, once a staple of anarchist ideology (Firth 2020), became a demotic, shared discourse, enacted through an ethos of horizontal and collective action. The digitally connected neighbourhood, even if physically isolated, turned into a site of care, but also of political awareness of the need for mutuality. Of course, the politicization of social media solidarity and its enactment on the urban street did not come out of nowhere. First of all, as discussed in the pages of this book, crisis and its liminalities generate radical possibilities. Second, social media, we know, do not by themselves produce practice, but the possibility to extend sharing and shared know-how between new and established activists does. Knowledge and tools of solidarity emerged collectively, as the various agents of the network either generated new knowledge or summoned knowledge that pre-existed, having been generated during years of radical political mobilization in the city. For example, the Covid-19 mutual aid groups adopted health emergency guidelines produced for the LGBTQI community by the grassroots Queercare well before the pandemic. Third, networks turned experience into solidarity because the dehumanizing conditions of inequality and isolation became so acute in crisis that for many people they were impossible to ignore.

While ephemeral, the politicization of everyday performativities of solidarity has left its mark over the city, though not unambiguously. In London, for example, some of the WhatsApp mutual aid groups eventually transformed themselves into reconfigured networks of solidarity for the post-pandemic but still deeply unequal city: they support food justice or migrant justice, for example. Others reoriented themselves towards the hyperlocal reaffirmation of class-based symbolic boundaries, with middle-class exchanges of sourdough recipes and gardening advice that replaced the discourse of mutuality and care.

In conclusion, the case of the mutual aid groups illustrates the possibility of collectively generating agentive capabilities designed to manage a dire dehumanization. The moment of crisis, which at the level of the neighbourhood was managed largely online, reflected, even if not exclusively, the liminal potentiality for transformation. The pandemic, qua crisis, produced an exacerbated state of liminality across cities, a state of suspension; and this liminal state also produced a suspension of the existing rules and norms (Thomassen 2012). Neighbours who used to consider isolation, alienation, and inequality as a given of urban life reshuffled the taken-for-grantedness of this order. Against the norms, crisis became generative of collective agency, the mutual aid networks engendering capabilities to act and imagine the city through solidarities that envisioned a shared humanity. Even if ephemerally, this was a moment of radical possibility, a moment of mobilizing collective agency to reimagine urban humanity through solidarity.

Zooming out of the hyperlocal space of mutual aid networks, we also see how digital cities have become anchoring points for the collective agency of the now transurban movements of #BLM, #RefugeesWelcome, and #MeToo. These movements are powerful examples of the transnationalization of claims to dignity and freedom; but they also reflect the fragility of collective agency, often appropriated within the political economies of the digital order.

Hashtag activism (Yang 2016) provides a powerful illustration of the ambivalence of collective agency: expanding and popularizing justice politics, it spread across crisis-ridden digital cities, shaping transurban imaginaries of shared goals and consequently collective capabilities to speak, if not to act, in togetherness, in solidarity. #BLM, #RefugeesWelcome, and #MeToo protests, online and offline, have articulated new expressions of humanistic imaginaries that challenge

Eurocentrism and patriarchy. For example, the progressive language of racial, gender, and environmental justice and collective mobilization has marked people's experience across university campuses, schools, and urban streets. I saw hashtags like #BLM originating in American cities, #ColstonStatue originating in Bristol, or #RhodesMustFall originating in Cape Town, graffitied on the walls of cities like Nicosia, New York, and London; and I also witnessed their appropriation as adornment on individual Instagram posts, T-shirts, and handbag merchandise sold in London and in Athens.

The collective agency produced by and producing the digital city comes with its own tensions. While attending protests in London and Los Angeles, I heard young people speaking passionately about the need to act against environmental, racial, and gender injustice. But I also repeatedly saw woke capitalism's '"feel good" and "positive" messages of female empowerment, LGBTQI pride, racial and religious diversity and inclusion, and environmental awareness' (Kanai and Gill 2020) in commercial initiatives, not least in the incorporation of the concept of 'collective' by Marks & Spencer, a major brand, into its M&S Collective marketing campaign.

The digital city is a site of agency, individual and collective. Its liminality, a product of crises as much as of the yet unfulfilled promises of technological responses to crises, produces moments of radical possibility that challenge its order. But, as this agency is, more often than not, generated and channelled through temporary and unstable networks, solidarities inevitably remain ephemeral. What the discussion on collective agency has tried to show is that the digital order will remain fragile, as long as urban humans collectively generate capabilities to demand freedom and justice. But it also showed that the solidarities that collective agency produces are themselves fragile, as they are embedded in the structures of inequality that the digital order disguises through the feel-good and commodified ambience of the city. This ambience unites humans as consumers, but rarely as equitable subjects of rights.

Conclusions: The struggle of becoming urban human

Demotic humanism, in its contradictions, reveals the struggle of being and becoming human in the digital city. For some, especially those in positions of relative privilege, demotic humanism is about being urban; for others, especially those who are constantly denied their humanity, it is about becoming human. Demotic humanism uncovers how ordinary uses of digital artefacts and infrastructures produce particular entanglements of the urban and the human, especially in cities that are surveilled, datafied, and commodified but are also lived and imagined as spaces of belonging and freedom. These cities, digital cities, in their diverse histories and material realities, differentially become sites of liminality, as the digital order's promise to reconcile control and freedom constantly clashes with the ambivalent meanings of digital uses. Promising to deliver cities that are diverse, open, and inclusive not despite datafication and commodification but precisely through them, the digital order encourages urban humans to reimagine and enact the self through it, individually and collectively. Investment into a better future is experiential, affective, and agentive. Hashtag activism, for example, indicates that individual visibility gains from performative commitment to a progressive politics; engagement with social media solidarities promises to enhance shared and inclusive cities; and learning digital skills promises to give work and dignity.

The many promises of the digital order, legitimized as they are through everyday uses of social media, public consent to surveilled cities, and investment in digital economies and infrastructures, open up spaces of possibility, perhaps of limitless possibilities for rehumanized cities and people. The open-endedness of the promise and its always deferred realization are also sustaining the liminality of the city and its people. This unending liminality implies a progressive openness, expressed in a set of two contradictory states of always becoming. First, the prospect of technologically induced freedoms that, urban humans are constantly reminded, comes at the cost of precarity and uncertainty against permanence and stability. Urban technologies, from smartphones to GPS navigations, can open unending opportunities for discovering the secret city, for acquiring new skills, and for connecting with different networks of romance, friendship, and solidarity. That possibility of living the city to the full by effectively maximizing one's chances of self-realization as an urban human comes with the requirement to be always willing to change, to adopt entrepreneurial skills, and to invest in technologies and their logics of surveilled and ephemeral connectivity. Second, the unending possibilities of discovery, freedom, and happiness come with a progressive social consciousness, which is integrated in the 'pop-up revolution' (Ferreri 2021) and the performative post-neoliberal embracement of environmental, feminist, and anti-racist values. After all, in digital cities these values are visible everywhere, on walls, on social media, in advertising. In the aesthetic and affective economies of the city, however, these values are primarily directed to acts of consumption – shopping local, shifting to plant-based diets, crowdsourcing the arts and the culture – and occasionally to ephemeral acts of citizenship (Isin 2002) – hashtag activism and performative solidarities that tackle racial, gender, and environmental injustice but are rarely linked to long-lasting political commitments against injustice. An urban collective consciousness is built through digitally mediated hyperlocal solidarities and transurban protests, but it is a consciousness that exists through its ephemerality. Liminality is generative, as it always implies hope and achievement of a new state; but if liminality's temporality becomes unending, it turns into insecurity and permanent suspension, an aspiration for something better to come but in the absence of any clear idea as to how to achieve that – apart from staying connected.

Thus demotic humanism, as I saw it emerge over many years of engagement with people and places, provides a frame for a critical epistemology that tells the story of the digital city through its humans and their practice. Against a top-down perspective privileging the corporate and state actors of digitization, the experiences and voices of those who are heard and of those who are silenced drive this analysis. Demotic humanism, we saw, unravels the intersubjective and intersectional making of digital cities and their humans through, with, and against inequalities and solidarities, through data and platforms and sometimes against them. The digital city is more than a category and a strategic policy of building infrastructures and systems of order; it's lived, sensed, and imagined differentially, both locally and globally. The transurban perspective that my discussion adopted aimed to emphasize the spatial and social diversities that divide cities, but also to illustrate the converging commonalities of the digital political and aesthetic economies that transnationalize particular conceptions of humanity, technology, and progress. As such, the lens of demotic humanism invites us to understand digital change through the multitude of actors, practices, and geographies that shape it and are shaped by it, avoiding binary interpretative frames of either technologized oppression or resistance.

By observing, listening, and reflecting on what happens when practice, values, and digitization come together in non-isomorphic and indeterminate constellations, demotic humanism empirically grounds conceptualizations of the city as an agonistic and lived space of order and disorder. Thus researching and analysing demotic humanism matters if we wish to understand the digital order – not as a command imposed from the top, but as an order that seems just (Boltanski and Chiapello 2005), rational (Wynter 2003), and ordinary (Wrong 1994). Unlike popular humanism and its identifiable, even if differing, tropes of a hegemonic vision of order, demotic humanism is messy, unpredictable, contradictory. It reflects the constant struggles around human life in cities torn by uncertainties and inequalities, but also in cities made through creativity, solidarity, and conviviality. Yet demotic humanism, precisely because it is mostly performed through ephemeral acts of solidarity and imagined through commodified visions of green, inclusive, and open cities, reproduces exclusions and does little to challenge the digital order and its fundamental consequences: an ordered urban humanity that rehumanizes some people sometimes, while sustaining conditions of racial, class, and gender dehumanization. What demotic humanism makes most apparent is the need to challenge the digital order at its core: the digital order calls for a critical humanism.

5
Critical Humanism
Against the Digital Order

To the urban flâneur's gaze, the digital city constantly reveals itself. The 4G and 5G towers have become ordinary urban signs, a new staple of city life, as newspaper stands once were. The old industrial estates have turned into carefully designed sites of convergent privilege and selective difference, most importantly staged so to be instagramable. Away go the factories, or they are pushed to the periphery, alongside the incinerators that burn the leftovers of overconsumption – reminders of the uncertain future of the urban world and of the predicament of perpetual demands for change, for the new. This is the communicative and infrastructural environment of the digital city.

If technologies of industrial capitalism – the factory and mechanical reproduction (Mason 2020) – and of colonialism – the telegraph and the slave ship (Towns 2022) – established a certain order of humanity, what particular order do technologies of digitization produce?

Let us remember that questions about who becomes human and how are not new, even if the advancement of digital economies, connected lives, and AI revived their relevance. In colonialism, the humanity of white Europeans, that is, of those who controlled transport and communication technologies, was unquestionable; yet colonized peoples, whose access to these technologies was strictly controlled, had to fight against the erasure of their claims to being human. In industrial capitalism, the humanity of the owners of the means of production was categorically superior to that of workers; workers had to resist for centuries their reduction to mere components of production chains. When it comes to the digital order, who are the ones deemed to be (to various degrees) human, and where do (or should) struggles against a hierarchical humanity take place?

I open this chapter with a reference to the technologies of modernity's prevailing orders – colonialism and industrial capitalism – so as to identify and place the digital order within the historical and technological trajectories of social control. These are continuing but also changing trajectories of regulation; humanity is constituted and performed within and against order, differentially, and through processes of selective humanization and dehumanization. I have highlighted, across the pages of this book, the conflicting claims to humanity made by different actors of the digital city. I aimed to speak to the connections between the current conjuncture of 'hyperconnectivity' (Brubaker 2023) and the past and present trajectories of the urban world made through histories of violence, extraction of value from life and from places, but also innovation and agency. Throughout the book I have also argued that we can understand the relationship between technology and power only by paying close attention to the human and to the constitution of humanity through and with technology. In this final chapter I conclude by focusing on the human not only as a category mobilized for control in the context of popular humanism, not only as a liminal subject of changing cities in the context of demotic humanism, but *both* as an analytical category *and* as an actor at the heart of contestations of the digital order. With Mosco (2019: 1), I ask what the democratizing and humanizing alternatives to cities are, when we do not assume that 'the answer begins and ends with technology'. I argue for an epistemological and political response that rethinks the human. I speak here of critical humanism.

Critical humanism represents the third dimension of the competing humanisms of the digital city. Popular humanism, we saw, mobilizes sociotechnical imaginaries of diversity, sustainability, and openness in order to reassure distrustful citizens that digital corporations and the state have people's well-being, rights, and freedom at heart. We also saw how important these values are for urban humans as, in everyday life, they mobilize their own experiential, affective, and agentive capabilities so as to manage change and crisis through a demotic humanism. Looking into the digital city, we have observed how urban humans have not let go of fundamental humanist values such as dignity, autonomy, and freedom; these still are, or become again, prominent ideals in sociotechnical imaginaries driven from the top and from the bottom of the city. Most importantly, we saw that many need these values – especially those at the urban margins and those who experience the intensity of a digitally generated violence managed through surveillance and interveillance: minoritized groups stereotyped, silenced, prosecuted on the basis of racial, gendered, and ability profiling enacted on the cities' material and digital streets. They need these values now as much as ever.

The initial, generative force behind this book came from my observations around the dynamic comeback of humanist values in and for the digital city. The return (or the new life) of humanist imagination may be a response to the rising mistrust of technology and its affordances of control, or to the ontological insecurities generated by the perpetual crises of neoliberal capitalism, or to the circulation of activist demands for respect for those who regularly suffer dehumanization – and possibly a variegated response to all of the above. Observing the rising appeal of humanism may be significant in its own right. But what the return of humanism(s) reveals and hides matters much more.

The argument at the heart of the book is that humanism matters. It matters when it mobilizes power (popular humanism), it matters when it normalizes power (demotic humanism), and it also matters when it contests power (critical humanism). At the centre of my discussion in this final chapter is precisely that contestation: critical humanism as a performative opening, a praxis, and an intellectual invitation, an epistemology for contesting the digital makings of a hierarchical humanity. Here I discuss critical humanism as praxis and as epistemology, in turn. I follow this dual pathway to emphasize that considering alternatives to the digital order is not merely a scholarly exercise but a committed political and intellectual stance. I also want to show how the epistemology of critical humanism draws its energy from a praxis that envisions and enacts democratic and inclusive digital cities. I thus deliberately start with the praxis of critical humanism, offering some insights into the many ways in which local, national, and transurban political action reclaims the city through, and occasionally against, technology. The projects I will refer to in illustrating critical humanist praxis are neither pure nor perfect but reflect a process of exploration of what humanist values for technologized cities could or should be; more than anything, these glimpses into critical humanist praxis capture particular moments within sociotechnical imaginaries and political practices mobilized against the dehumanization of digitally ordered cities. They show how the city itself generates critical humanist responses to the co-optation and contradictions of popular humanism and demotic humanism. After discussing critical humanist praxis, I move to reflecting on a critical humanist epistemology and propose that we pay serious attention to the values of justice and freedom when researching technology, urbanism, and power.

Critical humanism as praxis

Cities are hotspots of technological innovation, but also of inequalities. Against these, or precisely because of them, cities 'hold out the promise of democracy' (Mosco 2019: 6). This is not a new promise. Historically, the city has been the epicentre of a politics of discontent and resistance against authoritarianism and exploitation (Harvey 1996, 2009; Marcuse et al. 2021). The urban trajectories of dissent are finding new expressions in the city, pushing forward political claims for justice and the right to the city (Cardullo et al. 2019; Kitchin 2019a, 2019b) through, or in response to, digital urbanism. This politics takes multiscalar expressions, observable in local, national, and transurban mobilizations that propose alternatives to the commodified, controlling, and discriminatory urbanism of the digital order.

I briefly discuss here three different kinds of praxis that challenge the digital order and its hierarchical humanity. In terms of scale I will use local, national, and transurban examples, each speaking of a politics of voice, care, and public good. Each of those cases involves a range of diverse actors and differential performances of the right to the digital city (Cardullo et al. 2019). What they all share is a performative enactment of resistance against the divisive order that mobilizes technologies for the selective rehumanization of certain constituencies in the city and for the perpetual dehumanization of others.

I start this multiscalar snapshot of the praxis of critical humanism at the level of the local, precisely because the micro-scale of the neighbourhood reveals what the large-scale politics of urban and platform governance hides, sometimes deliberately: the small acts of reclaiming and hacking the commodified digital spaces of visibility. Against the dehumanization of migrants through racial profiling, exclusion, and the hostile environment that the British government has created against them (Gentleman 2023), the North London grassroots Haringey Welcome inaugurated in 2023 a podcast series titled *No Small Victories*. Through a series of interviews with local activists and migrants in the London Borough of Haringey, *No Small Victories* claims its space across the commodified podcast spaces of voice, to demand not large audiences but migrant justice. Put together by local volunteers and activists, this is just one small and particular expression of a wider culture of political praxis – an urban example of micro-scale activism, which digitally generates and circulates voices from the margins in cities that suffer the effects of surveillance and deep inequalities.

The podcast series focuses specifically on a praxis of voice: opening up a co-creative space where the voices from the margins – 'a sound nobody wants to hear' (hooks 1989: 16) – gain centre-stage. As *No Small Victories* is available on all mainstream podcast platforms, the social capacity built collectively around it reminds us of how hooks (1989) refers to the margins as a site of radical possibility. Of course, *No Small Victories* is unlikely to attract the most devoted Spotify users, whom the platform's algorithmic order privileges, supporting them to buy more and to listen to more (profit-generating) sounds. However, for the praxis of critical humanism this is of lesser importance. Just as Guma speaks of the informal and transient structures that generate collective life, work, and a way of being at the peripheries of African digital cities, infrastructures of voice also generated at the periphery of the global city 'instigate a mode of practice that speaks to different ways of being-in-the-world' (Guma 2021: 2). What the podcast technology does in this case is to amplify voices from the margins – not by making them heard by many others elsewhere, but by making it possible to speak to the collective urban self from there, from elsewhere, from everywhere – from the digital space that the podcast platforms open; this space is affectively proximate but also part of a (digital) societal whole. In hooks' (1989: 20) words, '[t]o be in the margins is to be part of the whole but outside the main body'. The sociotechnical imaginary of the city becomes not just one of selective inclusion of the few but, at least momentarily, one of presence and recognition, where 'place-specific innovations and [the] ingenuity of ordinary residents' (Guma and Mwaura 2021: 14) place their humanity centre-stage against the symbolic boundaries of the digital economies of racism and discrimination.

Digital infrastructures provide platforms of control but also, no less importantly, platforms of voice, as seen in this initiative. The name of the podcasts itself – *No Small Victories* – emphasizes how it is not only the scale that matters in a politics of resistance; the act of claiming dignity and freedom is invaluable in its own right. *No Small Victories* is an example of the ordinary acts of citizenship (Isin 2002) that generate collective capabilities to demand an unconditional recognition of pluriversality (Escobar 2020) for the city that is connected to networks not only of power but also of life and resistance.

Such claims to pluriversal humanity are not just hyper-local; they have grown as coordinated activism on a national and transurban scale. At the national level, the case of the Joint Council for the Welfare of Immigrants in the UK (JCWI) and its demand for digital justice for migrants destabilizes imaginaries of universally applied rights across the nation. JCWI is only one of the many campaign groups in the country, and also across Europe and beyond, that have recently elevated digital justice as a fundamental right by placing it at the core of their activism. The aim of this and similar campaigns is to generate public awareness of how racist politics is increasingly enacted through digital systems of control. 'A key part of the Hostile Environment is a swathe of datasharing arrangements between different public agencies that allow the Home Office to access people's personal information for the purpose of immigration enforcement', the group highlights in its campaign (JCWI 2023). At the heart of this campaign is human vulnerability – how migrants can be 'switched off', made invisible, or deemed to be dangerous through data classifications: 'A digital-only status that provides migrants with no physical documentation risks allowing the Home Office to "switch off" a person's status and entitlement to services when it decides – rightly or wrongly – that a person no longer has the right to be in the UK' (JCWI 2023). As migrants' being and becoming humans with rights increasingly depends on their data classification, the digital border expands into their cities of residence (Chouliaraki and Georgiou 2022). Through perpetual data profiling, every day and every city effectively turn into sites of making and unmaking humanity. But not without resistance. The Digital Justice Toolkit, developed by a wider coalition (Open Rights Group 2022) that includes JCWI, aims to raise awareness about the dehumanizing technologies of migration governance and to offer tangible tools to refuse digital control, but also to advance the ethics of digital care. Offering information on how to resist digital control, this toolkit sets forth the language of digital rights in order to turn harm into benefit; this is a politics of peripheral care that aims at 'undoing harm' (Simone 2018: 122) with and through the digital. The digital is not just a technological apparatus of control, we are being reminded. Most importantly, constituencies that are pushed out of the mainstream political and media spaces, with no or little space of recognition within them, have no choice but to direct claim-making through the digital.

Summoning the language of rights, activists such as those behind the Digital Justice Toolkit expound a politics of care – working at the juncture of hyperlocal grassroots activism and national campaigning to contest the governmentality of migrant lives in various quarters of the city. The language of digital rights has gained transurban prominence, too, not least through progressive local governments' contestations of digital inequalities and injustices.

At the transurban level, pressures against the lack of accountability surrounding the use of personal data by corporations and the state to classify individuals and groups have spilled outside the field of activism, occasionally generating policy change. Most significantly, the growing municipalist movements (Russell 2019; Thompson 2021), with their progressive and sometimes radical commitment to the right to the city, have brought digital justice claims into urban policymaking. The most prominent example is that of the Cities Coalition for Digital Rights, a coalition of fifty cities, mostly in Europe and North America, proclaiming their commitment to a vision of digital cities that prioritizes their humans and their environment. This is also a commitment to

> promoting and defending digital rights in urban context through city action, to resolve common digital challenges

and work towards legal, ethical and operational frameworks to advance human rights in digital environments ... The Cities Coalition for Digital Rights bring [sic] together cities committed to harnessing technology to improve the lives of people and support communities in cities by providing trustworthy and secure digital services and infrastructure. (Cities Coalition for Digital Rights 2022)

The Cities Coalition for Digital Rights, as a mayor-led transurban initiative, aims to amplify debates that have grown across cities, themselves revealing the ethical maturity (Mhlambi 2020) of a progressive policy that proposes 'a deeply normative vision for smart cities that is rooted in ideas of citizenship, social justice, the public good, and the right to the city that needs to be developed in conjunction with citizens' (Kitchin 2019a: 193). Such municipal initiatives also uncover the crisis of the digital sublime (Mosco 2005) – the mythologies that have driven power conceptions and applications of digital cities for so long (Mosco 2005, 2019; Mackinnon, Burns, and Fast 2022).

As the fragility of mythologies of technologically induced urban betterment and shared benefits of digital transformation becomes more apparent, so does the demand for accountability and the effort of progressive municipalism to offer 'democratic alternatives' (Mosco 2019: 1) and to introduce systems of regulation and accountability against the full intrusion of Big Tech in systems of health, education, and public services. Of course, the stories of different cities vary and these differences matter to the kinds of life and order within each one of them. Yet the decentralized approach to the city offered here aims to capture key ethico-political expressions of resistance and alternative pathways for urban futures vis-à-vis the digital order. This is a reminder that not only hegemonic visions of digital cities circulate globally, but also their opposites and alternative versions. Demands for cities driven by respect for life rather than by profit (Brenner et al. 2012; Greenfield 2017; Kotkin 2016) are not local exceptions but widely circulated challenges to

Big Tech's domination and to the failed promises of corporations, media, and the state to tackle inequalities through a depoliticized vision of technosolutionism.

These glimpses into just a few among the many manifestations of critical humanism's praxis at local, national, and transurban level indicate that the bizarre humancentrism generated in centres of power is confronted by a different kind of humanism in progressive and radical politics. To the growing realization that the digital order functions as an opaque system of ordering and othering (Van Houtum and Van Naerssen 2002), the cases discussed here add a pluriversal imagination of being and becoming urban human: these are glimpses into the many pathways that various constituencies need to follow if they are to claim open, diverse, and inclusive cities, which are against, but also within, the digital and social structures of technologized cities.

Epistemological blind spots: Why we need a humanist reading of the digital city

> The premise is to change the terms and not just the content of the conversation.
> Mignolo 2009: 20

I read the digital city through a critical humanist lens, following my own observations, but also as I try to respond to what may be considered epistemological blind spots in the current research on digitization, power, and the city. If we start our interrogation of urban change through theories of datafication and digitization and through methodologies that privilege objects of study such as data, AI, and algorithms, what and whom are we pushing to the margins of our scholarship? Who is silenced and whose agency and affect are ignored or misunderstood? Put in Foucauldian terms (see Foucault 1978), what is the cognitive order created through policy and corporate discourse, but also through academic discourse – a contemporary episteme that ties the present and the future of cities and of humanity to technology, both by celebrating and by critiquing its implications? Is it possible that this episteme effectively acts as a normalizing force of existing power relations in urban societies that transition from neoliberalism to post-neoliberalism?

As we saw, the neoliberal promise of individual success and economic growth becomes less and less convincing for most urban humans; as capitalism faces its crises, its episteme mutates (Foucault 1970). Through the analysis of the digital cities' competing humanisms, we have come to grasp the limits of a broad-brush framing of digitization as a mere realization of neoliberal domination (with Big Tech deciding and profiteering and humans adapting to corporate command). As actors that range from corporations to national and local governments and to citizens and non-citizens mobilize a range of diverse and contradictory humanist imaginaries to advance their competing stakes, we get to know that neoliberalism is more than 'a transmission belt from some ethereal sphere of greater forces' (Massey 2007: 11). Neoliberalism is in trouble and at the same time reinvents itself, showing in its revamped popular humanism that different agents and their actions matter.

In the 1970s, when neoliberalism was making its initial advance, Wynter argued that capitalism is sustained not through the modes of production alone but through 'the economic conception of the human – *Man* – that is produced by the disciplinary discourse of our now planetary system of academia as the first purely secular and operational public identity in human history' (Wynter 2000: 160); this is an identity, Wynter continues, that 'unifies us as a species in *economically* ... absolute terms'. The concept of *Homo economicus* dominated society and academia for a long time, but its current decline is accompanied by the rising currency of digital posthumanism. A possibly better, possibly more fragile human, constituted through technology rather than economy, comes centre-stage in imaginaries of urban futures. We can see this imaginary manifested in public investment that prioritizes digital infrastructures of health against investment in medical staff, popular representations that visualize humans as cyborgs, and scholarship that focuses simultaneously on the potential of AI and datafication to improve life conditions and on the threats they pose to human autonomy and life more generally.

Like *Homo economicus*, the concept of the posthuman now works as a normative frame for understanding humanity, its constitution, and its trajectories. The connected (wo)man as a conception of the human (or posthuman, for that matter) dominates academic thought, unravelling a new order of discourse that brings under the digital everything and everyone that matters. Yet seeing the world through the deterministic force of technology reflects the continuing currency of a Eurocentric episteme – one driven by economic and technological rationalities, and one that sets norms and regulations about what and how to conduct research. Against these rationalities, a critical humanist response is urgent.

Scholars such as Eubanks (2018), Benjamin (2019a, 2019b), and Noble (2018) have already questioned this episteme by discussing how data-driven and data-controlled governance of the lifeworld reproduces and enhances racial, gendered, and class hierarchies. Alongside the processes discussed in that literature of classifying humanity according to economic risk and value, what the digital city further reveals is the complication of racial, class, and gender hierarchies, as urban humanity is divided anew, within a technologically managed dehumanization–rehumanization continuum. Those who already are privileged benefit from technologies of convenience that mediate work, sociality, and even self-discovery (Beatty 2020); those without privilege are promised rehumanization against the dehumanizing conditions of marginality, as long as they can embrace digitization by consenting to control, by developing entrepreneurial skills relevant to the digital economy, and by finding capital to spend, spend, and spend within it. This is a process that does not match neatly the categories of class, race, and gender (or those of ability, sexuality, and geography), but instead makes hierarchies opaque through the promise of 'digital inclusion'. How do we understand that movement of being and becoming human, or of being denied being and becoming human, through the promises and the rules of the digital order? Do we have the language, the tools, the research interest, and the ethical orientation to see why the human – as a category and as an actor – matters to the digital order?

For a critical humanism

I have been reminded through my research and readings that the most compelling claims to humanism come from those who experience dehumanization. Arendt's humanism unravels the brutality of concentration camps, Wynter's humanism responds to the suffering and resistance of the Black diaspora, hooks' humanism speaks to the intersectional violation of humanity at the racialized margins of the urban world. These humanist approaches remind us that claims to humanity do not represent a mere intellectual debate but a need of the dehumanized to be seen, heard, and recognized. We may need to remember what these claims represent, historically and in present times, when platformization and advances in AI – and even in machine intuition – raise scepticism about the relevance of the human: who needs to be seen as human, and what for, anyway? – some ask. As certain humanities are yet again brushed aside in the arms race that accelerates order through investment, diffusion and normalization of platforms and AI across all elements of life, from learning to health and to communicating, new and longstanding claims to recognition gain urgency. The longstanding ones come from those who have historically experienced dehumanization repeatedly. Exploitative and extractive economies, or even sophisticated systems of surveillance, are not digital capitalism's inventions, as those at the margins of the urban world know well. After all, racial profiling, intense surveillance, racism, misogyny, and classism have been fundamental dimensions of the ever-expanding geographies of exclusion and the violent reproduction of order – violent albeit unseen by those with privilege. Alongside these old, longstanding claims against the dehumanizing technologies of colonialism and capitalism, new claims emerge at present. Many of those who have long enjoyed the privileges of the racial, class, and gender order are now becoming exposed to insecurities that those at the margins have experienced for so long. This happens as individuals' data profiles evaluate everything and everyone on the basis of risk; more and more individuals are now becoming exposed to the possibility of losing access to work, housing, and health, as automated decision-making could at any time deem them a risk on account of ill health, income, or even family relations changes (Eubanks 2018). This also means that the constituencies in need of tools, methods, and institutions that can control the surveillance systems themselves and protect the ownership of individual and collective data keep growing exponentially.

If it is from the margins that we can see most clearly how the technologies of extraction and control work, it is also from the margins that we can best comprehend the possibilities of resisting the digital order and its selective humanization. Tactics of hacking the digital order – sharing one's Wi-Fi with those who cannot afford connectivity, or using social media to organize acts of commoning, such as squatting for the homeless – remind us why being human in the digital city matters. They also remind us that being and becoming urban humans is an always incomplete process and takes its meaning at the juncture of human and human–non-human assemblages and under conditions of intertwined changes: technological, social, economic, cultural.

With these observations in mind, one can see that the critical humanism proposed here pushes the boundaries in understanding urban life beyond the core arguments in digital urbanism. The conception of critical humanism outlined in this book emerges in dialogue with postcolonial, transnational, and feminist theory and activism, a dialogue that challenges the project of a unitary human as much as the notion of a single technologized future. Critical humanism opens up a critical space of engagement with the city, technology, and power. This is most necessary at the present, when the human is claimed by the most powerful actors as the driving and legitimizing force of the rehumanizing–dehumanizing continuum that drives the transformation of cities into datafied, surveillant, and discriminatory spaces for profit and that of humans into aggregated data and commodities.

Against presentism and technodeterminism

If we are to challenge the digital order effectively, we need to put the values of dignity, autonomy, and freedom back at the heart of intellectual and political responses to it; we need to recognize the need for a critical humanism against the dehumanizing workings of the digital order. This is not a new claim, of course. Black humanists such as W. E. B. Du Bois, Frantz Fanon, and Sylvia Wynter integrated humanist ideals into their radical political claims, contesting white European elites' claim of ownership of humanism. Humanist claims centred on struggles against inequality are not new but are part of complex histories of humanism; these are claims that historically coexist with a justified suspicion of Enlightenment humanism and its association with colonial violence. In critical data studies and posthumanism, the split between the humanist and the antihumanist trajectories has taken a new turn. Posthumanism and some critiques of digital capitalism have once again displaced claims of being human – sometimes fiercely, often wrongly.

The 'death of the human' has two blind spots. First, it assumes an (imaginary) past, where 'the human' existed as a stable and essential category, unlike now. We know, of course – through Black, feminist, postcolonial, and indigenous theorizations of the human as well as through empirical evidence on ethics, politics, and traditions from across the world – that being human, with dignity, autonomy, and freedom, has always been about claims for and against power.

We also know that humanism is not limited to Europe, since dignity, autonomy, and freedom are moral and political values circulating across the world, as can be seen in African Ubuntu, Black humanism, or Confucianism. Second, 'the death of the human' as a critique of digital capitalism is often driven by the fallacy of presentism (Chernilo 2017: 11). Digital capitalism, it is argued, is so dehumanizing that what makes us humans – agency, autonomy, and the desire for freedom – has been so comprehensively corrupted and colonized by platforms, data, and their political economy that it is now redundant. Such technoderministic presentism, however, erases long histories of struggles against the many dehumanizing economies and technologies of control. To the dehumanizing trajectories of capitalism and its current digital incarnations, the death of the human offers unsatisfactory answers.

This displacement of the human in critical readings of digital lives and digital cities thus becomes doubly problematic: politically, it emboldens those in power to claim the human against antihumanist critiques of technology; conceptually, it gives answers to urban digital futures by displacing the humans, and thus meaning-making within digital change – underestimating what it actually means to live so much of everyday life on platforms and through apps, to be surveilled on the street and on the screen, to be part of human and non-human digital assemblages, and effectively to channel one's needs and desires through these assemblages.

Humanist values are not the problem (and not the solution either – or not in their own right). The desire to be human is not an outdated problematic; digital capitalism's overwriting the human is not the endpoint. Beyond these polarizations, we need to see what the revival of humanism requires. Claims to or against humanity, yet again, have become a site of struggle. We witnessed in Chapter 3 the incorporation of humanist values into the sociotechnical imaginaries advanced by those who occupy the city's centres of authority; we saw how those at the centre of power, who also feel the fragility of neoliberalism, mobilize those values to speak on behalf of an idealized and connected humanity in their strategic communication and consequently to advance their plans for urban transformations. We also saw in Chapter 4 that many of those who populate urban streets and neighbourhoods experiment with new and old ways of being human with others, and sometimes against them, by mobilizing technologies that enhance pleasure and work opportunities, but also the surveillance of the most vulnerable. These competing humanisms matter – both separately and together, for research and for politics alike. They matter if we want to understand what is at stake when competing claims are made for and on behalf of urban humanity. And they matter if we want to invalidate the appropriation of humans for profit and to encourage a politics of hope and freedom.

What popular humanism and demotic humanism demand is a response to the digital order: a critical humanism. This response needs to decouple human progress from technological innovation, so as to 'effectively denaturalise' this relationship (Mansell and Steinmuller 2022), and to consider human autonomy and freedom together with, but sometimes also beyond, technology. It needs to decentre technology and recentre justice, autonomy, and freedom against what might look like progress but in reality compromises life (human and non-human).

The values of critical humanism

Critical humanism is not offering a mere collection of established humanist values; it engages with an epistemology and a praxis that speak to those values in new ways and at the juncture of power, technology, and the city. I want to conclude this conversation not with a closure of argument but with an opening – an invitation to think about cities beyond the digital order, through a set of nine values that I came to identify during the research that generated this book project. This is an attempt to open rather than close a conversation on the ethics, the politics, and in effect the relevance of the research we conduct with cities and urban humans.

Critical humanism is radical: It represents an epistemological commitment to understanding being and becoming human as an always incomplete process situated at the juncture of the past (with its histories of knowledge production and inequalities), the present (with its experiences of change and order), and the future (with its individual and collective imaginings of what is to come or ought to come). This means (1) recognizing the diverse trajectories within and across humanity that contest universalizing conceptions of the human as a unique and normative biological and cognitive entity that rationally defines progress; (2) decentring conceptions of actors that matter by seeing and speaking to experiences of those who claim humanity beyond that of the familiar subject – usually beyond being western, white, and middle-class; and (3) contesting the epistemic rationality of Eurocentrism, which habitually reproduces linear conceptions of change, in this case digitization, as an undeviating process that either releases or crushes human freedom. Instead, critical humanism recognizes the longer trajectories of capitalist accumulation and technological innovation, and how digitization becomes embedded in current and particular technological, cultural, and economic conditions of human life. Furthermore, critical humanism adopts an intersectional and transnational approach to recognizing and critiquing power as well as its contestations. This requires sensibilities for simultaneously identifying and speaking to the technological and structural injustices *and* the 'radical interventions' (Mignolo 2009: 11) in the life of the city that open the 'possibility of our eventual emancipation, of our eventual full autonomy, as humans' (Wynter 2000: 195).

Critical humanism is pluriversal: Humanist values contest the digital order only when they speak to technological change through the lens of a pluriversality (Escobar 2020).

Only when driven by a pluriversal conception (Escobar 2020) of urban humanity that provincializes knowledge (Bhambra 2014; Willems 2014a, 2014b) do these values recognize the many voices, experiences, and indeed humanities that a democratic city can enable, sometimes against the potentials and limits of technology. A pluriversal approach challenges the universalist idealism of 'all humans are the same' approaches, as this idealism effectively reproduces privilege among those who have long been recognized for their humanity and leaves behind those whose experiences and voices, on and off platforms, have been marginalized and even pathologized. What this means is that visions of humane (digital) futures demand a recognition of the particular pathways through which different urban constituencies need to gain access to what all humans in the whole urban world need: dignity, autonomy, and freedom.

Critical humanism is political: The claim to being human is a political claim, a claim that Benjamin (2019a) also emphasizes as being fundamental to both understanding and contesting power and order. In her critique of the racial dimensions of technology, Benjamin (2019b: 32) emphasizes the idea that architectures of power are shaped as 'different genres of humanity are constructed in the process'. Freire, in his pedagogy of the oppressed, also speaks of the different genres of humanity, ordered not only through exclusion but also through the selectively applied promise of rehumanization that erases certain humanities. In the digital city, those historically dehumanized are promised rehumanization if they integrate into the structures and cultures of consent, into the violence of the same (Han 2018), into surveillance and the commodification of all forms of life. But those who need rehumanization 'may discover through existential experience that their present way of life is irreconcilable with their vocation to become fully human' (Freire 1996: 61). What is needed, Freire emphasizes, is not integration 'into the structure of oppression' but rather the transformation of that structure, so that the excluded 'can become "beings for themselves'" (62). I argue, with Benjamin and Freire, that we need to see, not ignore, humans – in the plurality of their trajectories, which reflect the uneven distribution of rights and freedoms, historically constituted through uneven and unequal access to technologically produced and circulated systems of knowledge and urban resources. Only then can we talk of a (or any) humanism that destabilizes structures and cultures of oppression.

Critical humanism is not Luddite: Contesting the digital order is not contesting digital change. What I suggest is not a Luddite response to technology but a critique of the digital sorting of worthy and unworthy humanities. Critical humanism recognizes that infrastructural change and digital artefacts can, and often do, support a good life for many people, through opportunities for play, work, health, and acts of citizenship. In fact we need to be aware that, for those at the margins – often excluded from mainstream spaces of publicity and representation – voice and claims cannot but be routed digitally. Critical humanism need not call for 'switching off', for fully disconnecting, but instead for 'switching over' – finding pathways to reclaim spaces of freedom online as much as offline, to contest the power and domination of Big Tech and its logics of surveillance, often shared with the state. Thus digital change is desirable as long as it works in one of the pluriversal ways of being and becoming against the extractive normativity, single and monolithic, of the digital order. It becomes dangerous for the city and for the lives in it when offered as a solution to the problems caused by the same economies that generated it and created these problems in the first place. A critical humanist perspective does not dismiss political economic responses to digitization. On the contrary, it amplifies their significance: extractive and surveillant technologies of platformization and datafication are dangerous precisely because of the threats they present to humans (and many other forms of life, for that matter) when they reduce the value of life to data and profitable commodities, when they divide and classify people and places on the basis of their estimated profitability and the economic risk they may present. Critical humanism is not an alternative to but a lens on critical data studies and digital urbanism.

Critical humanism is situated: Critical humanism conceives of power and resistance in the temporalities and spatialities of an unequal but interconnected urban world, in the intimacies of continents (Lowe 2015) that unevenly tie the fate of some places and people to the fate of other places and people, proximate or distant. Situatedness is fundamental to conceiving of the urban world in its economic, but also in its human interconnectedness; it recognizes both the particular, transurban currency of technologically induced progress and freedom and its positionalities in legacies of colonialism and industrial capitalism. The situatedness of the human as a category of analysis and as an agent of change strives to 'prevent classification and ranking to justify domination and exploitation among people who are supposed to be equal by birth' (Mignolo 2009: 11) and contests the spatial and temporal universality of 'equal humans'. Thus critical humanism avoids *declaring* that the technological and economic power of digitization is universally relevant and applicable. Instead, it recognizes the situatedness of the digital order in local, national, and transurban spaces, in environments where humans and non-humans coexist and sometimes compete among themselves, and in the different landscapes that involve corporate, state, citizen, and non-citizen actors.

Critical humanism is dewesternizing: Critical humanism can be progressive only if it challenges assumptions about the normativity of rigid divides between the global North (where power sits) and the global South (where power is exercised). Critical humanism needs to be uncomfortable with systems of knowledge that reproduce singular, patriarchal, or Eurocentric conceptions of geography, humanity, and technology. Specifically, it needs to keep questioning old and new normative frameworks – such as that of posthumanism, which make claims by universalizing privilege and western systems of knowledge and experience – or western-centric political economy – which overlooks meaning-making processes generated from the margins, as migrants and urban subalterns connect with places and people across the world (López 2007). Datta (2023), using Chakrabarty's (2000) notion of provincialization, speaks to the need to recognize how alternative and plural systems of knowledge on digital cities are produced at the urban margins and by people historically excluded and misrecognized. Within digital cities, urban divides continue to be reproduced through unequal access to infrastructures and privacy; they are also reaffirmed through sociotechnical imaginaries that perceive urban divides of class, gender, and race as stable vis-à-vis technological (and determinant) change. However, critical epistemology requires an understanding of urban divides as shaped at the juncture of technological, racial, class, gender, and geographical relations, none of these being predetermined.

Critical humanism is historicized: A foundational grounding of a critical humanist perspective is the recognition of the long entanglement of technology with humanity. This is not new. Humanity, we now know, does not exist outside the discourse and practice of technologies that selectively recognize those who are human (or human enough). For a long time, media and communication technologies, through representations, have produced knowing and unknowing subjects, symbolically marking boundaries around humans who matter and deserve recognition, in contrast with those who don't. Even more, modernity's historical trajectories uncover how those in power have always mobilized technologies, not only to make but also to divide and debase humanity (Gilroy 2011). Humanity has never been about an essential, unchanged, or all-encompassing entity, either in the past or now. Thus the conception of the human in critical humanism is always under erasure and review. 'The traditional volitional, dispositional, affective and indeed moral connotations of the human are in need of permanent redefinition', argues Chernilo (2017: 13). A historical perspective also points out how order reveals but also hides its power when this is displaced by celebratory discourses of technological change. More specifically, the order of discourse (Foucault 1970) has for a long time produced a normativity that ties technological advancements to the optimal humans – namely those who become better humans because they have the cognitive and literacy capabilities to embrace technology, from controlling industrial machinery to living with wearable digital technologies. Those lacking these capabilities are often deemed by the market, the state, and the media as lesser humans, they are losing out, they are at fault. At the same time, the order's performative workings reveal what is usually hidden: that divides are not actually between the knowing and unknowing subjects but between the consenting subjects who sustain order and the ones who do not have the means or the desire to do so. The better human of the digital order is not the one who knows how to use, accept, celebrate, and benefit from technology but the one who consents to technology's perceived potential to improve societies and individuals. The establishment of a normative superiority of the technologically savvy subject is not new. But in the case of the digital order this normativity is more profound, not least because platforms, data, and AI are now integrated into all the aspects of work, pleasure, education, and health. At present we see those who consent to and, even more, those who celebrate the digital order, being rewarded with opportunities to socialize, to represent the self on social media, and to buy things that support well-being, productivity, and pleasure. But this recognition remains conditional on accepting the 'terms of reference' of platforms – more specifically, the many 'entrenched forms of technological dependence' (Huberman 2021: 342) and consent to surveilling the city. We know who the human of the digital order is, because we know who is *not*. We know who is included because we know who is *not*. The digital order after all renews, but also revamps, familiar colonial and capitalist tropes of assorting humans.

Critical urbanism is environmental: Critical humanism recognizes how the conditions of human and non-human life change not only through technological but also through environmental transformations. Thus it calls for accountability by identifying specific actors responsible for violence and destruction, instead of making generic condemnations of human domination over nature. Critical humanism questions the technologically driven promises for inclusive, diverse, and open cities not only because Big Tech's interests make these promises suspicious. The ongoing investment in digitization as a pathway for better cities, a vision embraced, albeit differently, by both the left and the right, pays little attention to the environmental consequences of cities organized around wireless networks, cloud computing, databanks, and algorithm-powered AI. The levels of energy emissions, digital material toxicity and waste, and aggregation of humans with non-human data points (Brevini 2022; Langlois and Elmer 2019), alongside the consequences of urban digital pollution for places and people in different parts of the world, cannot be ignored. The consequences of normative conceptions of progress through technology need to be debunked not only because of their dehumanizing consequences for urban humans, but also because of their dehumanizing and destructive consequences for places and different forms of life, human and non-human, all over the urban world and beyond.

Critical humanism is hopeful: Critical humanism offers a politics of hope against the selective and conditional rehumanization of the digital order. Against the digital order, it opens a space for imagining, enacting, and thinking of pluriversal urban worlds and urban humans' diverse pathways to humanization. It sustains and depends on a politics of hope (Mbembe 2021) whose precondition is 'dealing effectively with the spectres of the past' (Mbembe and Posel

2005: 283) and with the reproduction of current divisions of humanity into the (re)humanized, deemed digitally worthy, and the dehumanized, deemed digitally inferior or dangerous or irrelevant humans. Critical humanism recognizes and critiques the role of technology in discursively and affectively reproducing uneven dependencies. But its critique is also coupled with 'creative alternatives that bring to life liberating and joyful ways of living in and organizing our world' (Benjamin 2019b: 197). And while it understands how data and infrastructures fit in with state and corporate strategies to further profit and control, it does not lose heart.

Precisely because critical humanism does not relegate the human and life more generally to a second place but recognizes and respects them, it understands how and when digitization is about communication, community, connection; when the infrastructures of the digital are not the problem or the solution; and when promises for technologically induced progress do not advance profitable and anthropocentric cities, but the right to cities driven by equitable co-dependences and by new possibilities for claiming dignity, autonomy, and freedom.

Notes

NOTES TO CHAPTER 4

1 The research reported here is part of the project Youth Skills (ySKILLS) and received funding from the European Union's Horizon 2020 Research & Innovation Programme under Grant Agreement no. 870612. The team working on this project included, apart from myself, Alia Zaki in London, Leen d'Haenens, Veronica Donoso and Emilie Bossen in Belgium, and Ioanna Niaoti, who offered research support in Athens.
2 The project 'Resilient communities, resilient cities: Digital making of the city of refuge' was conducted from 2017 to 2019, mainly across three European cities – Athens, Berlin, and London – and secondarily in Hong Kong and Los Angeles. The team consisted of M. Georgiou (principal investigator), S. Hall (co-investigator), D. Dajani (research fellow), and K. Kolbe (research assistant). The project also benefited from fieldwork support from A. Koulaxi and P. Theorodopoulou in Athens and was supported by the Rockefeller Foundation in collaboration with the Institute of Global Affairs, LSE. The data were collected during creative workshops with migrants and civil society actors in each city (co-creative research tools were designed through collaboration with the studio Proboscis, where participants identified and discussed digital and material needs, resources, and obstacles that make or constrain the city of refuge) and during individual storytelling walks in the city

with migrants and civic actors. Participants were invited to narrate their experiences of migration throughout the city by taking us to the places that mattered to them and by driving the narrative in their storytelling; our role was primarily to listen rather than to frame the conversation. The walk storytelling methodology developed in collaboration with Counterpoints Arts and, specifically, with the photographer Marcia Chandra; its creative outputs are available at www.digitalcityofrefuge.com).

Bibliography

Administrative Capital for Urban Development. (2021). *The Capital Egypt: Smarter Future*. ACUD. Retrieved 21 April, 2023 from http://www.acud.eg.

Agamben, G. (2005). On the metropolis, trans. by J. Gavroche and A. Bove. Autonomies. https://autonomies.org/2017/10/giorgio-agamben-on-the-metropolis.

Ahearne, J. (2007). *Michel de Certeau: Interpretation and Its Other*. Cambridge: Polity.

Ahmed, S. (2007). The language of diversity. *Ethnic and Racial Studies*, 30 (2), 235–56. https://doi.org/10.1080/01419870601143927.

Aiello, G. (2021). Communicating the 'world-class' city: A visual-material approach. *Social Semiotics*, 31 (1), 136–54. https://doi.org/10.1080/10350330.2020.1810551.

Aitkenhead, D. (2011). Rise up, rise up. *Guardian Weekend* magazine, 31 December, pp. 13–15.

Alinejad, D., Candidatu, L., Mevsimler, M., Minchilli, C., Ponzanesi, S., and Van der Vlist, F. N. (2018). Diaspora and mapping methodologies: Tracing transnational digital connections and 'mattering maps'. *Global Networks*, 19 (1), 21–43.

Alpopi, C., and Manole, C. (2013). Integrated urban regeneration: Solution for cities revitalize [sic]. *Procedia Economics and Finance*, 6, 178–85.

Altan-Olcay, Ö. (2014). Entrepreneurial subjectivities and gendered complexities: Neoliberal citizenship in Turkey. *Feminist*

Economics, 20 (4), 235–59. https://doi.org/10.1080/13545701.2014.950978.
Amin, A. (2007). Re-thinking the urban social. *City*, 11 (1), 100–14.
Amin, A., and Thrift, N. (2017). *Seeing like a City*. Cambridge: Polity.
Amsterdam Smart City. (2021). Home page. https://amsterdamsmartcity.com.
Arendt, H. (1958). *The Human Condition*. Chicago, IL: University of Chicago Press.
Bai, C., Dallasega, P., Orzes, G., and Sarkis, J. (2020). Industry 4.0 technologies assessment: A sustainability perspective. *International Journal of Production Economics*, 229. https://doi.org/10.1016/j.ijpe.2020.107776.
Banet-Weiser, S. (2018). *Empowered: Popular Feminism and Popular Misogyny*. Durham, NC: Duke University Press.
Banet-Weiser, S., Gill, R., and Rottenberg, C. (2020). Postfeminism, popular feminism and neoliberal feminism? Sarah Banet-Weiser, Rosalind Gill and Catherine Rottenberg in conversation. *Feminist Theory*, 21 (1), 3–24. https://doi.org/10.1177/1464700119842555.
Baraka, C. (2021). The failed promise of Kenya's smart city. *Rest of World*, 1 June. Retrieved 18 April 2023 from https://restofworld.org/2021/the-failed-promise-of-kenyas-smart-city.
Barns, S. (2020). *Platform Urbanism: Negotiating Platform Ecosystems in Connected Cities*. Basingstoke: Palgrave Macmillan.
BBC. (2016). EU Referendum results. *BBC News*. https://www.bbc.co.uk/news/politics/eu_referendum/results.
Beatty, J. S. (2020). Technologies of convenience. In S. Hrisova, S. Hong, and J. D. Slack, eds, *Algorithmic Culture: How Big Data and Artificial Intelligence Are Transforming Everyday Life*. Lanham, MD: Lexington Books.
Bender, T., and Cinar, A. (2007). *Urban Imaginaries: Locating the Modern City*. Minneapolis, MN: University of Minnesota.
Benjamin, R. (2019a). *Captivating Technology: Race, Carceral Technoscience and Liberatory Imagination in Everyday Life*. Durham, NC: Duke University Press.
Benjamin, R. (2019b). *Race after Technology*. Cambridge: Polity.
Benjamin, W. (1997). *One-Way Street and Other Writings*. London: Verso.
Berger, K. (2017). A decade of protest photography by George

P. Hickey. Crosscut, 27 September. Retrieved 21 April 2023 from https://web.archive.org/web/20210303090839/http://features.crosscut.com/seattle-protest-photos-george-hickey-street-marches.

Berlant, L. (2011). *Cruel Optimism*. Durham, NC: Duke University Press.

Berlin Partner. (2020). Home page. Retrieved 19 April 2023 from https://www.berlin-partner.de/en/the-berlin-location/smart-city-berlin.

Bhambra, G. K. (2014). *Connected Sociologies*. London: Bloomsbury.

Big Data for Humans. (2017). Home page. https://e27.co/startups/big-data-for-humans.

Bleiker, R., Campbell, D. K., Hutchison, E., and Nicholson, X. (2013). The visual dehumanisation of refugees. *Australian Journal of Political Science*, 48 (4), 398–416. https://doi.org/10.1080/10361146.2013.840769.

Bloomberg UK. (2019). The city versus the nation-state defined, 2019. https://www.bloomberg.com/opinion/articles/2019-12-19/cities-protested-their-own-governments-in-2019-and-will-in-2020?leadSource=uverify%20wall.

Boltanski, L., and Chiapello, E. (2005). The new spirit of capitalism. *International Journal of Politics, Culture, and Society*, 18 (3/4), 161–88. http://www.jstor.org/stable/20059681.

Bottero, W. (2010). Intersubjectivity and Bourdieusian approaches to 'identity'. *Cultural Sociology*, 4 (1), 3–22. https://doi.org/10.1177/1749975509356750.

Bourdieu, P. (1977). *Outline of a Theory of Practice*. Cambridge: Cambridge University Press.

Bourdieu, P. (1984). *Distinction: A Social Critique of the Judgement of Taste*. London: Routledge.

Bourdieu, P. (1985). The market of symbolic goods. *Poetics*, 14 (1–2), 13–44. https://doi.org/10.1016/0304-422x(85)90003-8.

Bourdieu, P. (1993). *The Field of Cultural Production*. Cambridge: Polity.

Boyer, M. C. (1996). *CyberCities: Visual Perception in the Age of Electronic Communication*. Princeton, NJ: Princeton Architectural Press.

Braidotti, R. (2006). Posthuman, all too human. *Theory, Culture & Society*, 23 (7–8), 197–208. https://doi.org/10.1177/0263276406069232.

Braidotti, R. (2013). *The Posthuman*. Cambridge: Polity.

Braudel, F. (1979). *Civilization and Capitalism: 15th–18th Century*, Vol. 3: *The Perspective of the World*. New York: Harper & Row.

Brenner, N., Marcuse, P., and Mayer, M., eds. (2012). *Cities for People, Not for Profit: Critical Urban Theory and the Right to the City*. London: Routledge.

Brenner, N., Peck, J., and Theodore, N. (2010). After neoliberalization? *Globalizations*, 7 (3), 327–45. https://doi.org/10.1080/14747731003669669.

Brevini, B. (2022). *Is AI Good for the Planet?* Cambridge: Polity.

Brewster, T. (2019). Immigration cops just spent a record $1 million on the world's most advanced iPhone hacking tech. *Forbes*, 8 May. https://www.forbes.com/sites/thomasbrewster/2019/05/08/immigration-just-spent-a-record-1-million-on-the-worlds-most-advanced-iphone-hacking-tech.

Bridge, G. (2004). *Reason in the City of Difference*. London: Routledge.

Brubaker, R. (2023). *Hyperconnectivity and Its Discontents*. Cambridge: Polity.

Burbano, L. (2022). Africa and smart cities: Between a necessity and an emergency. *Tomorrow City*. https://tomorrow.city/a/africa-and-smart-cities.

Burns, R., Fast, V., and Mackinnon, D. (2023). Introduction: Towards urban digital justice: The smart city as an empty signifier. In D. Mackinnon, R. Burns, and V. Fast, eds, *Digital (In)justice in the Smart City*. Toronto: University of Toronto Press.

Business Insider. (2020). Social Media Users Report. *Business Insider*. https://www.businessinsider.com/global-social-network-users-report?r=US&IR=T.

Butler, J. (2006). *Gender Trouble*. London: Routledge.

Calhoun, C., and Sennett, R. (2007). Introduction. In C. Calhoun and R. Sennett, eds, *Practicing Culture*. London: Routledge.

Cammaerts, B. (2021). The new-new social movements: Are social media changing the ontology of social movements? *Mobilization*, 26 (3), 343–58. https://doi.org/10.17813/1086-671x-26-3-343.

Campano, G., Ghiso, M., and Sánchez, L. (2013). 'Nobody knows the... amount of a person': Elementary students critiquing dehumanization through organic critical literacies. *Research in the Teaching of English*, 48 (1), 98–125. http://www.jstor.org/stable/24398648.

Campbell, D. (1996). Political processes, transversal politics, and the anarchical world. In M. J. Shapiro and H. Alker, eds, *Challenging Boundaries*. Minneapolis: University of Minnesota Press.

Cardullo, P., Di Feliciantonio, C., and Kitchin, R., eds. (2019). *The Right to the Smart City*. Bingley: Emerald.

Castells, M. (1989). *The Informational City: Information Technology, Economic Restructuring and the Urban-Regional Process*. Oxford: Blackwell.

Castoriadis, C. (1987). *The Imaginary Institutions of Society*. Cambridge, MA: MIT Press.

Cecco, L. (2021). Toronto swaps Google-backed, not-so-smart city plans for people-centred vision. *Guardian*, 12 March. https://www.theguardian.com/world/2021/mar/12/toronto-canada-quayside-urban-centre.

Centre for London. (2021). London futures: Building a new vision for London to 2050 and beyond. Centre for London. Retrieved 21 April 2023 from https://www.centreforlondon.org/project/london-futures.

Chakrabarty, D. (2000). *Provincializing Europe: Postcolonial Thought and Historical Difference*. Princeton, NJ: Princeton University Press.

Cheney-Lippold, J. (2017). *We Are Data: Algorithms and the Making of Our Digital Selves*. New York: New York University Press.

Chernilo, D. (2017). *Debating Humanity: Towards a Philosophical Sociology*. Cambridge: Cambridge University Press.

Chouliaraki, L., and Georgiou, M. (2022). *The Digital Border: Migration, Technology, Power*. New York: New York University Press.

Christensen, M., and Jansson, A. (2015). Complicit surveillance, interveillance, and the question of cosmopolitanism: Toward a phenomenological understanding of mediatization. *New Media & Society*, 17 (9), 1473–91. https://doi.org/10.1177/1461444814528678.

Chun, W. H. K. (2016). *Updating to Remain the Same: Habitual New Media*. Cambridge, MA: MIT Press.

Cielemęcka, O., and Daigle, C. (2019). Posthuman sustainability: An ethos for our anthropocenic future. *Theory, Culture & Society*, 36 (7–8), 67–87. https://doi.org/10.1177/0263276419873710.

Cities Coalition for Digital Rights. (2022). About us. Cities for Digital Rights. https://citiesfordigitalrights.org/thecoalition.

City Possible. (2021). What is City Possible? City Possible. https://citypossible.com/cpuserportal/public/cpuserui/home.

Collier, C. (2019). Lonely people in big cities: How technology is both creating and solving the isolation crisis. *Smart Cities Connect.* https://smartcitiesconnect.org/lonely-people-in-big-cities-how-technology-is-both-creating-and-solving-the-isolation-crisis.

Couldry, N. (2000). *The Place of Media Power: Pilgrims and Witnesses of the Media Age.* London: Routledge.

Couldry, N. (2004). Theorising media as practice. *Social Semiotics,* 14 (2), 115–32. https://doi.org/10.1080/1035033042000238295.

Couldry, N. (2012). *Media, Society, World: Social Theory and Digital Media Practice.* Cambridge: Polity.

Couldry, N., and Hepp, A. (2017). *The Mediated Construction of Reality.* Cambridge: Polity.

Couldry, N., and Mejias, U. A. (2019). *The Costs of Connection: How Data Is Colonizing Human Life and Appropriating It for Capitalism.* Stanford, CA: Stanford University Press.

Cowen, D. (2020). Following the infrastructures of empire: Notes on cities, settler colonialism, and method. *Urban Geography,* 41 (4), 469–86. https://doi.org/10.1080/02723638.2019.1677990.

D'Amico, G., L'Abbate, P., Liao, W., Yigitcanlar, T., and Ioppolo, G. (2020). Understanding sensor cities: Insights from technology giant company driven smart urbanism practices. *Sensors,* 20 (16), 4391. https://doi.org/10.3390/s20164391.

Damiani, E., Kowalczyk, R., and Parr, G. (2017). Extending the outreach. *ACM Transactions on Internet Technology,* 18 (1), 1–7. https://doi.org/10.1145/3140543.

Datta, A. (2020). The 'smart safe city': Gendered time, speed, and violence in the margins of India's urban age. *Annals of the American Association of Geographers,* 110 (5), 1318–34. https://doi.org/10.1080/24694452.2019.1687279.

Datta, A. (2023). A dialogue with Ayona Datta. In D. Mackinnon, R. Burns, and V. Fast, eds, *Digital (In)justice in the Smart City.* Toronto: University of Toronto Press.

Davies, W. J., and Gane, N. (2021). Post-neoliberalism? An introduction. *Theory, Culture & Society,* 38 (6), 3–28. https://doi.org/10.1177/02632764211036722.

Dayan, D., and Katz, E. (1992). *Media Events.* Cambridge, MA: Harvard University Press.

de Certeau, M. (1984). Walking in the city. In M. de Certeau, *The Practice of Everyday Life.* Los Angeles, CA: University of California Press.

de Certeau, M. (1988). *The Writing of History*. New York: Columbia University Press.

de Certeau, M. (1997). *Culture in the Plural*. Minneapolis, MN: University of Minnesota Press.

Degen, M., and Rose, G. (2022). *The New Urban Aesthetic*. London: Bloomsbury.

Deleuze, G. (1995). *Negotiations, 1972–1990*. New York: Columbia University Press.

Deleuze, G., and Guattari, F. (2013). *A Thousand Plateaus: Capitalism and Schizophrenia*. London: Bloomsbury.

Deliveroo. (2020). About. Deliveroo. https://uk.deliveroo.news/about.

Dell. (2018). Digital cities. Dell Technologies. https://www.dell.com/content/dam/uwaem/production-design-assets/en/microsites/digital-cities/pdf/Digital_Cities_Whitepaper.pdf.

Deloitte. (2015). Africa is ready to leapfrog the competition through smart cities technology. Deloitte, Johannesburg. https://www2.deloitte.com/content/dam/Deloitte/za/Documents/risk/ZA_SMARTCITIESA4(VIEW)_020615.pdf.

Derickson, K. D. (2018). Urban geography III: Anthropocene urbanism. *Progress in Human Geography*, 42 (3), 425–35. https://doi.org/10.1177/0309132516686012.

De Sousa Santos, B. (2005). Beyond neoliberal governance: The world social forum as subaltern cosmopolitan politics. In B. De Sousa Santos and C. Rodriguez-Garavito, eds, *Law and Globalization from Below*. Cambridge: Cambridge University Press.

Devadas, V. (2021). Gendered technologies: Youth, gender and mobile phones in Chennai City. *Indian Journal of Gender Studies*, 29 (1), 5–75. https://doi.org/10.1177/09715215211056802.

Dillabough, J.-A., and Kennelly, J. (2010). *Lost Youth in the Global City: Class, Culture and the Urban Imaginary*. London: Routledge.

Doughty, K. (2019). Rethinking musical cosmopolitanism as a visceral politics of sound. In K. Doughty, M. Duffy, and T. Harada, eds, *Sounding Places*. Cheltenham: Edward Elgar Publishing.

Douglass, M., Garbaye, R., and Ho, K. C. (2019). *The Rise of Progressive Cities East and West*. New York: Springer.

Dugan, E., and Syal, R. (2023). New hostile environment policies show Windrush lessons 'not been learned'. *Guardian*,

22 January. https://www.theguardian.com/uk-news/2023/jan/22/new-hostile-environment-policies-immigration-home-office.

Dutta, M. J., and Pal, M. (2020). Theorizing from the global South: Dismantling, resisting, and transforming communication theory. *Communication Theory*, 30 (4), 349–69. https://doi.org/10.1093/ct/qtaa010.

Ebbersmeyer, S. (2017). Humanism. In S. Golob and J. Timmermann, eds, *The Cambridge History of Moral Philosophy*. Cambridge: Cambridge University Press.

Economist Impact (2022) Digital Cities Index. https://impact.economist.com/projects/digital-cities/

Edelman. (2021). The 2021 Edelman Trust Barometer. https://www.edelman.com/trust/2021-trust-barometer.

Escobar, A. (2010). Latin America at a crossroads. *Cultural Studies*, 24 (1), 1–65. https://doi.org/10.1080/09502380903424208.

Escobar, A. (2020). *Pluriversal Politics: The Real and the Possible*. Durham, NJ: Duke University Press.

Esposito, R. (2012). *Third Person: Politics of Life and Philosophy of the Impersonal*. Cambridge: Polity.

Eubanks, V. (2018). *Automating Inequality: How High-Tech Tools Profile, Police, and Punish the Poor*. New York: St Martin's Press.

Fanon, F. (2004). Algeria unveiled. In P. Duara, ed., *Decolonization: Perspectives from Now and Then*. London: Routledge.

Fassin D. (2007). Humanitarianism as politics of life. *Public Culture*, 19, 499–520.

Fassin, D. (2019). Humanism: A critical reappraisal. *Critical Times*, 2 (1), 29–38. https://doi.org/10.1215/26410478-7769750.

Ferreri, M. (2021). *The Permanence of Temporary Urbanism: Normalising Precarity in Austerity London*. Amsterdam: Amsterdam University Press.

Ferris, G. (2022). Automated policing helped kill Chris Kaba. Novara Media, 14 September. https://novaramedia.com/2022/09/14/a-police-algorithm-helped-kill-chris-kaba.

Firth, R. (2020). Mutual aid, anarchist preparedness and Covid-19. In J. Preston and R. Firth, eds, *Coronavirus, Class and Mutual Aid in the United Kingdom*. Cham: Palgrave Macmillan.

Floridi, L. (2019). Translating principles into practices of digital ethics: Five risks of being unethical. *Philosophy & Technology*, 32 (2), 185–93. https://doi.org/10.1007/s13347-019-00354-x.

Foucault, M. (1970). *The Order of Things*. London: Tavistock Publications.
Foucault, M. (1978). *The History of Sexuality*, vol. 1: *An Introduction*. New York: Vintage Books.
Foucault, M. (1982). The subject and power. In M. F. Hubert, L. Dreyfus, and P. Rabinow, eds, *Michel Foucault: Beyond Structuralism and Hermeneutics*. Chicago, IL: University of Chicago Press. http://scholar.google.com/scholar?hl=en&btnG=Search&q=intitle:Beyond+Structuralism#9.
Foucault, M. (2007). *Security, Territory, Population: Lectures at the Collège de France, 1977–1978*. Basingstoke: Palgrave Macmillan.
Foucault, M. (2008). *The Birth of Biopolitics: Lectures at the Collège de France, 1978–1979*. New York: Palgrave Macmillan.
Fraser, N. (2003). Social justice in the age of identity politics: Redistribution, recognition and participation. In N. Fraser and A. Honneth, eds, *Redistribution or Recognition? A Political–Philosophical Exchange*. London: Verso.
Fraser, N. (2018). Recognition without ethics? In C. McKinnon and D. Castiglione, eds, *The Culture of Toleration in Diverse Societies*. Manchester: Manchester University Press.
France Digitale. (2023). Mark your calendars for 2023. France Digitale. https://francedigitale.org/agenda/talent-awards-2023.
Freire, P. (1996). *Pedagogy of the Oppressed*. London: Penguin.
Frosh, P., and Georgiou, M. (2022). Covid-19: The cultural constructions of a global crisis. *International Journal of Cultural Studies*, 25 (3/4), 233–52. https://doi.org/10.1177/13678779221095106.
Fukuda-Parr, S. (2003). The human development paradigm: Operationalizing Sen's ideas on capabilities. *Feminist Economics*, 9 (2/3), 301–17. https://doi.org/10.1080/1354570022000077980.
Gajjala, R., Rybas, N., and Altman, M. (2008). Racing and queering the interface: Producing global/local cyberselves. *Qualitative Inquiry*, 14 (7), 1110–33.
Galloway, A. (2004). Intimations of everyday life: Ubiquitous computing and the city. *Cultural Studies*, 18 (2/3), 384–408.
Gane, M. (2008). Foucault on governmentality and liberalism. *Theory, Culture & Society*, 25 (7/8), 353–63. https://doi.org/10.1177/0263276408097812.
García Canclini, N. (1997). Urban cultures at the end of the century: The anthropological perspective. *International Social Science Journal*, 153, 345–54.

Gentleman, A. (2023). UK's hostile environment policies 'disproportionately impact' people of colour. *Guardian*, 10 February. https://www.theguardian.com/uk-news/2023/feb/09/uks-hostile-environment-policies-disproportionately-impact-people-of-colour.

Georgiou, M. (2013). *Media and the City*. Cambridge: Polity.

Georgiou, M. (2017). Is London Open? Mediating and ordering cosmopolitanism in crisis. *International Communication Gazette*, 79 (6/7), 636–55. https://doi.org/10.1177/1748048517727175.

Georgiou, M. (2019). City of refuge or digital order? Refugee recognition and the digital governmentality of migration in the city. *Television & New Media*, 20 (6), 600–16. https://doi.org/10.1177/1527476419857683.

Georgiou, M., Hall, S., and Dajani, D. (2020). Suspension: Disabling the city of refuge? *Journal of Ethnic and Migration Studies*, 48 (9), 2006–22. https://doi.org/10.1080/1369183X.2020.1788379.

Georgiou, M., and Leurs, K. (2022). Smartphones as personal digital archives? Recentring migrant authority as curating and storytelling subjects. *Journalism: Theory, Practice & Criticism*, 23 (3), 668–89. https://doi.org/10.1177/14648849211060629.

Giddens, A. (1976). *New Rules of Sociological Method: A Positive Critique of Interpretative Sociologies*. London: Hutchinson.

Giddens, A. (1990). *The Consequences of Modernity*. Stanford, CA: Stanford University Press.

Gilbert, J. (2019). This conjuncture: For Stuart Hall. *New Formations: A Journal of Culture, Theory, Politics*, 96, 5–37. https://www.muse.jhu.edu/article/730832.

Gill, R. (2008). Culture and subjectivity in neoliberal and postfeminist times. *Subjectivity*, 25 (1), 432–45. https://doi.org/10.1057/sub.2008.28.

Gillespie, T. (2010). The politics of 'platforms'. *New Media & Society*, 12 (3), 347–64. https://doi.org/10.1177/1461444809342738.

Gilroy, P. (2004). *After Empire: Melancholia or Convivial Culture?* London: Routledge.

Gilroy, P. (2011). Fanon and Améry. *Theory, Culture & Society* 27 (7/8), 16–32. doi: 10.1177/0263276410383716.

Goldberg, D. H. (2019). Coding time. *Critical Times*, 2 (3), 353–69. https://doi.org/10.1215/26410478-7862517.

Google. (2021). Google careers: Berlin. Retrieved 2 February 2021 from https://careers.google.com/locations/berlin.

Google. (2023). Google Maps: Explore and navigate your world. Retrieved 5 January 2023 from https://www.google.co.uk/maps/about/#!.

Gordon, E. (2010). *The Urban Spectator: American Concept-Cities from Kodak to Google*. Lebanon, NH: Dartmouth College Press.

Gordon, L. R. (2014). Justice otherwise: Thoughts on Ubuntu. In L. Praeg and S. Magadla, eds, *Ubuntu: Curating the Archive*. Pietermaritzburg: University of KwaZulu-Natal Press.

Graham, D. A. (2017). Red state, blue city. *Atlantic*. https://www.theatlantic.com/magazine/archive/2017/03/red-state-blue-city/513857.

Graham, M. (2020). Regulate, replicate, and resist: The conjunctural geographies of platform urbanism. *Urban Geography*, 41 (3), 453–7. https://doi.org/10.1080/02723638.2020.1717028.

Graham, S. M., and Wood, D. A. (2003). Digitizing surveillance: Categorization, space, inequality. *Critical Social Policy*, 23 (2), 227–48. https://doi.org/10.1177/0261018303023002006.

Green, N. H. (2002). On the move: Technology, mobility, and the mediation of social time and space. *The Information Society*, 18 (4), 281–92. https://doi.org/10.1080/01972240290075129.

Greenfield, A. (2017). *Radical Technologies: The Design of Everyday Life*. London: Verso.

Guma, P. K. (2021). Recasting provisional urban worlds in the global South: Shacks, shanties and micro-stalls. *Planning Theory & Practice*, 22 (2), 211–26. https://doi.org/10.1080/14649357.2021.1894348.

Guma, P. K., and Mwaura, M. (2021). Infrastructural configurations of mobile telephony in urban Africa: Vignettes from Buru Buru, Nairobi. *Journal of Eastern African Studies*, 15 (4), 527–45. https://doi.org/10.1080/17531055.2021.1989138.

Gupta, N., and Ray, A. (2022). Probing 'instaworthiness': Siting the selfie. *Convergence*, 28 (3). https://doi.org/10.1177/13548565211048977.

Hackworth, J. (2013). *The Neoliberal City*. New York: Cornell University Press.

Halegoua, G. R. (2019). *The Digital City*. New York: New York University Press.

Hall, S. (1981). Notes on deconstructing 'the popular'. In R. Samuel, ed., *People's History and Socialist Theory*. London: Routledge & Kegan Paul.

Hall, S. (1997). Cultural identity and diaspora. In L. McDowell, ed., *Undoing Place: A Geographical Reader*. Hobocken, NJ: John Wiley & Sons.

Hall, S., Roberts, B., Clarke, J., Jefferson, T., and Critcher, T. (1978). *Policing the Crisis: Mugging, the State, and Law and Order*. Basingstoke: Macmillan.

Han, B.-C. (2018). *The Expulsion of the Other*. Cambridge: Polity.

Haraway, D. J. (1991). *Simians, Cyborgs and Women: The Reinvention of Nature*. London: Routledge.

Harvey, D. (1996). *Justice, Nature and the Geography of Difference*. Oxford: Blackwell.

Harvey, D. (2001). *Spaces of Capital: Towards a Critical Geography*. Edinburgh: Edinburgh University Press.

Harvey, D. (2009). *Cosmopolitanism and the Geographies of Freedom*. New York: Columbia University Press.

Hayles, N. K. (1999). *How We Became Posthuman: Virtual Bodies in Cybernetics, Literature, and Informatics*. Chicago, IL: University of Chicago Press.

Heater, B. (2018). HUD Complaint accuses Facebook ads of violating Fair Housing Act. TechCrunch, 19 August. https://techcrunch.com/2018/08/19/hud-complaint-accuses-facebook-ads-of-violating-fair-housing-act/?guccounter=2.

hooks, b. (1989). Choosing the margin as a space of radical openness. *Framework: The Journal of Cinema and Media*, 36, 15–23. http://www.jstor.org/stable/44111660.

Honneth, A. (2007). *Disrespect: The Normative Foundations of Critical Theory*. Cambridge: Polity.

Horan, T. A. (2000). *Digital Places: Building Our City of Bits*. Washington, DC: Urban Land Institute.

Hornborg, A. (2001). *The Power of the Machine: Global Inequalities of Economy, Technology, and Environment*. Walnut Creek, CA: AltaMira Press.

Huang, C.-C. (2010) *Humanism in East Asian Confucian Contexts*. Bielefeld: transcript Verlag. https://doi.org/10.1515/transcript.9783839415542

Huberman, J. (2021). Amazon Go, surveillance capitalism, and the ideology of convenience. *Economic Anthropology*, 8 (2), 337–49. https://doi.org/10.1002/sea2.12211.

Hutchinson, A. (2021). Survey finds a third of people don't trust social media companies with their data. *Social Media Today*, 16 March. https://www.socialmediatoday.com/news/survey-finds

-a-third-of-people-dont-trust-social-media-companies-with-thei/596830.
IBM. (2023). Smart city technology revolutionizes infrastructure. IBM. https://www.ibm.com/industries/government/infrastructure-citizen-services.
Ingold, T. (2006). Against human nature. In N. Gontier, J. P. Van Bendegem, and D. Aerts, eds, *Evolutionary Epistemology, Language and Culture: A Non-Adaptationist, Systems Theoretical Approach*. Basingstoke: Palgrave Macmillan. https://doi.org/10.1007/1-4020-3395-8_12.
Ingvarsson, J. (2020). Digital epistemology: An introduction. In J. Ingvarsson, *Towards a Digital Epistemology*. Cham: Palgrave Macmillan. https://doi.org/10.1007/978-3-030-56425-4_1.
Isin, E. (2002). *Being Political: Genealogies of Citizenship*. Minneapolis, MN: University of Minnesota.
Jackson, M. (2013). *The Politics of Storytelling: Variations on a Theme by Hannah Arendt*. Copenhagen: Museum Tusculanum Press.
Jacobs, K. (2022). Toronto wants to kill the smart city forever. *MIT Technology Review*, 22 June. https://www.technologyreview.com/2022/06/29/1054005/toronto-kill-the-smart-city.
Jali, L. (2022). Decoloniality, inclusivity and autonomy in reimagining cities of the future. *Journal of Inclusive Cities and Built Environment*, 2 (4), 67–76. https://doi.org/10.54030/2788-564x/2022/sp1v1a6.
Janoschka, M., and Mota, F. (2021). New municipalism *in action* or urban neoliberalisation *reloaded*? An analysis of governance change, stability and path dependence in Madrid (2015–2019). *Urban Studies*, 58 (13), 2814–30. https://doi.org/10.1177/0042098020925345.
Jasanoff, S. (2015). Future imperfect: Science, technology, and the imaginations of modernity. In S. Jasanoff and S. Kim, eds, *Dreamscapes of Modernity: Sociotechnical Imaginaries and the Fabrication of Power*. Chicago, IL: University of Chicago Press. https://doi.org/10.7208/chicago/9780226276663.003.0001.
Jasanoff, S., and Kim, S. H. (2009). Containing the atom: Sociotechnical imaginaries and nuclear power in the United States and South Korea. *Minerva*, 47, 119–46.
Jaywork, C. (2017). Sawant calls for removal of secret FBI cameras in Seattle. *Seattle Weekly*, 24 January. http://www.seattleweekly.com/news/sawant-calls-for-removal-of-secret-fbi-cameras-in-seattle.

JCWI. (2023). Briefing: Resisting the digital hostile environment. Joint Council for the Welfare of Immigrants. https://www.jcwi.org.uk/briefing-resisting-the-digital-hostile-environment.

Johnson, P. (2018). *Feminism as Radical Feminism*. London: Routledge.

Kanai, A., and Gill, R. (2020). Woke? Affect, neoliberalism, marginalised identities and consumer culture. *New Formations*, 102, 10–27. https://doi.org/10.3898/newf:102.01.2020.

Kelly, G., and McAdam, M. (2022). Scaffolding liminality: The lived experience of women entrepreneurs in digital spaces. *Technovation*, 118. https://doi.org/10.1016/j.technovation.2022.102537.

Kitchin, R. (2011). The programmable city. *Environment and Planning B: Planning and Design*, 38 (6), 945–51. https://doi.org/10.1068/b3806com.

Kitchin, R. (2019a). Toward a genuinely humanizing smart urbanism. In P. Cardullo, C. Di Feliciantonio, and R. Kitchin, eds, *The Right to the Smart City*. Bingley: Emerald Publishing.

Kitchin, R. (2019b). The timescape of smart cities. *Annals of the American Association of Geographers*, 109, 775–90. https://doi.org/10.1080/24694452.2018.1497475.

Kitchin, R., Cardullo, P., and Di Feliciantonio, C. (2019). Citizenship, justice, and the right to the smart city. In P. Cardullo, C. Di Feliciantonio, and R. Kitchin, eds, *The Right to the Smart City*. Bingley: Emerald Publishing.

Koch, R., and Miles, S. (2021). Inviting the stranger in: Intimacy, digital technology and new geographies of encounter. *Progress in Human Geography*, 45 (6), 1379–1401. https://doi.org/10.1177/0309132520961881.

Komarraju, S. A., Arora, P., and Raman, U. (2021). Agency and servitude in platform labour: A feminist analysis of blended cultures. *Media, Culture & Society*, 44 (4), 672–89. https://doi.org/10.1177/01634437211029890.

Konza Technopolis Development Authority. (2021). About us: Vision & mission. Konza Technopolis. https://konza.go.ke/vision-mission.

Kotkin, J. (2016). *The Human City: Urbanism for the Rest of Us*. Chicago, IL: Agate B2.

Kozlarek, O. (2021). From the humanism of critical theory to critical humanism. *European Journal of Social Theory*, 24 (2), 246–63. https://doi.org/10.1177/1368431020960958.

Krajina, Z. (2013). *Negotiating the Mediated City: Everyday Encounters with Public Screens*. London: Routledge.

Krajina, Z., Moores, S., and Morley, D. (2014). Non-media-centric media studies: A cross-generational conversation. *European Journal of Cultural Studies*, 17 (6), 682–700.

Krivý, M. (2016). Towards a critique of cybernetic urbanism: The smart city and the society of control. *Planning Theory*, 17, 8–30. https://doi.org/10.1177/1473095216645631.

LabGov. (2020). 'Songdo, we have a problem!': Promises and perils of a utopian smart city. The Urban Media Lab, 8 December. https://web.archive.org/web/20230226151726/https://labgov.city/theurbanmedialab/songdo-we-have-a-problem-promises-and-perils-of-a-utopian-smart-city.

Ladegaard, H. J. (2013). Demonising the cultural other: Legitimising dehumanisation of foreign domestic helpers in the Hong Kong press. *Discourse, Context & Media*, 2 (3), 131–40.

Ladouceur, D. (2019). The new normal is digital cities – not smart cities. *Forbes*, 19 November. https://www.forbes.com/sites/forbestechcouncil/2019/11/19/the-new-normal-is-digital-cities-not-smart-cities/?sh=5e826242231d.

Lamola, M. J. (2021). The future of artificial intelligence, posthumanism and the inflection of Pixley Isaka Seme's African humanism. *AI & Society*, 37 (1), 131–41. https://doi.org/10.1007/s00146-021-01191-3.

Langlois, G., and Elmer, G. (2019). Impersonal subjectivation from platforms to infrastructures. *Media, Culture & Society*, 41 (2), 236–51. https://doi.org/10.1177/0163443718818374.

Lara, A. P., Da Costa, E. P., Furlani, T. Z., and Yigitcanlar, T. (2016). Smartness that matters: Towards a comprehensive and human-centred characterisation of smart cities. *Journal of Open Innovation*, 2 (1). https://doi.org/10.1186/s40852-016-0034-z.

Larkin, B. (2013). The politics and poetics of infrastructure. *Annual Review of Anthropology*, 42 (1), 327–43. https://doi.org/10.1146/annurev-anthro-092412-155522.

Latonero, M. (2018). Governing artificial intelligence: Upholding human rights and dignity. Data & Society. https://datasociety.net/library/governing-artificial-intelligence.

Latour, B. (1993). *We Have Never Been Modern*. Cambridge, MA: Harvard University Press.

Law, J., and Singleton, V. (2013). ANT and politics: Working in and on the world. *Qualitative Sociology*, 36 (4), 485–502.

Lefebvre, H. (1991). *The Production of Space*. Oxford: Blackwell.
Lefebvre, H. (2013). *Rhythmanalysis: Space, Time and Everyday Life*. London: Bloomsbury.
Lemke, T. (2001). 'The birth of bio-politics': Michel Foucault's lecture at the Collège de France on neo-liberal governmentality. *Economy and Society*, 30 (2), 190–207.
Lin, W.-Y., Song, H., and Ball-Rokeach, S. J. (2010). Localizing the global: Exploring the transnational ties that bind in new immigrant communities. *Journal of Communication*, 60 (2), 205–29.
Linder, C. (2009). London undead: Screening/branding the empty city. In S. Hemelryk Donald, E. Kofman, and C. Kevin, eds, *Branding Cities: Cosmopolitanism, Parochialism and Social Change*. London: Routledge.
Lockie, S. (2004). Collective agency, non-human causality and environmental social movements: A case study of the Australian 'landcare movement'. *Journal of Sociology*, 40 (1), 41–57. https://doi.org/10.1177/1440783304040452.
Lockie, S. (2016). Sustainability and the future of environmental sociology. *Environmental Sociology*, 2 (1), 1–4. https://doi.org/10.1080/23251042.2016.1142692.
López, A. J. (2007). Introduction: The (post)global South. *The Global South*, 1(1), 1–11. http://www.jstor.org/stable/40339224.
Lott, T. L. (1999). *The Invention of Race: Black Culture and the Politics of Representation*. Oxford: Blackwell.
Loughnan, S., Haslam, N., Sutton, R. M., and Spencer, R. (2014). Dehumanization and social class. *Social Psychology*, 45 (1), 54–61.
Lowe, L. (2015). *The Intimacies of Four Continents*. Durham, NC: Duke University Press.
Lupton, D. (2020). Thinking with care about personal data profiling: A more-than-human approach. *International Journal of Communications*, 14, 3165–83.
Lurry, C. (2011). *Consumer Culture* (2nd edn). Cambridge: Polity.
Mac Sithigh, D., and Siems, M. M. (2019). The chinese social credit system: A model for other countries? *Modern Law Review*, 82 (6), 1034–71. https://doi.org/10.1111/1468-2230.12462.
Mackinnon, D., Burns, R., and Fast, V. (2022). *Digital (In)justice in the Smart City*. Toronto: University of Toronto Press.
Mackintosh, M. (2005). *London: The World in a City: DMAG Briefing*. London: Greater London Authority.

Mager, A., and Katzenbach, C. (2021). Future imaginaries in the making and governing of digital technology: Multiple, contested, commodified. *New Media & Society*, 23 (2), 223–36. https://doi.org/10.1177/1461444820929321.

Mansell, R. (2012). *Imagining the Internet: Communication, Innovation, and Governance.* Oxford: Oxford University Press.

Mansell, R., and Steinmueller, W. E. (2022). Denaturalizing digital platforms: Is mass individualization here to stay? *International Journal of Communication*, 16, 461–81.

M&S Collective. (2023). Home page. Retrieved 21 April 2023 from https://www.mandscollective.com.

Marcuse, P. (2002). The layered city. In P. Madsen and R. Pluntz, eds, *The Urban Lifeworld: Formation, Perception, Representation.* London: Routledge.

Marcuse, P., Harvey, D., and Akunon, K. (2021). *Take the City: Voices of Radical Municipalism.* Chicago, IL: Chicago University Press.

Marcuse, P., and van Kempen, R., eds (2000). *Globalizing Cities: A New Spatial Order?* Oxford: Blackwell.

Markham, T. (2020). *Digital Life.* Cambridge: Polity.

Marr, B. (2023). The best examples of what you can do with ChatGPT. *Forbes*, 1 March. https://www.forbes.com/sites/bernardmarr/2023/03/01/the-best-examples-of-what-you-can-do-with-chatgpt.

Martín-Barbero, J. (1993). *Communication, Culture and Hegemony: From the Media to Mediations.* London: SAGE.

Mason, P. (2020). *Clear Bright Future: A Radical Defence of the Human Being.* Milton Keynes: Penguin.

Massey, D. (2005). *For Space.* London: SAGE.

Massey, D. (2007). *World City.* Cambridge: Polity.

Mattern, S. (2017). A city is not a computer. *Places: A Forum of Environmental Design.* https://doi.org/10.22269/170207.

Mattern, S. (2018). Databodies in codespace. *Places: A Forum of Environmental Design.* https://doi.org/10.22269/180417.

Mattern, S. (2021). *A City Is Not a Computer: Other Urban Intelligences.* Princeton, NJ: Princeton University Press.

Mayor of London. (2018a). Mayor appoints London's first chief digital officer. Retrieved 19 April 2023 from https://www.london.gov.uk/press-releases/mayoral/mayor-appoints-chief-digital-officer.

Mayor of London (2018b). Mayor launches new £7m programme

to unearth London's digital talent. Mayor of London. https://www.london.gov.uk/press-releases/mayoral/mayor-launches-new-7m-scheme-to-find-tech-talent-0.

Mayor of London. (2021a). An emerging technology charter for London. Mayor of London, London Assembly. https://web.archive.org/web/20210616093726/https://www.london.gov.uk/publications/emerging-technology-charter-london-0.

Mayor of London. (2021b). Mission 1: More user-designed services. https://www.london.gov.uk/what-we-do/business-and-economy/supporting-londons-sectors/smart-london/mission-1-more-user-designed-services.

Mayor of London. (2021c). Priorities and programmes for 2021 and beyond. Mayor of London, London Assembly. https://www.london.gov.uk/programmes-strategies/business-and-economy/supporting-londons-sectors/smart-london/priorities-and-programmes-2021-and-beyond.

Mbembe, A. (2019). *Necropolitics*. Durham, NC: Duke University Press.

Mbembe, A. (2021). *Out of the Dark Night: Essays on Decolonization*. New York: Columbia University Press.

Mbembe, A., and Posel, D. (2005). A critical humanism. *Interventions: International Journal of Postcolonial Studies*, 7 (3), 283–6. https://doi.org/10.1080/13698010500267876.

McClary, S. (2003). Bessie Smith: 'Thinking Blues'. In M. Bull and L. Back, eds, *The Auditory Culture Reader*. Oxford: Berg.

McCullough, M. (2015). *Ambient Commons: Attention in the Age of Embodied Information*. Cambridge, MA: MIT Press.

McKinsey & Company. (2018a). Smart cities: Digital solutions for a more livable future: Executive summary. McKinsey Global Institute. https://www.mckinsey.com/~/media/McKinsey/Business%20Functions/Operations/Our%20Insights/Smart%20cities%20Digital%20solutions%20for%20a%20more%20livable%20future/MGI-Smart-Cities-Executive-summary.pdf.

McKinsey & Company. (2018b). Smart cities in Southeast Asia. https://www.mckinsey.com/business-functions/operations/our-insights/smart-cities-in-southeast-asia.

McKinsey & Company. (2019). Future of cities. https://www.mckinsey.com/featured-insights/future-of-cities.

McKinsey & Company. (2021). Infrastructure options for the future of cities. https://www.mckinsey.com/business-functions

/operations/our-insights/infrastructure-options-for-the-future-of-cities.

McLean, D., Rachal, M., and Zukowski, D. (2021). Smart city evolution: How cities have stepped back from a 'tech arms race'. Smart Cities Dive, 9 November. https://www.smartcitiesdive.com/news/smart-city-evolution-how-cities-have-stepped-back-from-a-tech-arms-race/609732.

McQuire, S. (2008). *The Media City: Media, Architecture and Urban Space*. London: SAGE.

McQuire, S. (2016). *Geomedia: Networked Cities and the Future of Public Space*. Cambridge: Polity.

McRobbie, A. (2016). *Be Creative: Making a Living in the New Culture*. Cambridge: Polity.

Meadway, J. (2020). Coronavirus is the greatest challenge capitalism has ever faced: Will a new system result? *New Statesman*. https://www.newstatesman.com/politics/2020/03/coronavirus-financial-economy-impact-labour-market.

Merrifield, A. (2014). *The New Urban Question*. London: Pluto.

Mhlambi, S. (2020). From rationality to relationality: Ubuntu as an ethical and human rights framework for artificial intelligence. Carr Center Discussion Paper Series, 2020-009. https://carrcenter.hks.harvard.edu/publications/rationality-relationality-ubuntu-ethical-and-human-rights-framework-artificial.

Mignolo, W. (2009). Who speaks for the 'human' in human rights? Human rights in Latin American and Iberian cultures. *Hispanic Issues on Line*, 5 (1), 7–24. https://hdl.handle.net/11299/182855.

Miles, S. (2012). The neoliberal city and the pro-active complicity of the citizen consumer. *Journal of Consumer Culture*, 12 (2), 216–30.

Mitchell, W. J. (1996). *City of Bits: Space, Place, and the Infobahn*. Cambridge, MA: MIT Press.

Mooney, G. (2000). Urban 'disorders'. In S. Pile, C. Brook, and G. Mooney, eds, *Unruly Cities? Order/Disorder*. London: Routledge.

Moore, B. A. (2012). Viewpoint: V for Vendetta and the rise of Anonymous. *BBC News*, 8 March. http://www.bbc.co.uk/news/technology-16968689.

Moore, J. W. (2016). Anthropocene or Capitalocene? Nature, history, and the crisis of capitalism. *Sociology Faculty Scholarship*, 1. https://orb.binghamton.edu/sociology_fac/1.

Moores, S. (2004). The doubling of place: Electronic media, time–space arrangements and social relationships. In N. Couldry and

A. McCarthy, eds, *Mediaspace: Place, Scale and Culture in a Media Age*. London: Routledge.

Moores, S. (2017). *Digital Orientations: Non-Media-Centric Media Studies and Non-Representational Theories of Practice*. New York: Peter Lang.

Mosco, V. (2005). *The Digital Sublime*. Cambridge, MA: MIT Press.

Mosco, V. (2019). *The Smart City in a Digital World*. Bingley: Emerald Publishing.

Murray, S. (2020). Digital literacy: What is it, and why does it matter? *Guardian*. https://web.archive.org/web/20210223165515/https://www.theguardian.com/tomorrows-campus-today/2020/may/21/digital-literacy-what-is-it-and-why-does-it-matter.

Nakashima, R. (2018). AP exclusive: Google tracks your movements, like it or not. AP NEWS, 13 August. https://apnews.com/828aefab64d4411bac257a07c1af0ecb/AP-Exclusive:-Google-tracks-your-movements,-like-it-or-not.

Napolitano, V., and Pratten, D. (2007). Michel de Certeau: Ethnography and the challenge of plurality. *Social Anthropology*, 15 (1), 1–12. https://doi.org/10.1111/j.1469-8676.2007.00005.x.

Nash, J. (2008). Re-thinking intersectionality. *Feminist Review*, 89 (1), 1–15. https://doi.org/10.1057/fr.2008.4.

Natale, S., and Guzman, A. L. (2022). Reclaiming the human in machine cultures: Introduction. *Media, Culture & Society*, 44 (4), 627–37. https://doi.org/10.1177/01634437221099614.

Nava, M. (2007). *Visceral Cosmopolitanism*. London: Bloomsbury.

New York City Office of Technology & Innovation. (2022). *Strategic Plan 2022*. https://www.nyc.gov/assets/oti/downloads/pdf/about/strategic-plan-2022.pdf.

New York State Comptroller, Thomas P. DiNapoli. (2022). Nearly 14% of New Yorkers live in poverty; surpasses national average for eight straight years. Office of the New York State Comptroller. https://www.osc.state.ny.us/press/releases/2022/12/dinapoli-nearly-14-percent-of-new-yorkers-live-poverty-surpasses-national-average-eight-straight-years.

Nijman, J., and Wei, Y. D. (2020). Urban inequalities in the 21st century economy. *Applied Geography*, 117, 102188. https://doi.org/10.1016/j.apgeog.2020.102188.

Noble, S. U. (2018). *Algorithms of Oppression: How Search Engines Reinforce Racism*. New York: New York University Press.

Noonan, J. (2012). Critical humanism. In L. M. Given, ed., *The

SAGE Encyclopaedia of Qualitative Research Methods. Thousand Oaks, CA: SAGE.

Noone, G. (2018). 'Sorry, I've only got my card': Can the homeless adapt to cashless society? *Guardian*, 27 February. https://www.theguardian.com/cities/2018/feb/27/card-cashless-society-homeless-contactless-payments-britain.

Nussbaum, M. C. (2011). *Creating Capabilities: The Human Development Approach*. Cambridge, MA: Harvard University Press.

O'Hagan, S. (2020). Chris Killip Obituary. *Guardian*. https://www.theguardian.com/artanddesign/2020/oct/16/chris-killip-obituary.

Open Rights Group. (2022). Migrant digital justice toolkit. Retrieved 21 April 2023 from https://www.openrightsgroup.org/blog/migrant-digital-justice-toolkit.

Owusu-Bempah A. (2017). Race and policing in historical context: Dehumanization and the policing of Black people in the 21st century. *Theoretical Criminology*, 21 (1), 23–34. https://doi.org/10.1177/1362480616677493.

Papacharissi, Z. (2021). *After Democracy: Imagining Our Political Future*. New Haven, CT: Yale University Press.

Papadopoulous, D. (2010). Insurgent posthumanism. *Ephemera: Theory & Politics in Organization*, 10 (2), 134–51.

Park, R. E. (1915). The city: Suggestions for the investigation of human behavior in the city environment. *American Journal of Sociology*, 20 (5), 577–612. https://doi.org/10.1086/212433.

Park, R. E., Burgess, E. W., and McKenzie, R. (2000). The city [1925], in M. Miles and T. Hall, with I. Borden, eds, *The City Reader* (3rd edn). London: Routledge.

Parnell, S., and Robinson, J. (2012). (Re)theorizing cities from the global South: Looking beyond neoliberalism. *Urban Geography*, 33 (4), 593–617. https://doi.org/10.2747/0272-3638.33.4.593.

Peck, J., Theodore, N., and Brenner, N. (2009). Neoliberal urbanism: Models, moments, mutations. *SAIS Review of International Affairs*, 29 (1), 49–66. http://doi.org/10.1353/sais.0.0028.

Pelenc, J., Bazile, D., and Ceruti, C. (2015). Collective capability and collective agency for sustainability: A case study. *Ecological Economics*, 118, 226–39. https://doi.org/10.1016/j.ecolecon.2015.07.001.

Phillips, A. (1997). *The Politics of Presence: The Political Representation of Gender, Ethnicity and Race*. Oxford: Oxford University Press.

Pipitone, N. (2021). How privacy concerns can derail a smart city. Propmodo. https://www.propmodo.com/how-privacy-concerns-can-derail-a-smart-city.

Pisani, F. (2015). *A Journey through Smart Cities: Between Datapolis and Participolis.* UNESCO Publishing. https://unesdoc.unesco.org/ark:/48223/pf0000234422.

Plummer, K. (2021). *Critical Humanism: A Manifesto for the 21st Century.* Cambridge: Polity.

Polaris. (2021). *Smart Cities Market Share, Size, Trends, Industry Analysis Report, by Application, by Smart Governance, by Smart Utilities, by Smart Transportation, by Regions: Segment Forecast, 2021–2028.* Polaris Market Research (No. PM1989). (Contents at https://www.polarismarketresearch.com/industry-analysis/smart-cities-market.)

Poole, S. (2014). The truth about smart cities: 'In the end, they will destroy democracy'. *Guardian,* 17 December. https://www.theguardian.com/cities/2014/dec/17/truth-smart-city-destroy-democracy-urban-thinkers-buzzphrase.

Poon, L. (2018). Sleepy in Songdo, Korea's smartest city. Bloomberg.com. https://www.bloomberg.com/news/articles/2018-06-22/songdo-south-korea-s-smartest-city-is-lonely.

Portal del Ciudadano de la Habana. (2022). Havana's digital transformation strategy presented. Portal del ciudadano de La Habana. https://www.lahabana.gob.cu/post_detalles/en/13093/presentan-estrategia-para-la-transformacion-digital-de-la-habana.

Powell, A. B. (2021). *Undoing Optimization: Civic Action in Smart Cities.* New Haven, CT: Yale University Press.

Prevost, L. (2018). Building a connected city from the ground up. *New York Times.* https://www.nytimes.com/2018/04/03/business/smart-city.html.

Punathambekar, A., and Mohan, S., eds. (2019). *Global Digital Cultures: Perspectives from South Asia.* Ann Arbor, MI: University of Michigan Press.

Qiu, J. L. (2022). Humanizing the posthuman: Digital labour, food delivery, and openings for the new human during the pandemic. *International Journal of Cultural Studies,* 25 (3/4). https://doi.org/10.1177/13678779211066608.

Rajdev, N. (2022). Smart cities are great: Human-centric cities are (again) the future. Quartz. https://qz.com/1088012/smart-cities-are-great-human-centric-cities-are-again-the-future.

Reyes, R., and Villarreal, E. (2016). Wanting the unwanted again:

Safeguarding against normalizing dehumanization and discardability of marginalized, 'unruly' English-learning Latinos in our schools. *Urban Review*, 48, 543–59. https://doi.org/10.1007/s11256-016-0367-8.

Rifkin, J. (2004). *The End of Labour: The Decline of the Global Labour Force and the Dawn of the Post-Market Era*. London: Penguin.

Rodgers, S., and Moore, S. (2018). Platform urbanism: An introduction. *Mediapolis*, 3 (4). https://www.mediapolisjournal.com/2018/10/platform-urbanism-an-introduction.

Rodgers, S., and Moore, S. (2020). Platform phenomenologies: Social media as experiential infrastructures of urban public life. In M. Hodson, J. Kasmire, A. McMeekin, J. G. Stehlin, and K. Ward, eds, *Urban Platforms and the Future City: Transformations in Infrastructure, Governance, Knowledge and Everyday Life*. London: Routledge.

Rofe, M. W. (2003). 'I want to be global': Theorising the gentrifying class as an emergent elite global community. *Urban Studies*, 40 (12), 2511–26.

Rose, G. (2020). Actually-existing sociality in a smart city. *City*, 24 (3/4), 512–29. https://doi.org/10.1080/13604813.2020.1781412.

Rose, G., Raghuram, P., Watson, S., and Wigley, E. (2021). Platform urbanism, smartphone applications and valuing data in a smart city. *Transactions of the Institute of British Geographers*, 46 (1), 59–72. https://doi.org/10.1111/tran.12400.

Russell, B. (2019). Beyond the local trap: New municipalism and the rise of the fearless city. *Antipode*, 51 (3), 989–1010.

Sack, R. (1997). *Homo Geographicus*. Baltimore, MD: John Hopkins University Press.

Sadowski, J. (2021). Who owns the future city? Phases of technological urbanism and shifts in sovereignty. *Urban Studies*, 58 (8), 1732–44. https://doi.org/10.1177/0042098020913427.

Safransky, S. (2019). Geographies of algorithmic violence: Reading the smart city. *International Journal of Urban and Regional Research*, 44 (2), 200–18.

Sartre, J.-P. (1961). Preface to Frantz Fanon's *Wretched of the Earth*. Marxists Internet Archive. https://www.marxists.org/reference/archive/sartre/1961/preface.htm.

Schiølin, K. (2020). Revolutionary dreams: Future essentialism and the sociotechnical imaginary of the fourth industrial revolution in Denmark. *Social Studies of Science*, 50 (4), 542–66. https://doi.org/10.1177/0306312719867768.

Scott, D. (2000). The re-enchantment of humanism: An interview with Sylvia Wynter. *Small Axe*, 8, 119–207. https://trueleappress.files.wordpress.com/2017/10/wynter-the-re-enchantment-of-humanism.pdf.

Scoville, C. (2016). George Orwell and ecological citizenship: Moral agency and modern estrangement. *Citizenship Studies*, 20 (6–7), 830–45. https://doi.org/10.1080/13621025.2016.1192105.

Seaver, N. (2017). Algorithms as culture: Some tactics for the ethnography of algorithmic systems. *Big Data & Society*, 4 (2). https://doi.org/10.1177/2053951717738104.

Sen, A. (1989). Development as capabilities expansion. *Journal of Development Planning*, 19, 41–58.

Sen, A. (1999). *Development as Freedom*. Oxford: Oxford University Press.

Sennett, R. (1970). *The Uses of Disorder: Personal Identity and City Life*. New Haven, CT: Yale University Press.

Sennett, R. (2013). *The Open City*. Richard Sennett. https://web.archive.org/web/20150501035829/https://www.richardsennett.com/site/senn/UploadedResources/The%20Open%20City.pdf.

Shaw, D. B. (2018). *Posthuman Urbanism: Mapping Bodies in Contemporary City Space*. London: Rowman & Littlefield.

Sheller, M., and Urry, J. (2003). Mobile transformations of 'public' and 'private' life. *Theory, Culture and Society*, 20 (3), 107–125.

Shelton, T., Zook, M., and Wiig, A. (2015). The 'Actually Existing Smart City.' *Cambridge Journal of Regions, Economy and Society*, 8 (1), 13–25. https://doi.org/10.1093/cjres/rsu026.

Signona, N. (2016). Everyday statelessness in Italy: Status, rights, and camps, *Ethnic and Racial Studies*, 39 (2), 263–279, https://doi.org/10.1080/01419870.2016.1105995.

Simone, A. M. (2018). *Improvised Lives: Rhythms of Endurance in an Urban South*. Cambridge: Polity.

Simonsen, K. (2013). In quest of a new humanism: Embodiment, experience and phenomenology as critical geography. *Progress in Human Geography*, 37 (1), 10–26. https://doi.org/10.1177/0309132512467573.

Simonsen, K., and Koefoed, L. (2020). *Geographies of Embodiment: Critical Phenomenology and the World of Strangers*. London: SAGE.

Sims, C. (2017). *Disruptive Fixation: School Reform and the Pitfalls of Techno-Idealism*. Princeton, NJ: Princeton University Press.

Singapore Together. (2021). Singapore Together. SG Together. https://www.singaporetogether.gov.sg/.

Smart Cities World. (2021). Our Mission. https://www.smartcitiesworld.net/about/about-us.

Smart Nation. (2021). LifeSG Initiative. Smart Nation Singapore. https://web.archive.org/web/20210612112246/https://www.smartnation.gov.sg/what-is-smart-nation/initiatives/Strategic-National-Projects/lifesg-initiative.

Smith, M. P. (2001). *Transnational Urbanism: Locating Globalization*. Oxford: Blackwell.

Srnicek, N. (2017). *Platform Capitalism*. Cambridge: Polity.

Suchman, L. A. (1987). *Plans and Situated Actions: The Problem of Human–Machine Communication*. Cambridge: Cambridge University Press.

Sundararajan, A. (2017). *The Sharing Economy: The End of Employment and the Rise of Crowd-Based Capitalism*. Cambridge, MA: MIT Press.

Taylor, C. (2004). *Modern Social Imaginaries*. Durham, NC: Duke University Press.

Telegraph. (2019). Of the people, by the people, for the people. https://web.archive.org/web/20220210181306/https://www.telegraph.co.uk/business/business-reporter/smart-cities-for-people.

Thomassen, B. (2012). Revisiting liminality: The danger of empty spaces. In H. Andrews and L. Roberts, eds, *Liminal Landscapes: Remapping the Field*. London: Routledge.

Thompson, M. (2021). What's so new about new municipalism? *Progress in Human Geography*, 45 (2), 317–42. https://doi.org/10.1177/0309132520909480.

Thrift, N. (2004). Driving in the city. *Theory, Culture & Society*, 21 (4/5), 41–59.

Ticktin, M. (2014). Transnational humanitarianism. *Annual Review of Anthropology*, 43 (1), 273–89.

Titley, G. (2020). The distribution of nationalist and racist discourse. *Journal of Multicultural Discourses*, 15 (3), 257–66. doi: 10.1080/17447143.2020.1780245.

Toh, A. (2023). Automated hardship. Human Rights Watch. https://www.hrw.org/report/2020/09/29/automated-hardship/how-tech-driven-overhaul-uks-social-security-system-worsens.

Tovar, M. (2001). The imaginary term in readings about modernity: Taylor and Castoriadis' conceptions. *Revista de Estudios Sociales*, 9, 31–38. http://journals.openedition.org/revestudsoc/28558.

Towns, A. R. (2022). Transporting Blackness: Black materialist media theory. In S. Sharma and R. Singh, eds, *Re-Understanding Media: Feminist Extensions of Marshall McLuhan*. Durham, NC: Duke University Press.

Trauth-Goik, A. (2021). Repudiating the fourth industrial revolution discourse: A new episteme of technological progress. *World Futures*, 77 (1), 55–78. https://doi:10.1080/02604027.2020.1788357.

Trust for London. (2023). London's poverty profile. https://www.trustforlondon.org.uk/data.

Tucker, S. (2015). *Instruments of War: Weapons and Technologies That Have Changed History*. Santa Barbara, CA: ABC-CLIO.

Tufekci, Z. (2012). We were always human. In N. L. Whitehead and M. Wesch, eds, *Human No More: Digital Subjectivities, Unhuman Subjects and the End of Anthropology*. Denver: University Press of Colorado.

Turner, G. (2009). *Ordinary People and the Media: The Demotic Turn*. London: SAGE.

Turner, V. W. (1969). *The Ritual Process: Structure and Anti-Structure*. Chicago, IL: Aldine Publishing.

Uber. (2020). Uber is now in over 10,000 cities globally. Uber Newsroom, 28 February. https://www.uber.com/newsroom/10000-cities.

UK Government Home Office. (2022). Home Secretary announces plans for contactless digital border. GOV.UK. https://www.gov.uk/government/news/home-secretary-announces-plans-for-contactless-digital-border.

UN Habitat. (2019). People-centred smart cities. UN Habitat. https://unhabitat.org/sites/default/files/2021/01/fp2-people-centered_smart_cities_04052020.pdf.

UN Habitat. (2020). The people-centered smart cities flagship programme. UN Habitat. https://unhabitat.org/programme/people-centered-smart-cities.

United Nations. (2010). Press release: 2009 Revision of world urbanization prospects. Available at http://esa.un.org/unpd/wup/Documents/WUP2009_Press-Release_Final_Rev1.pdf.

United Nations. (2022a). Reducing inequalities through digital public goods and youth collaboration for the SDGs. United

Nations Department of Economic and Social Affairs, 25 January. https://www.un.org/development/desa/dspd/2022/01/digital-public-goods-and-youth-collaboration-for-the-sdgs.

United Nations. (2022b). New urban agenda must be at heart of efforts to achieve sustainable development. United Nations Economic and Social Council. https://press.un.org/en/2022/ecosoc7077.doc.htm.

United Nations Economic and Social Council. (2022). Revitalizing the new urban agenda to fight rising inequalities: #NUA2030. United Nations Economic and Social Council. https://www.un.org/ecosoc/en/events/2022/revitalizing-new-urban-agenda-fight-rising-inequalities-nua2030.

UNESCO. (2019). Towards smart cities. *UNESCO Courier*. https://en.unesco.org/courier/2019-2/towards-smart-cities.

UNESCO and Netexplo Observatory. (2019). *Smart Cities: Shaping the Society of 2030*. Paris: UNESCO Publishing.

van der Graaf, S., and Ballon, P. (2019). Navigating platform urbanism. *Technological Forecasting and Social Change*, 142, 364–72. https://doi.org/10.1016/j.techfore.2018.07.027.

van Dijck, J., Poell, T., and de Waal, M. (2013). *The Platform Society*. Oxford: Oxford University Press.

Van Houtum, H., and Van Naerssen, T. (2002). Bordering, ordering and othering. *Tijdschrift voor economische en sociale geografie*, 93 (2), 125–36. https://doi.org/10.1111/1467-9663.00189.

Vaughan-Williams, N. (2014). 'We are not animals!' Humanitarian border security and zoopolitical spaces in Europe. *Political Geography*, 45, 1–10.

Weiss-Blatt, N. (2021). *The Techlash and Tech Crisis Communication*. Bingley: Emerald Publishing.

Whitehead, N., and Wesch, M. (2012). We were always human. In N. L. Whitehead and M. Wesch, eds, *Human No More: Digital Subjectivities, Unhuman Subjects and the End of Anthropology*. Denver: University Press of Colorado.

Willems, W. (2014a). Beyond normative dewesternization: Examining media culture from the vantage point of the global South. *Global South*, 8 (1), 7–23. https://www.muse.jhu.edu/article/581236.

Willems, W. (2014b). Provincializing hegemonic histories of media and communication studies: Toward a genealogy of epistemic resistance in Africa. *Communication Theory*, 24 (4): 415–34. https://doi.org/10.1111/comt.12043.

Williams, R. (1958). *Culture and Society: 1780–1950*. New York: Columbia University Press.
Winner, L. (1988). *The Whale and the Reactor: A Search for Limits in an Age of High Technology*. Chicago, IL: University of Chicago Press.
Wirth, L. (1938). Urbanism as a way of life. *American Journal of Sociology*, 44, 1–24.
Wrong, D. (1994). *The Problem of Order: What Unites and Divides Society*. New York: Free Press.
Wynter, S. (2000). Africa, the West and the analogy of culture: The cinematic text after man. In J. Givanni, ed., *Symbolic Narratives/African Cinema: Audiences, Theory and the Moving Image*. London: British Film Institute.
Wynter, S. (2003). Unsettling the coloniality of being/power/truth/freedom: Towards the human, after man, its overrepresentation: An argument. *CR: The New Centennial Review*, 3 (3), 257–337. https://doi.org/10.1353/ncr.2004.0015.
Yang, G. (2016). Narrative agency in hashtag activism: The case of #BlackLivesMatter. *Media and Communication*, 4 (4), 13–17. https://doi.org/10.17645/mac.v4i4.692.
Yates, J. S., and Bakker, K. (2014). Debating the 'post-neoliberal turn' in Latin America. *Progress in Human Geography*, 38 (1), 62–90. https://doi.org/10.1177/0309132513500372.
Yuval-Davis, N., Wemyss, G., and Cassidy, K. (2019). *Bordering*. Cambridge: Polity.
World Bank. (2023). Transparency & Accountability Initiative: Governance and institutions umbrella programs (video). World Bank. https://www.worldbank.org/nl/news/video/2023/01/20/transparency-accountability-initiative-governance-institutions-umbrella-programs.
Zuboff, S. (2019). *The Age of Surveillance Capitalism*. London: Public Affairs.

Index

#BLM (Black Lives Matter), 4–5, 12, 44, 62, 135–6
#ColstonStatue, 136
#LondonIsOpen, 119–22
#MeToo, 44, 62, 135
#RefugeesWelcome, 135

ability, 44, 48, 63, 94, 107, 143, 152
accountability, 30, 43, 73, 79–80, 148–9, 164
activism, 32, 44, 133–4, 143, 145–8, 154
  hashtag, 12, 32, 45, 135–8
actor–network theory (ANT), 59
advertising, 20, 22, 25, 40, 75, 81, 138
aesthetics, 32, 120–2, 138–9
affect, 34–5, 47–8, 52–5, 104, 108, 118–23, 126, 129, 150
agency, 18, 51, 102, 108, 129–36, 142, 150
  human, 42, 47–8, 80, 91–2, 94, 105, 121, 130, 156
  non-human, 59, 61, 68, 130
  political, 54, 65, 103

AI, 46, 55, 70, 73, 77, 105–6, 123–4, 141, 152–3, 163–4
Airbnb, 28
Alevi, 122–3
algorithm, 26, 28, 58, 60, 64, 69, 146, 150, 164
alienation, 53, 105–7, 122, 135
Amazon, 80
ambivalence, 33, 104, 106, 114, 119, 128–32, 135, 137
Amsterdam, 88
Anthropocene, 44
anthropocentrism, 42–3, 46, 63, 165
antihumanism, 9, 60, 155–6
anti-racism, 12, 31, 43, 72, 138
anxiety; *see* fear
app, 15, 20, 52, 116, 118, 123, 156
appropriation, 26, 123, 135–6, 157
Arabs, 126
Arendt, Hannah, 62, 153
Asia, 58, 83–4
asymmetry, 21, 25, 68, 100, 111–13

Index

AT&T, 80
Athens, 19, 21, 114–15, 125, 136
authenticity, 4, 52, 110
authoritarianism, 28, 72, 107, 145
authority, 77, 102, 104–5, 107, 156
automation, 11, 29, 58, 73, 125, 154
autonomy, 18, 35–6, 59, 83, 114–16, 124, 131, 143, 152, 155–9

Barcelona, 12
behaviour, 14, 48, 52, 88, 126
believability, 11–12, 29, 46, 81, 102, 106
belonging, 50, 78, 115, 121, 123, 137
Benjamin, Ruha, 57, 96, 152, 159–60
Berlin, 19, 21, 87, 94–5, 125–8, 130
betterment, 13, 19, 32, 71, 96, 107, 149
Big Data for Humans, 43
Big Tech, 60, 66, 75, 78, 118, 125, 149–51, 160, 164; *see also* corporation
Black, 32, 58, 91, 117, 125, 153, 155; *see also* #BLM
body, 35, 52, 98, 110, 128
border, 85, 110–11, 114–15, 118, 120, 123, 125, 147
Braidotti, Rosi, 59
Brexit, 120
Bristol, 136

camera, 15, 21, 24, 40, 97, 109–10, 125
campaign, 32, 44, 74–5, 87, 107, 147–8
   corporate, 43, 81, 136
   governmental, 75, 89, 93
   media, 32, 105, 120–1
capital, 73, 92, 110, 152
capitalism, 28–9, 35, 41–44, 46, 59–60, 87, 105, 107, 151, 158
   data, 36, 50
   digital, 60, 99, 123, 153, 155–6,
   industrial, 141–2, 161
   racial, 41–3, 50, 126
   surveillance, 86–7, 123–4, 126
   woke, 130, 136
care, 20, 44, 93–5, 121, 123, 133–5, 148
car, 47–8, 125
CCTV, 15, 21, 28, 105, 110
celebrity, 105, 120–2
censorship, 111
ChatGPT, 106
Chernilo, Daniel, 41, 58, 163
children, 78, 121
church, 115, 129
cinema, 52, 75, 84, 111, 121
Cities Coalition for Digital Rights, 29, 148–9
citizenship, 94, 99–100, 126, 132, 149; *see also* right (to citizenship)
   acts of, 108, 130, 138, 147, 160
city, 29–30, 45, 49–53, 72, 75, 86, 102, 120, 123–4, 144–5; *see also* right, ownership (of/to the city)
   controlled, 22, 27, 36, 57, 65, 71, 81, 96–7, 131
   corporatized, 36, 57, 71, 121, 124
   digital, 13–17, 70, 77–82, 89, 95, 106–7, 110–11, 116–19, 130, 136–9, 141

city (cont.)
  green(er), 31, 42–3, 105, 139
  humane, 22, 31, 76, 80
  neoliberal, 91, 94
  ordered, 15, 22, 36, 48–9, 79–80, 85, 89, 102, 144
  post-neoliberal, 48, 119
  progressive, 29–30, 71, 79, 87, 89, 148–9
  secret, 52, 116–17, 138
  shared, 131, 137
  smart, 14–15, 25, 54, 70–1, 73, 77–80, 83–8, 91–2, 107, 149
City Possible™, 82, 87
civil society, 11, 80
class, 55, 62, 109, 152
  middle, 34, 74, 92, 111, 116–17, 135, 158
  working, 67, 92, 95, 103, 121–2
classification, 35, 63, 107, 124, 126, 147–8, 160–1
climate, 30, 87, 89, 107
colonialism, 35, 47, 60–1, 83, 85, 91–2, 113, 141–2, 154–55, 164
commodification, 12, 54, 63, 112, 133, 136–7, 139, 145, 159
common good, 32, 46, 55, 89, 131, 145, 149
commonality, 99, 100–1, 110, 112, 139
communication, 21, 44, 47–8, 58, 86, 107, 109, 115, 126, 141
  strategic, 76, 81–2, 85, 89, 147
community, 79, 82, 87, 91, 93, 106, 115, 120–1, 133, 149, 165
competitiveness, 48, 83, 87
compliance, 49, 93–4, 97, 104
computer, 15, 39, 46, 50, 57, 62, 75
Confucianism, 58, 156
connection, 33–4, 60, 64, 105, 108, 111–13, 118, 128, 132–4, 138
connectivity, 16, 40, 43–5, 70, 79, 89, 100–1, 111–13, 118, 154
consensus, 4–5, 45, 55, 75, 79, 96
consent, 45, 76, 137, 152, 159, 163
consumerism, consumer, 31–2, 45–9, 53, 92, 94–6, 99–102, 110, 116–17, 121–3, 130–33
control, 31, 96–7, 103, 113, 118, 123–30, 141–2, 146–8, 152, 154; *see also* city (controlled)
  system(s) of, 16, 21, 40, 106, 115, 147
convenience, 101, 117–18, 152
corporation, 26, 31, 42–5, 72–88, 91–3, 96, 118, 124–5, 148, 150–1; *see also* Big Tech
Couldry, Nick, 27–8, 60
Covid-19 pandemic, 30, 79, 83, 89, 93, 132–5
creativity, 50–1, 54, 56, 91, 107, 121, 130, 139
crisis, 28, 31, 36, 44, 75, 89–90, 93–4, 132–6, 149; *see also* neoliberalism (crisis of)
  climate; *see* climate
  environmental; *see* environmentalism
  epidemiological; *see* Covid-19 pandemic
  financial (2008), 19, 74, 89
  migration (2015), 94, 125

Index

critical data studies, 26, 58–62, 64, 124–5, 132, 155, 161
culture, 43, 45, 47–8, 60, 68, 70, 112, 122–3, 138, 145
cyborg, 59, 152

data, 60, 73–4, 80–1, 96, 118, 123–4, 130, 147–8, 152, 155
  extraction, 26, 97, 105, 110, 112, 117, 123, 131, 160
  production, 26, 105, 116, 118
  profiling, 28, 34, 53, 64, 99–100, 124, 126, 147, 154; *see also* racial profiling
  protection, 79–80, 154
datafication, 28–9, 34, 60–61, 97, 110, 132, 137, 152, 160
decision-making, 26, 58, 80, 94, 97, 154
dehumanization, 46–7, 50, 108, 118, 124, 134–5, 145, 153–4, 156; *see also* rehumanization–dehumanization continuum
Delhi, 83
Dell, 81–2, 97
Deloitte, 91–2
democracy, 9, 12, 26, 72, 85–6, 90, 144, 149, 159
democratization, 74, 83, 97, 142
dependence, 27, 32, 47, 85, 112–13, 129, 163, 165
deprivation, 54, 94, 110
desire, 49–50, 52, 77, 92, 96, 106, 119, 130–1, 156
desirability, 53, 74, 81, 89, 91, 96, 102, 117, 160
development, 83–6, 92, 107
difference, 32, 44, 48, 52–4, 95, 131, 141, 149
digital change, 23, 44, 60, 68, 76, 90, 95, 119, 139, 160

digital order, 27–35, 41–2, 45–50, 53–4, 84–5, 93–8, 101–6, 136–40, 154–55, 163–4
  affirmation of, 54, 61, 76, 96
  constitution of, 34–5, 48
  contestation of, 34, 49–50, 54, 61, 142, 158–60
  fragility of, 30, 36, 53, 104, 136
  legitimization of, 42, 55, 61, 72, 95, 102, 105, 123, 137
  normalization of, 42, 46, 55, 61, 70, 72, 102, 130
digital solutionism, 26, 44, 88, 150
digital strategy, 80, 85–8, 91
Digital Talent Programme (London), 91
digital transformation, 27, 42, 45, 51, 73, 83, 90, 96–7, 149
digital urbanism, 23–4, 35, 56, 71, 77–8, 83–5, 119, 145, 161
digitization, 28, 42–3, 45, 52, 70, 101, 139, 141, 150–2, 158
dignity, 62, 116, 124, 132, 135, 137, 143, 155–6, 159
diNapoli, Thomas, 117
discontent, 36, 53, 64, 144
discourse, 22–3, 43, 52, 70–6, 80–5, 89–92, 95, 106, 129, 134–5; *see also* order of discourse
  corporate, 77, 82, 150
  hegemonic, 31–2, 49, 71–2, 75, 86, 95
  state, 89
discrimination, 60, 124, 145–6, 155
disobedience, 12, 65, 104

dissent, 32, 53, 65, 145
diversity, 29–31, 45–8, 52–3, 75–6, 88–90, 95, 119–122, 129–30, 136–7, 164
Douglass, Frederick, 58
drone, 21, 25, 118
Du Bois, W. E. B., 58, 155

economy, 13, 31, 34, 45, 60, 85, 112, 151, 156
  affective, 120–3, 138
  cultural, 52, 120–1
  digital, 19, 34, 47–8, 63, 91, 93–4, 112, 125, 137, 146
  extractivist, 26, 60, 142, 153
  market, 14, 48, 88, 90, 106
  political, 65, 74, 117–18, 125, 135, 139, 156, 160, 162
education, 74, 94, 96, 115, 129, 149, 163
Eko Atlantic City, 84
elderly, 89, 93, 95, 101
elite, 10, 14, 45, 49, 72, 90, 97, 155
emissions, 20, 84, 107, 164
employment, 28, 51, 53, 91, 94, 96, 99–100, 115, 124–5
Enlightenment, 41, 56, 58, 155
entertainment, 51, 92, 111
entrepreneurship, 42, 74, 77, 82, 88, 92–3, 106, 119, 125, 138
environment (social), 92, 109, 114, 119, 128, 131, 141, 145, 147–9, 161
environmentalism, 32, 43–6, 72, 83–5, 90, 94, 105, 136, 164
ephemerality, 105, 108, 133–6, 138–9
equality, 43, 46–7, 56, 62, 88, 95, 122, 161
equity, 42–3, 56, 61, 73–4, 79, 85, 88, 136, 165

ethics, 42, 56, 58, 64, 71, 75, 87–8, 90, 122, 148–9
  ethical consumption, 32, 47–8
ethnicity, 20, 32, 89, 120, 122,
Eurocentrism, 41, 46–7, 58–61, 63, 66, 72, 136, 152, 158, 161
Europe, 12, 19, 29, 56, 58, 114, 141, 147–8, 155–6
European Renaissance, 58
exclusion, 46, 48, 87, 90, 92, 116–17, 133, 140, 145, 154
experience, 33–5, 51–2, 57, 60, 102, 108–10, 113–15, 117–19, 123–4, 134
experimentation, 52, 106–7, 132, 157
exploitation, 60, 74–5, 85, 145, 153, 161
Extinction Rebellion, 44, 62

Facebook, 21, 121–3, 125, 133
factory, 20, 42, 141
family, 14, 33–4, 78, 94, 110, 115, 118, 121, 128–30, 154
Fanon, Frantz, 41, 155
fashion, 32, 47–8, 92, 107, 128, 136
fear, 75, 98, 106, 116, 119, 124, 126, 128–9, 132
feminism, 12, 31, 43, 45–6, 107, 138, 154–55
Floyd, George, 30
food, 31–2, 48, 92, 107, 127, 130, 133–5, 138
forms of life, 13, 36, 42, 56, 59, 61, 64, 159, 160, 164
Foucault, Michel, 27, 30, 71, 150
fragility, 4–5, 50, 82, 85, 110, 135–6, 149, 151; *see also* digital order, neoliberalism (fragility of)

Index

France Digitale, 43
freedom, 43–6, 56–8, 61–2, 65, 85, 94, 103, 116–17, 120–2, 135–8, 155–61
Freire, Paulo, 159–160
friendship, 33, 105, 138

gender, 43–6, 60, 72, 95, 107, 126–9, 136, 138, 152–4, 162
gentrification, 4, 11
Ghana, 84
global North, 2, 18, 28, 41, 66–8, 82–3, 113, 161
global South, 18–19, 66–8, 83, 91, 113, 161
globalization, 19, 65
Google, 2, 28, 73, 77–8, 80–1, 118
Google Maps, 28, 114, 118
governance, 13–14, 34, 45, 87, 89, 97, 117, 125, 148, 152
  digital, 89
  urban, 21, 24–6, 81–2, 145
government, 13–16, 29–32, 72, 74, 76, 82–4, 87–8, 96–7, 145, 148
governmentality, 14, 47, 89, 148
graffiti, 1, 32, 136
group, 27, 130–1, 133–5, 147–8
growth, 11, 29, 45, 60, 74, 85, 151

hacking, hacker, 67, 125, 145, 154
Hall, Stuart, 43, 62, 103
happiness, 52, 105, 107, 110, 119–21, 123, 130, 138
Haraway, Donna, 59
Haringey Welcome (London), 145–6
hashtag, 62, 107; *see also* activism (hashtag)
Havana, 19, 109–12, 119
health, 30, 53, 74, 84, 94, 96–7, 124, 130, 149, 151–4
hierarchy, 56, 74, 76, 152; *see also* humanity (hierarchical)
history, 53, 62–3, 95, 103, 110
Holm, Jeanne, 79
homelessness, 92, 122, 154
hooks, bell, 54, 100, 102, 132, 146, 153
HOPE City, 84
hope, 9–10, 36, 41, 47, 54, 57, 75, 138, 157, 164
housing, 22, 92, 109, 121, 124, 126, 154
Hudson Yards (New York), 73
'Human', 56, 59, 61, 63
human (being and becoming), 36, 55–8, 62–3, 100–2, 108, 111–13, 137, 141, 147, 153–9
  urban, 101, 108, 113–14, 137, 150, 154
humancentrism, 11, 23, 42, 49, 63, 71, 77, 90, 96, 97, 150; *see also* people-centrism
humanism, 5–6, 8–9, 56–8, 142–4, 150–1, 153, 155–7; *see also* values (humanist)
  Black, 58, 155–6
  critical, 35–6, 54–8, 61–9, 141–50, 153–65
  demotic, 43, 49–51, 54–56, 61, 99–105, 109–10, 118, 130, 134, 137–40
  liberal, 63
  popular, 41–56, 61, 70–6, 79–83, 86–7, 90–8, 101–2, 130, 151
humanity, 44, 57–65, 76–7, 89–90, 95, 124, 141–2, 146–7, 156–9, 162
  desired, 127

humanity (*cont.*)
　hierarchical, 46–7, 54, 100, 108, 142, 144–5
　selective, 61, 95
　shared, 86, 101, 133, 135
　urban, 44, 46–7, 83, 90–1, 100–1, 108, 110–13, 120, 133, 140

IBM, 97
idealism, 85, 159
identity, 24, 50, 59, 90, 102, 107, 111–14, 118, 128, 151
imaginary, 41, 47, 49, 71–82, 95–7, 104, 130, 135, 146–7, 151
imperialism, 87, 112
inclusion, 30, 79, 82, 86–7, 90, 104, 120, 136–7, 146, 153
India, 16, 84,
indigenous peoples, 14, 155
individualism, 31–2, 45, 48, 119, 131
Industry 4.0, 100, 104
inequality, 33, 41, 45–7, 72, 83, 87, 94–7, 105–7, 133–6, 139, 144
　digital, 45, 148
influencer, 25, 67, 71, 75
information and communication technology (ICT), 40–1, 86
infrastructure, 25–6, 41, 64, 80–1, 87, 89, 108–9, 111–13, 162
　digital, 13–14, 43, 50–1, 74, 84, 105, 128, 137, 146, 151
innovation, 32, 70–1, 76–9, 81–5, 87–90, 144, 146, 157–8
Instagram, 50, 107, 136, 141
institution, 27, 32, 72, 74–6, 87, 104, 119, 154
integration, 30, 39, 47, 49, 94, 125, 127, 159

Internet, 40, 64, 79–80, 106, 109, 111–12
intersectionality, 34, 128, 139, 153, 158
investment, 22, 31, 43, 73, 80–4, 96, 101, 106, 137–8, 151–2

JBG Smith, 80
Joint Council for the Welfare of Immigrants (JCWI), 147–8
justice, 29–30, 44, 72, 97, 130, 134–6, 138, 144–9, 157
　digital, 80, 89, 147–8
　social, 65, 72, 149

Kaba, Chris, 125–6
Kenya, 84–5
Khan, Sadiq, 122
Kigali, Kigali Innovation City, 83–4, 91
Killip, Chris, 103
knowledge, 34, 56–7, 66, 8s5, 103, 111, 114, 116, 118, 134
　production, 18, 51, 57, 63, 69, 110, 158
　system(s) of, 27–8, 71, 75, 160–2
Konza Technopolis, 84–5
Korea, 73

labour union, 133
language, 29, 76, 85–6, 88–90, 127, 134, 136, 148
Latin America, 12, 19, 115
Latinx, 115
law, 35, 97, 149
learning, 21, 46, 78, 101, 106, 113–14, 127, 137, 153
LGBTQI, 5, 12, 134, 136
liberalism, 31, 45, 73, 94
libertarianism, 31

Index

life, 30, 57, 66, 91, 93–4, 121–3, 130, 149, 160
  everyday, 26, 33, 43, 51, 60, 98, 101, 104, 143, 156
  digital, 17, 34, 50, 63, 69, 99–100, 114, 156
  quality of, 77, 85
  social, 11, 25, 27, 33, 74, 103
  urban, 45, 52, 73, 75, 96, 100, 123, 135, 141
LifeSG (Singapore), 89
liminality, 49, 102, 104–8, 119, 128, 134–8
literacy, 80, 126, 163
  digital, 62, 79, 96
London, 19–21, 88, 91, 116–17, 119–23, 125–6, 130, 134, 136, 145
loneliness, 40, 105, 107
Los Angeles, 12, 19, 21, 79, 115, 129–30, 136
love, 21, 33–4, 75, 105, 109, 111, 123, 126–9, 138

machine, 10, 35, 40, 46, 59, 61, 64, 68, 90, 153
machinery (industrial), 11, 163
mainstream, 53, 79, 85, 119, 146, 148, 160
marginality, marginalization, 44, 47, 53–55, 59–61, 91, 100, 113–16, 122–5, 146, 152–4
market (economics), 30–32, 47–8, 56, 74, 76, 81, 87–91, 94, 96, 163
market (physical), 52, 111
Marks & Spencer, 136
MaRS, 77
Martin, Kevin, 79–80
Marx, Karl, 11, 131
Mastercard, 82
mayor, 91, 120–3, 149
Mbembe, Achille, 36, 41, 54, 58

McKinsey & Company, 83–4, 97
meaning making, 10, 17, 33, 35, 59, 104, 156, 162
media, 25, 32, 64, 71–2, 75–9, 86–7, 96, 106, 111, 148
  digital, 14, 79, 127
  print, 1–2, 75, 78, 141
  social, 28, 31–2, 52, 64, 75, 105, 107, 109–10, 120–1, 126–38
mediation, 46, 52, 71–2, 75–6, 96, 108–12, 114, 126, 132–3, 152
men, masculinity, 56, 74, 126
Messenger, 34
Mhlambi, Sabelo, 46, 64
Microsoft, 125
migration, 18–19, 100, 114–15, 129, 132, 147–8; *see also* crisis (migration)
minorities, 12, 14, 32, 60, 67, 91, 104, 120, 122, 124
mobility, 84, 114–15, 121
modernity, 11, 15–16, 24, 46, 59, 61, 75, 142, 162
Modi, Narendra, 84
monetization, 25, 118, 123
morality, 44, 48, 50, 56–7, 61, 79, 90, 94, 96–7, 130
multiculturalism, 45, 127
municipalism, 87, 148–9
Muslim, 122, 126

narrative, 43, 46, 70–1, 79–2, 88–9, 94, 96–7, 105–6, 118–19, 127
nation, 29, 36, 45, 56, 72, 87, 120, 126, 147
National Landing (Virginia, US), 80–1
nationalism, 11, 29, 45, 120–1
nature, 44, 89, 164

navigation, 21, 28, 113–18, 123, 138
needs, 40, 46, 73, 78, 82, 87–9, 92–3, 96, 106, 130, 156
negotiation, 43, 49, 95, 98, 102, 111
neighbourhood, 45, 115, 125, 127, 130, 133–5, 145
neocolonialism, 91
neoliberalism, 30, 45, 74, 81–2, 87, 89, 91, 93–4, 119, 130, 151
  crisis of, 29–30, 55–6, 64, 71–4, 97, 130, 143, 151
  fragility of, 30, 158
network, 27, 31, 50, 58–60, 64, 74, 76, 93, 130, 133–6
  5G, 70, 105, 141
  fibre-optic, 13, 105
  wireless, Wi-Fi, 13–14, 16, 20, 109, 154, 164
New York, 19, 73, 88, 116–17, 136
Nextdoor, 133
non-humans, 43, 47, 51, 56–62, 108, 111–12, 119, 130, 154–7, 164
normativity, 43, 46–8, 54–5, 60–1, 71–4, 90, 93, 149, 152, 160–4
North America, 19, 77, 148

OpenAI, 106
openness, 31–2, 47, 52, 82, 103, 107, 119–22, 129, 132, 137
opposition, 41, 44, 47, 58, 65, 81, 95, 98
oppression, 26, 57, 61, 104, 110, 127, 139, 159–60
optimism, 105, 119, 122, 129
optimization, 16, 73, 82, 97, 108, 118

order, 24–28, 34, 45, 55–6, 81, 139, 141–2, 153–4, 163
  algorithmic, 60, 146
  capitalist, 43, 53, 124
  corporate, 43
  digital; *see* digital order
  economic, 75, 123
  neoliberal, 30, 73, 82, 89
  post-neoliberal, 104
  social, 27, 35, 47, 72, 74, 101
  urban, 24, 76, 112
order of discourse, 27, 54, 71, 75, 96, 152, 163
ordinary, 51–2, 54, 56, 100–18, 121, 123, 128, 133, 137–9, 146–7
ordoliberalism, 30
Other, other, 34–5, 48, 50–3, 56–8, 63, 108, 157
othering, 32, 150
ownership, 47, 96, 128, 142, 154
  of the city, 53, 64, 117

participation, 64, 86, 91, 95, 125
patriarchy, 35, 42, 46–7, 56, 59–61, 63, 72, 124, 136, 161
people-centrism, 78, 81–2, 86, 97
photography, 20, 24, 103, 110
placemaking, 25, 50
platformization, 10, 20, 60, 110, 125, 132, 153, 160
platform, 47, 60, 64–5, 76, 88, 99–104, 112, 139, 145–6, 163
play, 34, 48, 50, 52, 160
Plummer, Ken, 41, 58
plurality, 63, 68, 160
pluriversality, 44, 63, 65, 147, 150, 158–60, 164
podcast, 145–6
Poland, 30

Index

policing, 16, 21, 72, 94, 115, 129; *see also* violence (police)
   predictive, 11, 100, 125–6
policy, 71–2, 75, 79–80, 85, 87, 89, 93–4, 116, 148–50
political party, 133
politicization, 55, 61, 134
politics, 29–30, 33, 44–5, 112, 116, 123–4, 135, 144–50, 164
pollution, 87, 106, 164
populism, 11, 29, 43, 72, 74
Portland, 79
Posel, Deborah, 54, 58
possibility, 28, 71, 75, 100, 104, 129, 137–8, 154, 158
   conditions of, 122–3, 126, 128
   radical, 54, 133–6, 146
postcolonialism, 41, 64, 83, 91, 113, 154–55
posthumanism, 9 57–61, 64, 103, 151–2, 155, 162
post-neoliberalism, 29–31, 45, 48–9, 64, 72, 87–8, 106, 119–21, 138
poverty, 4, 41, 60, 84, 91–2, 104–5, 112, 116, 122, 124, 134
power, 42–3, 48–9, 71, 76, 101–4, 110–13, 116, 128, 132, 143–4, 155–61; *see also* visibility (of power)
   corporate, Big Tech, 60, 75, 88, 160
   economic, 19, 26, 113, 118, 161
   infrastructural, 26, 36
   political, 110, 118
   symbolic, 10–11, 19, 22, 24–5, 73, 90
   technological, 113, 161
precarity, 122, 129, 138
prediction, 46, 55, 73, 119, 124; *see also* policing (predictive)
presentism, 155–6
privacy, 80–1, 90, 94, 110, 116, 162
privilege, 34–5, 67, 110, 112, 129, 137, 152, 154, 159, 162
productivity, 106, 163
profit, 26, 29, 45, 48, 60, 80–1, 96–7, 123, 149, 155
profiteering, 9, 34, 84, 151
promise, 41–6, 49, 73, 81–5, 90–2, 104–7, 122–3, 137, 144, 150–3
   digital, 20, 23, 53, 63–4
   of progress, 33, 43, 46, 55, 104
prosperity, 74, 83, 90, 101
protest, 52, 75, 107, 135–6, 138
public good; *see* common good

Quayside (Toronto); *see* Toronto

race, 53–6, 60, 95, 107, 109–10, 124–6, 140, 152–4, 162; *see also* capitalism (racial)
racial justice, 30, 72, 89, 132, 135–6, 138
racial profiling, 143, 145, 153; *see also* data (profiling)
racism, 29, 41, 46, 115–16, 146–7, 153
rationality, 28, 30, 41, 46, 49, 57, 64–5, 104, 125, 152
recognition, 46–8, 53, 58–9, 65, 91, 95, 124, 146–8, 162–3
refugees, 9, 67, 94–5, 99–100, 114–15, 125–8; *see also* #RefugeesWelcome
   Afghan, 95, 115, 126
   Iraqi, 115
   Mali, 114
   Syrian, 99, 114, 126–8

Index

regulation, 13, 21–2, 30–1, 62, 89, 97, 142, 149
rehumanization, 43, 71, 76, 83, 88, 94, 137
rehumanization–dehumanization continuum, 46–9, 57, 64, 73, 104–6, 112–14, 117, 120–1, 124–5, 128–9, 152
religion, 101, 133, 136
representation, 32, 54, 64, 75, 89, 110, 116, 120–1, 160, 162
resistance, 43, 54, 104, 132, 139, 142, 144–5, 147–9, 153–4
resources, 55–8, 62, 80, 94, 96, 105, 109–10, 115, 160
   natural, 74, 87
   symbolic, 56, 74, 115
responsibility, 36, 53, 57–8, 65, 82, 89–90, 93–7, 131, 164
richness, 73, 112, 118
right(s), 29, 58, 61, 76, 85–6, 94, 110, 116–18, 124, 136
   to citizenship, settlement, 94, 99–100, 126, 147
   to the city, 25, 54, 97, 109, 117, 145, 148–9, 165
   digital, 29, 148–9
   human, 80–1, 88, 149
risk, 35, 115, 124, 126, 128–9, 147, 154, 161
roles, 52, 64, 90, 103
Rwanda, 84

safety, 21, 35, 44, 70, 74, 118
school, 22, 101, 125, 127, 136
science and technology studies (STS), 26, 59, 103
securitization, 47, 125
security, 81, 97, 107–8, 110, 118–19, 123, 125, 129, 138, 143, 154

segregation, 36, 87
Self, self, 34–6, 42, 47, 50–2, 57, 108, 110, 112, 128, 137, 152
selfie, 4, 52, 99, 109, 111
self-making, 52, 64, 100, 104–5, 131
self-realization, 45, 50, 52, 138
self-reliance, 49, 125
Senegal, 84
Seoul, 19, 21
services, 13, 16, 70, 73, 82, 88–9, 149
   public, 11, 22, 74, 79, 101, 147, 149
sexuality, 20, 44, 63, 107, 152
shared working spaces, 20, 45
sharing, 16, 20, 32, 45, 48, 109, 129, 134, 154; *see also* city, humanity (shared)
Sidewalk Labs, 73, 78
Singapore, 89, 91, 93
situatedness, 15–19, 25, 28, 33–4, 44, 62, 95, 112, 161
skills, 106, 138, 152
   digital, 49, 93–5, 125, 137
small business, 31, 77
Smart Cities World (network), 87
Smart City Berlin, 87
Smart City PDX (Portland), 79
Smart Nation Together (Singapore), 89
smartcitization, 2, 22–3, 81; *see also* city (smart)
Smarter London Together, 88
smartphone, 25, 50–2, 64, 75, 99, 111, 114–17, 126, 128–9
social movement, 12, 29–30, 32, 44, 62, 75, 86, 89, 135, 148
social peace, 3–4, 45

Index

sociality, 5, 33, 45, 53–4, 152
socializing, 14, 21, 42, 101, 163
society, 30, 41, 48–9, 64, 71, 75, 93, 145, 163
solidarity, 35, 44, 130, 132–9
Songdo, 19, 73, 81, 118
sovereignty, 15, 37, 57
sponsorship, 12, 125
Spotify, 146
stability, 27–9, 31, 41, 44, 48, 55, 74, 138
start-up, 32, 43, 88
state, 44–6, 51, 73–6, 84–9, 93–4, 111, 118, 124–6, 143, 150,
subjectivity, 48–9, 105, 108, 131
surveillance, 53, 81, 93, 97, 112–13, 116, 118, 123–9, 153–4, 160; *see also* capitalism (surveillance)
suspension, 104, 107, 135, 138
suspicion, 28, 53, 65, 74, 78, 155, 164
sustainability, 30, 43–5, 53, 64, 70, 81–7, 95, 97, 119

technocentrism, 25, 29, 42, 57, 66, 71, 78, 90, 97
technocracy, 11, 71, 74, 78
technodeterminism, 11, 22, 32, 73, 155
technologization, 11, 15, 22, 24, 49, 78–9, 81, 92, 96, 123
technology, 40–44, 55, 70–81, 87–8, 106, 113–14, 123–4, 128–30, 141–5, 157
 green, 31–2, 46
 haptic, 1, 20, 35, 75
 smart, 20, 31, 43, 128
 wearable, 1, 106, 163
threat, 35, 44, 65, 72, 80–1, 83, 115, 160

TikTok, 6, 21, 75, 107
TmplTalks, 40
togetherness, 56, 88–90, 93, 101, 131–2, 135
Tomorrow's Cities (research fund), 91
Toronto, 28–9, 73, 77–8, 80–1
tourism, 109–10, 112
tracking / tracing, 15, 35, 51, 89, 93, 128
traffic, 84, 92
transgender, 3, 127
transparency, 43, 80
trust, 28–9, 42, 44–5, 48, 72, 80–1, 87, 94, 143, 149

Uber, 28
Ubuntu, 58, 156
uncertainty, 104, 107, 129, 138
United Kingdom, 16, 99–100, 116, 120, 133, 145, 147
 UK Home Office, 100, 147
United Nations, 40–1, 85–7
United States, 12, 29–30, 79, 111, 114–15, 136
 US Immigration and Customs Enforcement (ICE), 115, 129
universalism, 63, 112, 159
users, 25, 34, 43, 88, 96, 102, 104–7, 116, 118
utopia, 80, 85, 105

values, 28, 31–2, 45, 85, 106, 108, 113, 118–20, 129–32, 138–9; *see also* neoliberalism, post-neoliberalism
 humanist, 40–1, 50–1, 58, 61, 82, 85, 122, 143–4, 156–8
 progressive, 42, 44, 46, 54, 72, 104, 119
videos, 48, 75, 120–2

violence, 35, 53–4, 56, 59–60, 93, 117, 123–5, 129, 154–5, 159
  police, 35, 52, 115, 126
visibility, 57, 66–7, 91, 94–5, 107, 112, 120, 128, 137, 145, 147
  of order, 31, 47, 70, 76, 95–7, 102, 110, 118, 150, 152
  of power, 95
  of technology, 21, 28, 75, 77
voice, 53–4, 59–60, 80, 102–3, 128, 132, 139, 145–6, 159–60
volunteering, 100, 145
voting, 29, 101
vulnerability, 32, 115, 124, 147, 157

Wakanda (real Wakanda, Ethiopia), 84
war, 9, 118, 123, 127

Weibo, 21
well-being, 43–4, 74, 90, 105, 123, 143, 163
West, western, 34, 41, 59, 66, 69, 84, 92, 109, 158, 161–2
WhatsApp, 21, 34, 133–4
white, whiteness, 34, 43, 48, 56, 74, 117, 141, 155, 158
Williams, Raymond, 43
witnessing, 15, 52, 54
women, 32, 44, 91, 95, 122, 128–9, 136
work, 9, 34, 45, 49–50, 78, 96, 126, 137; *see also* employment
  digital, 17, 108
Wu, Yung, 77–8
Wynter, Sylvia, 151, 153, 155

young people, 89, 109, 114, 116, 101, 122–3, 126, 136
YouTube, 105